Effort·Less Marketing

FOR FINANCIAL ADVISORS

5 Steps to a Super-Profitable Business and a Wonderful Life

Effort·Less Marketing

FOR FINANCIAL ADVISORS

5 Steps to a
Super-Profitable Business
and a Wonderful Life

Steve Moeller

AMERICAN BUSINESS VISIONS
Tustin, California

American Business Visions
1131 East Main St., Suite 203
Tustin, CA 92780
www.businessvisions.com
bizviz@businessvisions.com

First edition 1999
Fifth printing 2005

Designed and typeset by Robert Mott & Associates • Keswick, VA
Illustrated by Tom Klare • San Diego, CA
Printed in the United States of America

ISBN: 0-9672059-0-5

I dedicate this book to

the two people most important to me:

my wife, Brooke, who makes my life effort-less

and fills it with love;

and my mother, Betty,

who taught me to always look at

the positive side of life.

Contents

Introduction

As a highly motivated new producer for a well-known brokerage firm, my good friend Larry was so successful that he won a trip to Spain. The month after he returned, his production was down.

His manager said to him, "Larry, I know you built your business cold calling, and you're really good at it. But the day you stop cold calling is the day your business stops."

Larry told me later that those words had sent chills down his spine. He'd realized then that his work would never get easier and he'd be cold calling for the rest of his career. The operating principle seemed to be this: *Do what you hate and the money will follow.* Somehow, that didn't seem quite right. So Larry left the industry to find work he could enjoy.

Now a successful author and writing coach for the financial services industry, Larry has a passion for his work, and it seems almost effortless because it's so natural for him. Larry tells me writing energizes him, he's making tons of money, and he's having lots of fun now that his work requires less effort.

He was on to something: Massive, random activity is too much effort! In the past, you could survive—and maybe make a decent living—with traditional mass marketing techniques. Today, random prospecting, such as cold calling, is becoming less and less rewarding. To prosper in this new era, advisors must focus their energies on high payoff niches.

Look what this strategy has done for my friend, Hal. He's got it all: a loving wife, three wonderful kids, and a big house in one of the nicest areas of town. He drives a Lexus 400, enjoys his boat on weekends, and vacations in Europe. He earns $750,000 a year and has a multimillion-dollar net worth.

On top of all this, Hal works only 35 hours a week and takes six weeks off every year. He coaches his kids' soccer teams and spends lots of time with his family. At the age of 42—in the midst of a new phase in our industry—Hal has achieved the American dream: financial independence, personal freedom, and a high quality of life. He is one of the fortunate few.

Yet Hal wasn't born with a silver spoon in his mouth. He's not a senior executive in a high-tech company or a highly paid surgeon. Hal used to be a school teacher. Now he's a successful financial advisor—one of the new breed of independent entrepreneurs.

In the last years of the twentieth century, the financial services industry experienced rapid change. Today, major shifts continue to occur in the minds of your wealthy clients and prospects. Financial consumers are demanding much more for far less. Many of them are starting to seriously question whether traditional financial advisors add or subtract value. Many of them are deciding to manage their money themselves, trading their own accounts on the Internet.

Do you know how to harness this fundamental change? Or, as these winds of change blow against you, are you just rowing harder?

Most highly motivated financial professionals continue to market their products and services the same old way. They rely on endless hours of cold calling and expensive mass marketing campaigns. These tactics were always labor-intensive, but in today's more competitive marketplace, they're far less effective than alternative strategies. Because traditional marketing tactics require so much effort, many advisors decide to do nothing and just hope they get enough referrals to pay the bills.

The bottom line? If you continue to employ obsolete marketing strategies, you'll end up sacrificing your quality of life and your financial future. Or you'll decide, like Larry, to get out of the profession altogether because life as a financial advisor is just too hard.

Yet it doesn't have to be so difficult! In this book you'll learn how to harness the natural forces of the marketplace—improving your income and quality of life. Following my proven five-step strategy, you'll dominate your market while building a super-profitable financial services business and a wonderful life.

It's really very simple. There's only one marketing strategy uniquely suited for today's financial services market: *relationship-based niche marketing.* This book offers you an easy-to-follow approach for implementing this strategy. Follow the five-step process, and you will be successful.

How do I know? I've studied and lived marketing and sales for 25 years—nearly 18 of them in the financial services industry. For the first 15 years I marketed and sold everything from hot tubs to limited partnerships to charitable remainder trusts. I've always worked with sophisticated clients and financial advisors. For the last decade, I've worked one on one with successful advisors, helping them build stronger businesses and more rewarding lives. I've watched them as they implemented each step of the process, gradually building marketing machines that consistently generate a steady flow of qualified, motivated families who want and need their services—and are willing to pay for them.

The result: The advisors saw a tremendous boost in gross revenue. But just as important, they now enjoy an enhanced quality of life, free from the stress of long hours and arduous "grind it out" marketing. This book will save you a vast amount of time and energy. Invest a little time up front—to establish new processes—and your marketing will require much less effort during the rest of your career.

Who This Book Is For

This book is for seasoned successful financial professionals who want to systematically mine the most lucrative niches in their communities. It's also intended to be a training tool for newer financial professionals who are considering marketing for the first time, as well as a road map for those who've been marketing the hard way.

I wrote this book for those savvy advisors who are willing to transform their businesses to stay in alignment with the rapidly evolving consumer marketplace. If they follow this advice, they will reach greater success than they ever imagined. Advisors who already use these strategies are overwhelmed with opportunity.

Many of the advisors who work with me are surprised how truly easy our processes are to implement. In fact, they're frequently surprised by early results. All we are doing is getting into alignment with normal consumer behavior. Prospects' motivations and natural habits are the energy that drives our marketing machine.

It's important to point out, however, that these techniques are not for everyone. Although this book offers an easy-to-follow prescription for marketing, not every financial professional will complete the exercises and systemize the processes presented in this book. Advisors who are completely transaction-focused or excessively product- or performance-oriented may have a difficult time implementing this new approach (not that this means they shouldn't try).

What Effort-Less Marketing Can Do For You

The purpose of this book is to make you highly referable so you will consistently draw ideal new clients to your firm. My goal is to make you irresistibly attractive to your ideal clients, to make your marketing easier, requiring less of you—to make it *effort-less*. The book shows you how to do this by taking you through a five-step process. I'll introduce it in Chapter 2 and explain it in depth throughout the rest of the book. As you work your way through it, you'll reduce the barriers and increase your opportunities to consistently meet with friendly, eager, and ideal prospects.

The old way of thinking is that you have to work hard, pay your dues, make a lot of calls, and badger people to get them to buy your products. But this isn't the business you're in anymore. "How do we get people to buy the product?" is gradually being replaced with "How do we better serve our clients?"

The five-step process will give you a methodology for clarifying your personal values and goals, which will create the true north on your map to success. Clarity of purpose and values are powerful business assets.

You'll also learn a methodology for understanding the values and goals of your ideal clients. Then you'll learn the importance of putting the two in alignment. This process is a core competency: Align your interests, values, and resources with your targeted clients. Once you've mastered this, you're on your way to effort-less marketing.

If you follow the procedures I've set forth, not only will you transform your business, but you'll elevate the industry as well. Product pushing and commission-based selling are things of the past. My process takes that into account. It's based on the premise that fee-based advising is the model for a successful financial services business in the new millennium. In the pages that follow, you'll learn how to harness the market forces to drive your business to unimagined success.

To do that, you'll have to take your whole business to a new level of thinking.

In the future, I see financial advisors becoming "vision coaches" for their clients. This new breed of advisors will help clients define their life experiences by identifying core values and beliefs, determining the client's central purpose, setting goals, and formulating plans for the future. Then, using the financial and information resources available to them, these advisors will help their clients to turn their visions into reality.

This scenario is not as far in the future as it may sound. And best of all, you'll be there first . . . where the real action is . . . ahead of your competition!

Defining "Financial Advisor"

Throughout the book, I use the terms *financial professional* and *financial advisor* to represent a wide range of financial service providers. The traditional labels—stockbroker, insurance agent, financial planner, or investment advisor—are based on the products you sell. But we're going to use universal terms to remind us that your expertise, coaching, discipline, relationships, and service are the primary ways you add value for your clients. No matter which is your background, if you're client-centered, you'll come to the same conclusion about how you should design your business: It will be focused on your clients' wants and needs—not products.

How This Book Works for You

This book is designed to work on three levels. On first read, you'll begin to alter your thinking about your clients and your business. You'll absorb new information about what it takes to harness the market forces. You'll begin to visualize your future business.

The real value will come from the second level of understanding. The concepts will truly come alive as you go back and work through the exercises in each chapter.

The third level of value comes when you use the book as a reference as you begin to systemize the knowledge and processes into your business.

This book presents a series of short stories and analogies that illustrate either lessons I taught my clients or lessons my clients have taught me. The first half of the book explains the first four steps in the five-step process. These are the strategic, "getting ready" steps. The second half of the book focuses on step five: the tactical processes of communicating your benefits and attracting great new clients. These are the "taking action" tactics. You'll notice a shift from a more conceptual approach in the first half to a more hands-on, "how to" approach in the second half.

No doubt you deal with information overload on a daily basis. To make your life easier, this book shares with you the results of exhaustive research I've conducted over the last 25 years. I've worked with hundreds of top-producing financial advisors who have super-profitable businesses and wonderful lives.

You'll learn key success factors that highly innovative financial marketers have taught me. You'll also benefit from my extensive knowledge about wealthy niche markets and prospects. For example, you'll take advantage of my investigation of 400 occupations as you select your target market segments from the top 20 I recommend.

Don't let the information provided to describe these niches overwhelm you. As you take your first pass, feel free to skip over data that relates to markets that don't interest you. The information will always be there for reference.

Also in the interest of preventing further information overload, since you're already experienced with the sales process, this book does not tell you how to deliver a sales presentation. Instead, it tells you everything you need to do and say up until that point. In other words, the book tells you how to identify and attract qualified, motivated prospects.

Implement the Strategies Over Time

You may want to do a few specific exercises right away and save other exercises for later. This is fine if you want to implement this process gradually. If you consistently implement these ideas over a two- to three-year period, it will totally transform your business.

But keep one point in mind: If you do the tactical steps (the exercises) without the strategic (the thinking and planning), the process won't be nearly as effective. The same goes for the other way around. But when you combine the exercises with the thinking, your business will experience a fundamental change: It will become effort-less.

Also be patient. It takes a while to make everything work—as long as a year or even two to get through all five steps. So don't become discouraged if it seems like you're not getting anywhere at first. You're just experiencing the learning curve. Often you must expend 80 percent of the energy to get 20 percent of the desired results. Then by completing the final 20 percent, you generate the remaining 80 percent of the results.

People often feel resistance when learning something new. A little voice says, "This will never work," or "This is too hard," or "I just can't see myself doing that." This feeling of discomfort is actually a good sign because, to get radically different results, you need radically different strategies and tactics. That voice is telling you that you're challenging yourself to do something different.

So persevere! It'll start slowly and build and build and build. In the end, you'll make more money and have more fun than you ever imagined possible. You'll partner with your clients so you can both achieve your respective goals. You'll reduce the barriers for people doing business with you. You'll release your brakes, removing internal blocks that can keep you from being successful. And you'll never have to work hard for meager results again. Business will come to you effort-lessly.

I know I'm promising a lot. But my associates and I consistently transform our clients' businesses and their lives in 12 to 18 months using these processes in our coaching program. Try, and you will prevail. I'll be by your side, and the market forces will be with us.

Let's get started!

Discover the Secret of Effort-Less Marketing

I n ancient times, Mediterranean fishermen built simple boats to conduct trade between city-states. But rowing heavily laden vessels was strenuous work, especially when the prevailing winds were strong.

Harness the market forces.

Then around 2000 B.C., the Phoenicians learned how to harness the wind using sails. With this addition, their sailing vessels transported goods to faraway ports with little effort, and the new technology enabled them to dominate their trade area. *They became wealthy beyond measure by under-standing and using natural forces.*

In short, they discovered how to work smarter rather than harder. Today's financial professionals can learn a valuable lesson from the Phoenicians: Less effort can actually result in greater power. In our industry's terms, *effort-less* equals more efficient production success.

Section Preview

- Learn the three stages through which all industries evolve.
- Know which stage the financial services industry is now entering.
- Discover how old marketing and sales tactics are becoming obsolete.

- Work with the forces, rather than against them, to develop your business "effort-lessly."
- Preview the "5 Steps to a Super-Profitable Business and a Wonderful Life."

Powerful Forces Are Reshaping the Industry

It is not the strongest of the species that survives, nor the most intelligent; it is the one that is most adaptable to change.

—Charles Darwin, 19th-century English naturalist and author, *The Origin of Species*

In 1981, the "rookie of the year" in my office built his business by mass-mailing postcards to upscale neighborhoods. His simple mailer featured a tax-free bond fund and tear-off reply card prospects could mail back to request more information. The flood of bounce-back cards generated from this marketing tactic laid the foundation of my colleague's early success.

Almost 15 years later, a financial advisor in the same city used exactly the same mailer and a similar mailing list. But the postcard bombed! He made zero sales and collected only a few unqualified leads. Most telling, six angry prospects demanded to be taken off his mailing list.

What happened? Why do many marketing tactics fail today after having worked extremely well in the past?

A fundamental change is taking place in the financial services industry. In today's more demanding marketplace, traditional marketing tactics are out of date. Mass marketing, public seminars, and cold calling are expensive and require a great deal of effort. What's more, these tactics often yield a meager harvest of low-quality prospects and time-wasting information seekers.

Why? Financial consumers today are more sophisticated than they were 10 or 15 years ago. They know more, and they demand greater value. Many of them are gun-shy after being burned by big promises in the past.

Changing consumer demand drives industry evolution. What causes consumers to change their attitudes and perceptions? Two things. First, they gain more shopping experience and product knowledge. Second, an increase in the supply of products and services gives them more power. If you understand these phenomena, you can capitalize on them. You can stay on the leading edge of the value curve. If you don't keep up, your margins and clients will both disappear.

How the Industry Life Cycle Works

All consumers become more critical as they become better informed users of the services or products they're buying. Some purchasers experience buyer's remorse, the pang of doubt that makes them wonder if they got the best deal or bought the right product. Typically, this post-purchase angst and evaluation makes them more cautious consumers in the future.

An interesting parallel to consumer behavior in the financial services industry can be found in the computer industry. When did you buy your first personal computer? Back in the mid-1980s? Didn't you need a substantial amount of help from salespeople to determine exactly which computer to buy?

You've probably purchased a couple of computers since then. You've learned that the brands are essentially the same. They all get the job done. If you're like most consumers, when you buy your next computer, you'll probably look primarily for the best price.

In your mind, the computer is a commodity and the salesperson is a time waster. You already know what you want: reliable, cheap computer

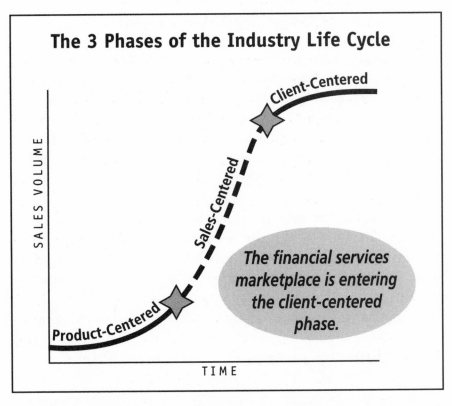

The 3 Phases of the Industry Life Cycle

SALES VOLUME

Client-Centered

Sales-Centered

Product-Centered

The financial services marketplace is entering the client-centered phase.

TIME

power. The specific products aren't important. But getting your network to run smoothly is extremely important.

What has become valuable is the expertise of the computer network technicians. They have the brainpower to provide the total solution to your computer needs. That's what we all want: someone to help us competently and completely. That's where the value is today. Not in the product, but in the expert guidance, advice, management and information systems, as well as personal service.

As consumers move through the learning curve, they start to behave in new ways, driving an industry through different phases. (See "Do You Recognize Today's Market?" on page 13 for an overview.) All industries go through three major phases: the product-centered phase, the sales-centered phase, and the client-centered phase. It doesn't matter whether you're selling computers, financial services, or anything else.

The Product-Centered Phase

In phase one, companies begin by focusing on creating a viable product. During this *product-centered phase*, management must focus on production: working the bugs out and "building a better mousetrap."

When manufacturers (or service providers) hit on products their customers want, their businesses take off. Demand outstrips supply. Just having a decent product puts the manufacturer in the power position. Consumers take what they can get, paying whatever the manufacturer demands.

Case in point: Consider the popularity of the Ford Model T. Henry Ford said, "You can have any color you want—as long as it's black." Closer to home, another example is the Brooklyn bond-closing technique: "Mrs. Jones, the bonds are paying seven percent. Do you want the bonds, or what?"

The product-centered phase of the modern financial services industry started in the early 1980s. You may remember the good old days of tax shelters and have fond memories of the time when financial planning and tax sheltering investments pretty much sold themselves. The reason life was so easy: tantalizing product benefits, such as three-to-one tax write-offs. If you could take orders, you could make money.

During those heady times, the most effective marketing strategy for financial professionals was to stress economic benefits. Advisors showed how their products and services could improve their clients' bottom lines. The color charts and graphs these advisors used were too compelling for most prospects to resist.

In the United States, the Tax Reform Act of 1986 brought this phase of the tax shelter industry to a screeching halt. But the American financial services industry (including financial planners, insurance agents, and stockbrokers) was on a roll. There was an army of salespeople on the lookout for a *hot new product* to sell. The bull market in stocks made mutual funds the obvious candidate.

The Sales-Centered Phase

As an industry grows, consumers have more options. In phase two of its life cycle, competition forces manufacturers to aggressively seek new customers, and smart companies focus on sales and distribution. During this *sales-centered phase*, the salesperson is king. Delivering the product to the end user takes up most of the industry's energy. A rush to grab marketshare dominates conversations in the boardrooms of the product manufacturers.

In the 1980s, evidence in our industry of the shift from product-centered to sales-centered strategies was staggering. Almost overnight the industry exploded with mutual fund offerings.

At the time, I was on the front lines doing marketing for a financial planning and investment advisory firm in Phoenix, Arizona. Our strong direct-response newspaper ads packed our seminars and filled my associates' appointment calendars. Our biggest challenge was convincing reticent prospects that our products were going to outperform their existing holdings. Potential clients already knew the economic benefits, so we competed on product features and performance.

The product-centered phase had ended, but we didn't know it. Most of us made the transition without realizing it. Our focus simply moved from one product to another. But we could no longer just take orders, we actually had to sell. The people who couldn't sell left the industry.

There was a side-effect to this shift in products: Tax shelters were designed for the elite, but mutual funds and annuities were for everyone. Our little industry exploded and woke up the slumbering insurance and mutual fund industries. Financial services blossomed into a mass-market phenomenon. We had a new version of Henry Ford's dream of "a car in every garage"; we hoped to put a mutual fund in every portfolio.

Savvy marketers used mass media and direct mail to get the message to as many people as possible. In the sales-centered phase, the successful salespeople were transaction-focused. They compared product features and performance specs. They used technical expertise to close deals. And if they could offer a wide range of hot products, they stood to earn high incomes. It's great to be a super-salesperson in this phase of the cycle.

The Client-Centered Phase

As any market expands, increased volume, competition and new technology push down prices. In phase three of the industry life cycle, with lower prices come increased consumption until the market is saturated. Distribution channels clog, inventories back up, and profits drop.

Once supply slightly exceeds demand, the power shifts from the producers to the consumers. This marks the beginning of the *client-centered phase*. During this phase, consumers seek the best deal. Products are driven to extremely low margins, and consumers are well aware that salespeople are paid to sell.

Product-oriented salespeople in any industry lose their clout during the client-centered phase. Technicians don't add much value because product information is readily available to everyone. With the help of the Internet, serious consumers know almost as much as the most experienced sales professionals.

And once these savvy customers have purchased a specific product four or five times, they start to wonder why they need a salesperson at all. They know they can save a few bucks by going direct to the manufacturer—trading on the Internet, for example. In the client-centered phase, the sales force that was taught to "always be closing" finds their best prospects are "always avoiding salespeople."

At this stage, smart manufacturers and salespeople shift their focus from products to customers. In the client-centered phase, salespeople can no longer make above-average incomes by simply distributing products. So the traditional product salesperson must look for new ways to add value.

But different consumers define value in different ways. When markets reach saturation, prospects tend to divide into two major segments: 1) those who want the lowest price and 2) those who want the greatest value. Those who want the lowest price are content to interview numerous salespeople as a form of research and then buy a product based solely on price, often excluding every one of the salespeople they consulted.

In financial services, the low-price seekers are no-load buyers and financial do-it-yourselfers. They are turning to the World Wide Web for advice and to purchase financial products.

On the other hand, financial consumers who want the greatest value will pay for products and services when a salesperson (or advisor) demonstrates the ability to add value beyond the core product. Clearly, the concept of added value has already been introduced with mutual funds. That's why so many advisors are now offering asset allocation and investment management services. They are actually giving the products away for free and charging for their advice and ongoing services.

The very best clients—those with a lot of money who are willing to pay for your services—want a trustworthy advisor who puts clients' interests first. And today's savvy financial consumers want more than just investment and insurance products. They want a total solution to their financial problems, and they want to be pampered in some meaningful way that enhances their life.

This is why the new concept in financial services is *comprehensive wealth management*. This evolving business model encompasses investment management, financial planning, estate planning, business coaching, and a host of other professional services. My good friend, John Bowen, president and CEO of Assante Capital Management, Inc., U.S., refers to this business model as becoming your clients' "personal CFO" (chief financial officer).

Align With Your Clients— Grow Deep Roots in Fertile Soil

In 1984, I overheard one broker say to another, "Gee, I'm kind of out of ideas. What are you working on?" The second broker told him about a bond from Paradise, California. He told him the maturity and the coupon rate. And the first broker said, "Ah, that's neat. I think I'll work on that after lunch."

I realized I had just eavesdropped on a high-level marketing planning meeting in the financial services industry. That type of product-centered cold calling approach worked at that time. In fact, a lot of people made a lot of money with that tactic back then. But today, it's wasted effort. Most wealthy clients won't even talk to cold callers.

I like to compare traditional mass marketing tactics to a hunting and gathering economy. I call this the "hoping to get lucky" school of marketing. There has never been a hunting and gathering society that's achieved great wealth. And just as many of those communities evolved over time into agricultural societies, successful advisors will make the transition to the client-centered phase.

An agricultural economy is more sophisticated than a hunting and gathering one. It requires more time and commitment to cut down the trees, till the earth, plant the seeds, and tend the garden. But this preparation enables you to grow deep roots in fertile soil and enjoy an abundant harvest year after year.

In today's marketplace, the gatherers have picked all the low hanging fruit. Those who settle for this approach will face pretty slim pickings from here on out.

Those financial advisors who have taken the time to develop their markets, cultivate relationships in targeted niches, build their expertise, and move to a more sophisticated approach are reaping an abundant harvest. They've planted deep roots in fertile soil. Now they are cultivating their niches. And they're marketing effort-lessly. They're having fun working with people they like and doing what they love doing. Wealthy clients are lining up to do business with them.

Making the transition from the product-centered phase to the sales-centered phase is relatively easy because the focus stays internal and product-oriented. Reengineering a sales-centered business into a client-centered business, however, is an enormous undertaking. This transition forces the industry to turn its attention away from the product and start focusing on its clients. This shift requires a new way of thinking and acting.

The shift is so extreme that no industry has ever made it without major denial, resistance, and upheaval. In fact, no industry has ever moved into the client-centered phase voluntarily.

A classic example is the U.S. automobile industry. For years it resisted asking clients what they wanted. Instead, it dictated to the customers what

Do You Recognize Today's Market?

	PRODUCT-CENTERED	SALES-CENTERED	CLIENT-CENTERED
The Product	"Ours is the only one."	"Ours will outperform," and "We have a product for everyone."	"Ours comes with value-added service."
Supply and Demand	Demand exceeds supply (clients are a captive audience).	Supply and demand are in equilibrium.	Supply exceeds demand.
Margins	Margins are high.	Margins drop; consumers begin to cut out intermediaries.	Margins are low or nonexistent.
Key Driver	Consumers have unmet demands.	Consumers have options and they're more experienced; they want a better deal.	Consumers are more sophisticated. Now they want either 1) the lowest price or 2) the greatest value.
Primary Focus	Create a viable product; tweak features; produce.	Sell as many units as possible; distribute; use new technology.	Strengthen relationship; get larger share of wallet.
Key Value	Product (Stress availability.)	Sales/distribution (Stress product benefits.)	Personalized service and emotional payoffs (Stress total solution.)
Salespeople	Order-takers	Aggressive, always closing, hungry	Advisors, counselors, coaches, behavior modifiers
Marketing	Minimal (People who can benefit will find you.)	Mass marketing	Referrals and niche-focused

cars they could buy. It was clearly product- and sales-centered. Then the Japanese competition came in, listened to customers, gave them what they wanted, and grabbed a huge chunk of marketshare. In response, the U.S. auto industry is becoming client-centered.

The market ultimately dictates that you either change or suffer a rapid and painful decline. The transformation of our industry will precipitate tremendous structural shifts in the very foundation of financial services. Everything is on the table. Fortunes will be made and lost as we navigate the most profound changes in the modern financial services industry.

To thrive in the client-centered phase, you must make the transition from product-centered selling to client-centered marketing. You must design your business around the wants and needs of your ideal clients— not around your need to generate income.

Today, much of the value you add is in your knowledge, caring, coaching, disciplined structure, and ability to make your clients feel everything is under control. This is often difficult for a product-oriented salesperson to understand. While the salesperson focuses on the fine points of passive versus active management, modern portfolio theory, and other esoteric issues, the client wants peace of mind, a feeling of security, and freedom from the responsibilities of dealing with the complexities of his or her personal finances.

No matter how difficult it is at first, you have to make the transition from being sales-centered to being client-centered. To compete in today's market, you must overhaul your business and align your marketing with the wants and needs of your prospects and clients.

Remember: Harness the Market Forces

Buckminster Fuller was a brilliant designer of the early twentieth century. He is best known for dubbing our planet "Spaceship Earth" and for designing the geodesic dome, which is a roundish structure. You've probably seen the one at Epcot Center in Orlando, Florida.

What's important about the geodesic dome is its construction is the only one known to mankind that gets stronger as it gets larger. Fuller created this amazing structure by figuring out how to apply weight and gravity to his advantage instead of working to defeat them. Based on what he learned in building it, he wisely counseled, "Use the forces. Don't fight them."

Effort-less marketing works on the same principle. What are the dominant forces in today's financial services market? You saw them in "Do You Recognize Today's Market?" on page 13. All of the descriptors of the client-centered phase are at play here. In short, the customer is king, and clients value exceptional service, relationships, professional advice, and emotional payoffs above product features.

When you start with these assumptions, it makes sense to build a business focused on your clients. You may think you already have such a business. But the truth is you probably don't even know what your individual clients want most out of life and from their money. You may not even be aware of what truly motivates you.

Think about this: Are you an expert in the products and services you sell? Does your sales process involve grinding through large numbers of strangers hoping to get lucky? Do you feel like your job mostly consists of chasing prospects? Are you still a salesperson?

Or have you carefully identified the types of people you truly enjoy helping? Are you an expert in the intimate details of your clients' wants and needs? Have you reconfigured your business to meet those wants and needs? Do you find your business automatically attracts ideal clients? Have you become a client-centered advisor?

If the first description sounds more like you, you're in the same boat with most financial advisors. But the good news is you're on the right track with this book. You'll learn how to revitalize your business model, aligning it with today's market forces. Then you'll be able to harness the tremendous power and motivation of investors and insurance consumers.

Today's Business Challenges

Market factors make it tough for financial advisors to achieve their goals by traditional means as the industry shifts from a sales-centered to a client-centered orientation. Three significant changes are starting to occur.

1. Increasing competition: Accounting firms offer asset management, banks sell annuities, online discount brokers' advertisements are everywhere—even airlines offer mutual funds. Financial consumers have more options and are more selective than ever. Competition has never been tougher, and it gets worse every day.

2. Declining commission compensation: Reduced income means financial advisors have to sell almost twice the volume of products today just to earn the same amount of money they did a few years ago. Factor in a small amount for ever-present inflation, and you'll find that advisors have to run hard just to stay in place.

3. Skeptical consumers: It seems the media and many consumers view most financial advisors as hustlers. This makes it difficult for knowledgeable, trustworthy advisors to break through the fear and reach the people who want and need their help.

These factors force advisors' incomes down while expenses keep going up. To create a super-profitable business in this client-centered phase, advisors must take their business model through a major shift.

Work Smarter, Not Harder

Even though the consumer market has shifted to the client-centered phase, most financial advisors, as well as the managers of many firms, haven't acknowledged the change yet. Most haven't recognized that a major structural transformation is taking place in the financial services industry. Companies must take radical actions to keep from being permanently left behind.

Advisors try to overcome these changes by working harder—making more calls, sending out more letters, placing more ads, and conducting more seminars. They're responding to the changes in the market with the same old tactics, only this time around they're spending more money and effort. These remnants of a past era are no longer cost- or energy-effective in the current market climate.

The traditional industry prescription for dealing with a difficult market is more effort. My prescription is to work smarter, not harder. My solution is to do some initial thinking and learning, and then design an intelligent plan based on market information. It's a strategic approach rather than a tactical approach. What the client-centered market requires is a fundamental change in the retail financial services business model. If you make the change—essentially shifting your focus from products to clients—you'll find yourself with an *effort-less* marketing plan rather than one that's *effort-ful.*

In the old days it was a lot easier. Even if you had an inefficient approach to marketing, it worked. Today, because it's a tougher market, you have to work smarter. Working harder isn't going to get the job done.

You have to be more sophisticated for all the reasons noted in "Today's Business Challenges" on the previous page. Increasing competition, declining commissions, and rising skepticism among consumers means you have to be far more productive today than ever before just to make the same money. And it's just about impossible to make any real progress with obsolete tactics.

The five steps outlined in the next chapter are the solution you're looking for.

5 Rules You Need to Know

Today's financial advisors fail to understand five marketing mandates. All companies—from mom-and-pop shops to Fortune 500 corporations—need to abide by these marketing rules. These rules embody the new challenges encountered as an industry enters the client-centered phase of the industry life cycle. These marketing rules, of course, need to be customized for each particular industry. For the financial services industry, the rules can be applied as follows.

1. Develop a long-term vision and plan. Most advisors focus on short-term prospecting activities instead of long-term business-building strategies. They hunt for the next hot product that will propel them to success. But success comes only when you have a clear vision of what you want and an intelligent plan to achieve it. It comes from the inside, not the outside.

2. Establish a systematic lead-generating process. A business lives or dies by its ability to attract customers or clients. Advisors who achieve the greatest success are often not the most technically competent or the best salespeople. They're the best marketers. Developing a process for consistently generating leads from ideal prospects is imperative.

3. Restructure to generate recurring revenue. All businesses have two goals: to maintain positive cash flow and to build equity for the future. Recurring revenue—predictable income that regenerates itself without further effort from you—can solve both challenges.

Running a commission-based business makes it impossible to establish recurring revenue. This compensation structure forces advisors to start with zero income at the beginning of every month. One advisor told me he was getting really tired of having to "kill something every month so I can feed my family."

4. **Focus on people rather than products.** Financial professionals have become product experts, but they don't study the subconscious hopes, dreams, and fears that motivate their clients to act. The next generation of financial service entrepreneurs will need to know much more about their customers.

5. **Specialize in a target niche.** In many professions, such as law and medicine, practitioners have responded to information overload by specializing. But most financial advisors are still generalists. They believe the key to success is to be all things to all people. This mass-market mentality is a prescription for mediocrity and ultimately failure in the client-centered marketplace.

If you want to specialize in such services as estate planning or qualified plans, that's fine. But you must focus your marketing efforts on the specific groups of people or niches that can benefit most from your specialized services.

The Opportunity Gap

The client-centered phase of the industry life cycle offers unique challenges to financial advisors. But these challenges can be met. Hal (the friend I wrote about in the introduction) is proof that there's huge growth potential for client-focused financial service professionals.

Never before have so many people controlled so much money as right now. Downsizing, rollovers, stock options, IPOs, inheritances, business sales, and stock market performance have driven worldwide wealth through the roof.

According to some experts, one new millionaire is created every four minutes in the United States. Couple this explosion of new wealth with the fact that more than 76 million baby boomers need to invest for their retirement. You can see there's a tremendous demand for personal financial advice.

This market of the newly rich and those approaching retirement is comprised of tens of millions of people. Many of them want and need help planning and implementing the best investment and insurance strategies for their unique situations. And the more money they have, the more help they need from a competent financial advisor.

The financial services industry is the only industry I know that allows a person with little or no capital to create any income level and any lifestyle he or she chooses. What a tremendous opportunity! That's what makes the financial services industry one of the most rewarding on earth.

Despite the challenges, right now is a great time to be a financial advisor. By capitalizing on current conditions, it's certainly possible for you to make your fortune. Then why, in the middle of this huge explosion of opportunity, do so many financial advisors fail to achieve their income potential? Some of the failure can be blamed on not fulfilling client expectations. But the lion's share of the blame should be placed on ineffective marketing practices.

If you apply all five steps outlined in this book, you'll reduce the resistance that keeps wealthy clients from working with you. You'll harness the market forces to attract ideal clients effort-lessly, they'll surrender their business to you, and you won't have to chase them anymore.

Chapter at a Glance

Many professionals in the insurance and securities industries are still mentally in the product-centered and sales-centered phases. But their best clients are moving into the client-centered phase.

It's important to understand that you can't escape these monumental changes. They're driven by human nature and consumer behavior. Consumers drive all industries through these three major phases: 1) product-centered, 2) sales-centered, and 3) client-centered. There are powerful market forces at work here that you simply cannot ignore.

At the same time, there's huge opportunity today for competent, client-centered financial advisors. The market of wealthy financial service consumers is growing rapidly. You can create any type of business and any lifestyle you want in the fast-changing financial services industry. But first there are some real challenges you must overcome.

Despite the amazing opportunity that exists for financial professionals, many never achieve true success. And many others who do make it, achieve success by sacrificing their quality of life. Advisors are underachieving because they're using outdated marketing tactics. Issues that limit success include

- no long-term business vision,
- focusing on products rather than people and relationships,
- failure to specialize or to become attractive,
- no systematic qualified lead generating processes, and
- little or no recurring revenue.

By aligning your business with market forces rather than resisting them, you can overcome these limitations. If you understand consumer behavior and the impact it has on the financial services industry, you can ride each successive phase to ever-higher levels of success.

Turn to the next chapter to learn how.

5 Steps to a Super-Profitable Business and a Wonderful Life

Sales is trying to get people to want what you have. Marketing is having what people want.

—Don Hobbs, chairman, Hobbs Herder Advertising

ow is it that some people seem to attract success, while others constantly pursue it ? One part of the equation is the difference between marketing and selling. The marketer strategizes and effort-lessly attracts great clients; the salesperson endlessly chases them.

Approaching your business from a marketing point of view means that if you are offering what your ideal clients want—and they know it—*they* will contact *you*. Their motivations and not yours will drive the sales process.

It's important to respect the market forces throughout the stages of the industry life cycle. But truly responding to these forces becomes mandatory in the client-centered phase. When offering value-added service to clients is the name of the game, you must know what motivates people. Sales tactics alone will not work. The real challenge lies in identifying and attracting new clients who are both wealthy and predisposed to see value in your service.

By following the five steps introduced in this chapter, you'll be able to work with the types of people you enjoy most. You'll vacation when and where you want. And you'll have total control over your life and your time.

Marketing vs. Sales

Many financial advisors confuse marketing with selling. Although they are related, they are substantially different. For our purposes, marketing is everything that happens before advisors come face to face with a prospect. It's about developing strategies to identify and attract specifically targeted prospects. Marketing is also about offering what those ideal prospects want.

Selling, on the other hand, is the act of persuading prospects to want what you are offering. Selling often involves "chasing" reluctant prospects and convincing them to buy. Traditional selling is a one-on-one process of helping a prospect make a decision and take action.

The following example clarifies this critical difference. The sales manager asks, "How can I move this product?" The marketing manager asks, "How can I best serve this group of people?"

Introducing the 5 Steps

After years of watching financial advisors at work, I've found that the most successful ones have a common method for consistently getting face to face with qualified, motivated prospects. They may not know it, but they all go through five steps.

I developed this model during my first 13 years in the business after looking for the most successful strategies of top producers. I then analyzed and refined the strategies over the past five years as I worked with financial professionals in my coaching program. The advisors who work with me fondly refer to it as "The Moeller Method." I like to call it "The Five Steps to a Super-Profitable Business and a Wonderful Life."

If you're looking for a silver bullet or a magic wand to bring you success, my method is the closest thing you'll ever find. I firmly believe the methods you are about to learn are the most effective available.

These five steps create the foundation for a successful client acquisition and satisfaction plan. You'll need to work through all of them, possibly over the course of a year or two or even more, to complete the program. But by the time you finish, you will see a dramatic change in your business. Wealthy, motivated new clients will come to you effort-lessly.

We will cover each of the five marketing steps in detail in Chapters 3 through 19. But to get started, here's a summary of the steps in the process.

1. Create Your Inspiring Vision of Success

Walt Disney once said, "When your values are clear, your decisions are easy." Having a clear, inspiring mission and written goals are two critical tools for success. Visualizing desired outcomes helps you establish direction and criteria for effective decision making. By looking into the future and planning backward, you can build your business with a distinct purpose in mind. Doing what you're good at while focusing on a distant goal is the surest way to maintain forward progress to success.

2. Target Profitable Niches

One of the keys to success is to select your clients carefully. Not everyone will enjoy the same level of benefits from your services and products. By focusing on the top five to ten percent of the households, you can selectively work with the clients who will benefit the most. These are the well-to-do clients who face major financial challenges and need the help and guidance of a financial professional.

You'll find these qualified, motivated prospects in thousands of "rich niches." But you won't find them just anywhere. In fact, if you don't target profitable niches, you'll end up trying to be all things to all people. And you'll end up with an inefficient business that may be more of a liability than an asset.

3. Research to Discover
New Opportunities

Market intelligence is your secret weapon. Before you can capitalize on opportunities, you must first find them. By identifying where wealth is concentrated, being transferred, or being gathered, you can focus your marketing resources where they'll generate the highest return. Specialized knowledge allows you to create compelling messages that attract your ideal prospects. In this section, you'll learn how to gather the information you need by conducting research interviews with your clients, centers of influence, and referrals.

4. Position to Attract
Ideal New Clients

Positioning is the art of controlling perceptions. It's also a promise of the benefits you provide. As you move from selling products to selling yourself, your clients' perceptions are critical.

Consumers often lump all financial advisors into the category of product pushers. If you want to be perceived as different from and better than your competitors, you'll need to out-position them.

The ideal position is to be seen as a knowledgeable, trustworthy advisor with specialized problem-solving skills.

5. Communicate Your Benefits Effectively

Once you have targeted profitable niches, identified specific opportunities, and positioned yourself to attract your predetermined prospects, you need to let them know about you and your wonderful services. Your goal is to get the right message sent through the right channels to the right people at the right time. If you can promise and deliver what your ideal clients want, the market will provide rich rewards far beyond the effort you invest.

Where to Begin

Most successful advisors want to start at step five, of course. They want to get right to the point and start communicating.

If you're inclined to agree, let me stop you for a moment. I have two questions: What do you want to say? Who do you want to say it to?

When you decide to invest your time and money to market your business, you must make some important decisions. Unfortunately, there are no shortcuts. The five-step process is the fastest and easiest way to build a super-successful business, which is far better than just making sales.

The process is like building a high-rise office tower. The first thing the builders do is dig a hole in the ground. A person who isn't familiar with the building process may well say, "Hey, you're going about this the wrong way! You've been working for three weeks, and all you have is a hole in the ground." But, when the builders get to the right depth, they'll pour a solid foundation.

In the same way, the first four steps of the effort-less marketing process create a solid foundation for successfully designing and positioning your business. These steps are largely concerned with helping you focus your business on your clients.

To conduct your marketing effort-lessly—in other words, to work with the current consumer behavior instead of against it—you *must* be client-centered. In the sales-centered phase, you drove the process through your desire to make a commission. In the client-centered phase, it's the client's eagerness for payoffs and results that drives the process.

But *effort-less marketing* does not mean that you put in zero effort. It simply means that you use your effort more efficiently. Just as in gardening, there's preparation and effort before there is reward.

Chapter at a Glance

Marketing is a strategy for identifying and attracting qualified, motivated prospects. *Sales* is the process of converting these prospects into clients. Most advisors are trying to sell without any effective marketing plans. Break away from this old way of thinking. Study consumer behavior and the market forces at work. Build these factors into your marketing plan. Harness them to build your business.

To effort-lessly build a super-profitable business, you must follow the five-step process for attracting qualified, motivated prospects:

1. Create your inspiring vision of success.
2. Target profitable niches.
3. Research to discover new opportunities.
4. Position yourself to attract ideal new clients.
5. Communicate your benefits effectively to your targeted prospects.

Step 1

Create Your Inspiring Vision of Success

When Alice came to the fork in the road, she asked the Cheshire cat, "Would you tell me, please, which way I ought to go from here?"

"That depends a good deal on where you want to get to," said the cat.

"I don't much care where," said Alice.

"Then it doesn't matter which way you go," said the cat.

If you don't know where you're going, don't be surprised if you end up somewhere you didn't expect. Most advisors don't know where they want to end up, so they ask, "Which is the easy road?" That's the wrong question if you want to build a super-profitable business and a wonderful life. In this book, you'll learn to ask yourself, *Where do I want to end up, and which road will take me where I want to go?*

You'll always know which road to take.

The most important thing you can do to grow your business is to develop clarity of purpose. You need to take some time to visualize your future in specific detail. Then, once you've fixed on the image of your future, it will become a beacon directing you to your dreams. I call the image your emotional lighthouse. With it you'll always know which road to take on your personal journey to success.

You'll learn about this first step in Chapter 3, "Live Your Life on Purpose." Once you've worked through the exercises in this chapter, you'll be amazed to discover you have developed a set of personal values and objectives that will inspire you far more than any sales goal ever could.

Section Preview

- Clarify what you want from your business life and your personal life.

- See how your vision can be an emotional lighthouse to guide you toward your ideal future.

- Understand how *living life on purpose* is much less stressful than *living life by chance*.

- Make informed decisions—including which clients to work with and which projects and strategies represent the best use of your time and resources.

Live Your Life
on Purpose

Catch the dream. See your own success.
Think in ideals. Envision a good future.
And it will happen.

—Lou Tice, American management expert and success coach

I n the mid-1980s, an advisor I knew built a large financial planning firm in the midwestern U.S. At one point, he had five offices, 25 employees, and was grossing more than $1 million a year. He was constantly winning production awards from his broker/dealer. But he wasn't having any fun.

In fact, he was working more than 90 hours a week, was completely stressed out, and his family life was in shambles. On top of all that, he was netting only $75,000 a year. He was sacrificing his quality of life to his business. But his business was never satisfied. It kept wanting more and more of him.

My friend eventually walked away from his dysfunctional business and left it to his partner. He was happy just to get out from under all the liabilities.

Dan, another advisor, built a company that nets him more than $300,000 a year. His business is worth well over $600,000. He works out of an executive suite and has no employees. He works short weeks and has plenty of spare time. In fact, in the five years since he started his business, he has earned an MBA from a major university.

Dan's business is thriving because he started with a vision. He had a clear idea of a sound business model that would support his ideal life experience. His vision has become a reality. Dan is now able to do the things he likes most.

After working with hundreds of financial advisors for more than a decade, I have learned that the *structure* and *design* of a business are critical. Some business models work extremely well. But the majority of business models in use today will never generate the financial independence, personal freedom, and quality of life their owners seek.

Set a Course for the Future of Your Choice

What's the difference between a financial advisor who works for years and eventually burns out and an advisor who creates a super-profitable business that supports a wonderful life? The difference lies in the ability to exercise a unique attribute only human beings have: *creative imagination.*

You possess the most wonderful computer in the world right between your ears. But without a clear and inspiring vision of success, you won't be able to tap its tremendous power. Your creative imagination gives you the ability to decide ahead of time what success looks and feels like—for you.

The ability to define the possibilities, and then see those possibilities grow into an ideal situation, is a uniquely human gift. When you have a clear path to follow, each success leads you closer to your ultimate goal. You build on a growing foundation of relationships, resources, markets, knowledge, and goodwill. You are the master of your own destiny, the builder of a legacy.

Advisors who don't have a clear vision of the type of business they want will often sell anything just to make a buck. This "easy" approach actually requires a great deal of effort.

My father is a perfect example of someone who didn't have a clear vision of what he wanted out of life. He lived his days based on what he assumed other people wanted from him.

Dad was an orthodontist and hated almost every minute of his career. Yet he pursued that occupation because he didn't think my mother's parents would respect him if he followed his passion and became an architect and builder.

After 20 years of doing work that stressed him out, Dad developed rheumatoid arthritis in his hands and was forced to sell his practice. He died five years later, cutting short his freedom from a profession that had held him down all of his adult life. Since he hadn't identified what he really wanted, he'd ended up living for other people—working toward someone else's goals.

Find Your Endorphin Zone™

It doesn't have to be this way. If you're "in alignment" with who you are, with what you're supposed to be doing, and with how you're supposed to be helping people, finding success and happiness is not hard. Once you discover the authentic you, life becomes easier. It flows. Everything works the way it's supposed to work. Solving problems becomes intuitive. You know exactly what to do.

When you are doing the things you're naturally good at, life is easy and fun. When you have the sense that everything is working the way it should and you're feeling no stress, no worries, and no pain, when you're in alignment with your natural talents, I call that the "Endorphin Zone." Instead of stress, you experience a calming sense of peace and even joy.

The concept of an Endorphin Zone is a take-off on the feeling athletes experience when they achieve a runner's high. All of a sudden, their pain goes away and they have a wonderful sense of peace and calm. Most important, what once seemed difficult now seems easy or effort-less.

Your work and your life can be a great source of joy and happiness—or of stress. It's up to you. You create your life experience with the choices you make (or don't make).

Success Starts With an Inspiring Vision

Without a clear and inspiring picture of the results you want to achieve and the life you want to live, you'll never reach your true potential to live in your Endorphin Zone. With clarity of purpose comes commitment, and with commitment come results.

Many people make a good income, but they sacrifice their quality of life in the process. This happened to me. I tripled my income in one year as an investment wholesaler, but the work was extremely hard and not meaningful to me. I had the money, but I didn't have the personal payoff. Then I started my company, American Business Visions. It was slow going at first, but now I have both the money *and* the sense of meaning and purpose. I live in my Endorphin Zone.

You can make a modest living just being yourself, making friends, and helping them get what they want out of life. But you don't have to settle for just getting by. You can create the business success and life experience you want.

You live in a world of abundance. All you have to do is define what you want, focus on it, work for it, and it will come to pass. I guarantee it.

In the next four sections of this chapter, you'll visualize and describe your ideal future from both a personal perspective and a business perspective. You'll be asked to

1. visualize your ideal life experience,
2. clarify your personal mission,
3. determine your business purpose, and
4. design your ideal new business model.

This is just a start. Defining what success means to you is a lifelong project. But now is a great time to begin. As you think through the exercises in each of these upcoming sections, you'll begin to craft your own inspiring vision of success. Don't worry if you can't answer all these questions now. Feel free to come back and refine or add to them later.

Your Ideal Life Experience

Your business can be a vehicle for you to achieve financial security for yourself and your family. But it's only a means to an end. The "end" is a wonderful life. Your business should be fun to run and provide you with a means to support your ideal life experience. So start by defining your *ideal life experience*.

Clarity of purpose is one of your most powerful assets. It's the foundation for meaningful success. If you don't have an inspiring vision of personal success, you'll focus on money-making activities instead of life-enhancing results. You'll take the easy road. This is a major mistake. It leads to careers that meander—to achieving financial success but not *total personal success*. Values and vision are the navigational tools that will help you stay on course to a wonderful life.

Answer the questions on the following page. They will help you develop an image of your ideal life experience.

Your Personal Mission

You've started to define what kind of life experience you want to have. Now it's time to define your *personal mission*.

First, identify what you value in life—what's important to you. Consider what unique talents or abilities you have. Then think about the people you want to help and how you want to help them. Articulate how you want to make a difference in the world. Your personal mission statement should embody your highest aspirations. Be careful not to aim too low.

As an example, consider my personal mission statement: "to play a major role in the evolution of human consciousness."

That's a huge mission, and it inspires me every minute of every day as a coach and agent for personal change and world transformation. My work is centered on helping people see the possibilities and then inspiring them to apply new and better ways to get what they want out of life.

Define Your Ideal Life Experience

Here are 20 questions to get you thinking about the life experience you want to create.

1. How do I envision success? (Define your values, payoffs, and motivations.)
2. How do I want to serve others and society? (Consider whether it's important for you to be in an occupation that adds value to others or makes a contribution to society.)
3. What types of clients and friends do I want to have? (Describe relationships, values, ideas, and entertainment.)
4. What type of house(s) do I want to own? (Think about self-expression, comfort, convenience, and beauty.)
5. Where do I want to live? (Visualize the community, your status, life experience, friends, and beliefs.)
6. How many weeks of vacation do I want to take each year? (Consider things such as adventure and family bonding.)
7. Where do I want to go on my vacations? (Picture fun, beauty, and adventure.)
8. How many hours do I want to work each week? (Think about balance, recharging yourself, and personal growth.)
9. What do I want to do when I'm not working? (List hobbies and other interests.)
10. Where do I want my children to go to school? (Address parental values and desired child experiences.)
11. How much net income will I need to support my ideal life experience? (List your ideal compensation range.)
12. At what age do I want work to become optional? (Visualize leisure activities.)
13. How much money will I need to retire comfortably? (Evaluate financial independence.)
14. How much money will I need to invest each year to achieve my retirement goals? (Describe money habits.)

15. Where do I want to live when I retire? (Consider weather and beauty.)

16. What do I want to do with my time when I retire? (Think about health, vitality, and fun.)

17. What type of conversations do I want to have? (What is the ideal conversation to have with friends and clients?)

18. What do I want to do to keep healthy? (Describe your ideal exercise program and the time it will take.)

19. What type of legacy do I want to leave for my family and my favorite causes when I die? (Describe meaning, purpose, and mission.)

20. What type of role model do I want to be for my children and my friends?

It's a good idea to go over these questions with your spouse or someone else close to you. If you turn your responses to these questions into goals, these goals will become an emotional lighthouse for you. If they're truly inspiring, they'll keep you focused and motivated. They are the foundation for your definition of a wonderful life, the true purpose of building a super-profitable business.

I'm not a financial advisor, so my example should give you a sense of tone but is certainly not a boilerplate for your mission. You need to develop a personal mission statement that's inspiring to no one else but you. Each person must develop his or her own. When you get your personal mission statement right, you'll own it. And it will own you. You won't have to look it up. You'll be able to recite it instantly. It'll be a statement of your most deeply held values, beliefs, and life goals. It will clarify your reason for living.

This may sound a little out there to some readers. But clarifying what you truly value is the key to building a super-profitable business *and* a wonderful life.

Define Your Personal Mission

Work through this exercise to help you start thinking about your mission in life. It may take you a while to phrase your answers so they're inspiring to you. Revise your mission as you read through this book and do the exercises. When your mission is expressed in terms that inspire you, it will be a powerful motivator for you. Read it daily and commit it to memory. It's your life's work.

1. My four highest values are . . .

2. My unique abilities are . . .

3. I like helping others to . . .

4. My mission is to . . .

Your Business Purpose

Everyone wants to feel that his or her work has significance and meaning. Just working to feed your family, pay the rent, and stay out of debt isn't very meaningful.

In the book *Built to Last: Successful Habits of Visionary Companies* (Harperbusiness, 1997) James C. Collins and Jerry I. Porras clearly demonstrate that the most financially successful companies are founded on solid values and belief systems. They have a higher purpose than just making money. Research by Collins and Porras shows that the values-based companies they studied were 15 times more successful in increasing their stock value than the general market.

It turns out the key to building a super-profitable business is to base it on solid values. These come from the personal values and belief systems of the key managers; in this case, that's you. The business then becomes a vehicle to express your deepest values and beliefs. If there's any question in your mind about the relationship of your personal mission, values, and beliefs to your business success, read *Built to Last*. It's one of the most important business books of our time.

Now that you've started to clarify your personal mission, you can start to develop your *business purpose*. Some people call this a "business mission." I like the term *business purpose* better because I believe it's clearer.

Your business purpose is constructed from your unique set of personal values, beliefs, and interests. It should focus on how you'll generate revenue and build a business by expressing your personal values and mission. In short, your business purpose should fulfill your personal mission in a commercial way.

Your personal mission can be a bit spiritual (like mine), but your business purpose must be grounded in the realities of the marketplace. When your business purpose is in alignment with what the market wants, you can't help but make tons of money. Most people don't understand this. They think they have to work harder to earn more. They think the only purpose of their business is to make money. These are mistaken beliefs that come from a limited understanding of business.

To be super-successful financially, your business must have a higher purpose. A powerful purpose will not only help focus you and your staff on your top priorities, but it will also guide and motivate you, your staff, and your clients. By creating an inspiring *business purpose* you can create meaning where it didn't exist before. You may be doing the same activities, but you and your employees will do them with greater heart, passion, and enthusiasm.

Your purpose should be big enough to inspire you but not so big that it's unfocused. Here's an example: The purpose of American Business Visions is "to inspire people to imagine and create a more joyful life for themselves and, ultimately, a better world for all."

We accomplish this by helping individuals clarify their vision, values, and goals. That's the most important thing we do for our clients. Once we have helped our clients define what they really want in life, then we help them implement step-by-step processes for making their visions a reality.

This book is an important contribution to fulfilling my personal mission and our business purpose. (See "The Purpose, Values, and Beliefs of American Business Visions" on page 43 for an expanded overview.)

Define Your Business Purpose

Use the following questions to start crafting your business
purpose.

1. How will my business help me fulfill my personal mission?
2. What values and principles do I want my business to express?
3. What principles will guide my business?
4. How will my business help people?
5. What needs and wants of my clients is my business primarily designed to fulfill?
6. What business do I really want to be in?

Our business purpose works like an emotional lighthouse in my company. All my employees know what we're working to accomplish. Making money simply is a result of fulfilling our purpose. It's how we keep score. Our mission and purpose are much more inspiring and motivating to us than just making money.

Your Ideal Business Model

Once you're clear on how your business purpose is going to support your personal values, beliefs, mission, and life experience, you need to determine what type of *business model* will help you accomplish your business goals.

Always remember that you are not your business. Your business is one key aspect of your life experience. To maintain a balance between your personal life and your professional life, you must regard your business as a separate entity.

Ideally, your business should be a self-sustaining system that can run smoothly and independently without you. You must start with that outcome in mind, or your business will soon control you. Ask yourself this key question: *How can I employ my talents to make the greatest contribution to my clients through my business?*

The Purpose, Values, and Beliefs of American Business Visions

The staff at my company, American Business Visions, is committed to our set of values and beliefs. We defined our values and beliefs by first clarifying our individual values and *personal missions*. Once this was accomplished, we developed our shared *business purpose*, which incorporated all our values and beliefs. The resulting document became our business constitution. Here's what it looks like.

Business Purpose

We inspire people to imagine and create a more joyful life for themselves and, ultimately, a better world for all.

Who We Are

- We are powerful agents for positive change and transformation.
- We are idea pioneers—we discover and act on new possibilities.
- We are early adopters—we embrace new information, technologies, resources, and actions that empower us to achieve our mission and our goals.
- We are transformational leaders—we lead by example— we walk our talk.

What We Do

- We inspire people to think big and to dream big dreams.
- We empower people to turn their dreams into reality so they can live with joy.
- We create value through imagination, creativity, and vision.
- We encourage people to trust and act on their intuition.
- We release pent-up psychic energy and then direct it with our ideas and processes.

continued next page

- We are building a community of people who are attracted by our purpose and who empower each other to bring it into reality.

Our Work Beliefs

- We see positive possibilities in every individual and in every situation.
- We experience joy and self-expression through work.
- We are committed to personal excellence: continuous learning and self-improvement.
- We value individual initiative and responsibility: We are highly productive and profitable.
- We value results over activities.
- We build strong relationships through honesty, integrity, respect, open communication, and understanding.
- Healthy profits and growth are essential because they make it possible to fulfill our personal missions, business purpose, and goals.

Other Values and Beliefs

- We believe all human beings have enormous untapped potential.
- We embrace peace, beauty, and balance.
- We make a positive impact on the world ecosystem.
- We support our fellow teammates in their expression of our company values and mission.

Financial services is really a people business. Of course, you'll set financial goals. But you'll attain those goals by building relationships with people. You'll help people clarify their visions of success and establish their goals. Then you'll help these people realize their dreams by providing financial products and services that will help them achieve their goals.

As you complete the exercises in this chapter, you'll quickly come to realize that the traditional transaction-based business is limited in its ability to support your ideal life experience. As mentioned earlier, any real business must generate current cash flow and build equity for the owner's retirement. Only a business with predictable, recurring revenue can take the financial pressure off you and create significant net worth. We'll explore this more in chapters to come.

Design Your Ideal Business Model

Answer these 16 questions about your ideal business structure and goals.

1. What is my ideal net income level?
2. What is the gross revenue of my ideal business?
3. What percentage of my revenue will come from transactions and what percentage from recurring fees?
4. How many clients will I have?
5. What types of clients do I want to serve?
6. What types of products and services will I offer?
7. Will I focus on reaching greater numbers of moderate income clients or attracting a smaller number of wealthy clients?
8. What will my average account (case) size be?
9. What types of knowledge and skills will my organization need to acquire in order to deliver value-added services?
10. How many employees will I need?
11. Where will I want to locate my office?
12. What type of office and equipment will I need?
13. Will I want to work on my own or in a branch office environment?
14. Will I run the office by myself or will I have a partner?
15. What strategic alliances will I need to develop to help solve my clients' problems?
16. What would I like my ideal business to be known for?

Big Goals Lead to Big Achievements

Once you've defined your ideal life experience, your personal mission, your business purpose, and your ideal business model, you've created your inspiring vision of success. You know what success looks like for you. That's something 95 percent of the population hasn't considered.

Many of your personal goals will be achieved only by meeting your business goals. Specific business goals are necessary to track your progress and keep you focused on the activities that will lead you to total success as you define it. Mission and purpose help you stay on the right road.

Goals help you determine where you are on your road to success. I learned an important lesson about setting business goals when I was an investment wholesaler. My boss asked me to give him a detailed breakdown of the production goals in my territory for the next year. He wanted specific sales figures for each broker/dealer, branch office, and individual producer.

I'd been working for only six months. I told him that I didn't have enough experience in the territory to make such detailed projections. His response left a lasting impression on me. He told me that I didn't understand how this process worked. Then he explained:

First you set your goals. Then you use your imagination and problem-solving skills to figure out how to reach those goals.

After I defined my goals, I wrote them on index cards. I silently read these goals to myself each morning and each night. I visualized myself achieving these goals. Within 18 months, I had improved my territory from last place out of 22 territories to third place. Without clear goals I would never have been so successful. And if I had set goals that I thought were realistic, I would never have risen so high so fast.

You *can* create any life you want. So dream big dreams. The most important part of any activity is using your imagination to clarify outcomes and to set inspiring goals. Don't let your past dictate your future. Design and live the life of your dreams.

Set Specific Client-Acquisition Goals

Here's a great way to set your basic business goals: First, set your income goal. Then determine how many client relationships you need to meet that income goal. For instance, let's say you decide to set your gross income goal at $1 million per year. How many clients will you need to achieve that income?

Here's how the math works: Let's assume you're a fee-based investment advisor and that your average clients will have $500,000 each to invest with you. To simplify our example, assume that you'll gross one percent each year from each client. That means you'll earn $5,000 per year from each client.

To gross $1 million you'll need 200 clients ($5,000 x 200 clients = $1 million). That should leave you with something around $350,000 to $750,000 of personal income, depending on your business model.

"Not a bad start," you might say. "But how can I get so many great clients?" Think about the following business concept for a moment.

Assume that over the next couple of years you establish strong relationships with ten successful and influential people in a few very specific niches. You select these niches because you know they have high concentrations of ideal prospects for your products and services.

Because these ten influential people know you, like you, and trust you, they recommend you whenever they come across anyone who could benefit from your services. Since almost everyone with whom these "centers of influence" come in contact could use your services, they send you a steady stream of qualified, motivated prospects. Let's assume each one of your original ten "influencers" sends you one ideal new client a quarter—or four new clients a year. Multiply that times ten and you get 40 new ideal clients a year.

If each new client has $500,000 in assets to invest, you'll capture $20 million a year. You'll achieve your goal of 200 clients in just five years. And that assumes no growth in their assets.

Of course, if these assumptions don't fit your business situation, you can change them. If your primary business is transaction-based, this model won't work so well. Think seriously about designing your business to establish value-added relationships so you can generate recurring revenue from your wealthy clients. Peter Drucker, the well-known management guru, wrote, "The purpose of a business is to make and keep a customer." If you're transaction-based, your business model drives you to create customers and then hope they don't need much service. But to create an effort-less business model, you need to attract great clients and then keep them for life. You need to focus on long-term relationships rather than one-shot sales. And you do that with a fee-based business rather than a transaction-based business, or with such other ongoing services as consulting or coaching.

The goal of 40 new, wealthy clients a year may seem high. And it is high if you use the traditional shotgun approach to marketing. You can't build a super-profitable business if you have to start from scratch at the beginning of each month. It takes a while to penetrate upscale market niches. Since it takes time to develop relationships with new people, it's important that your relationships pay off over the long haul. The real benefit of marketing to the wealthy resides in their ability to generate recurring income for you year after year after year.

The quickest way to an efficient, highly profitable business is to develop mutually beneficial relationships with people who are centers of influence who will send you clients. You'll learn how to generate these new clients each year from key centers of influence in the chapters ahead.

Your Informal Board of Advisors Supports Your Success

If your vision is truly inspiring, you'll become focused. As you become more focused you'll become more motivated. As you grow more motivated, you'll set bigger goals and make bigger plans. You can achieve whatever your mind can conceive, but you'll need help. You'll need a board of advisors. These are key clients, targeted centers of influence, and strategic alliance partners who support your business purpose and want your business to prosper. They must like you, trust you, understand how you help people, and know the types of people who will benefit most from your expertise.

An informal board of advisors usually consists of up to ten of the smartest and most influential people you know who are willing to invest some of their time in helping fulfill your mission and purpose. Usually, these board members don't meet formally. In my case, I simply call or e-mail my advisors and ask them specific questions on an informal basis.

If your board members are willing to support your business purpose and personal success, they'll share their valuable knowledge, perceptions, and insights with you. They can also help you build your business through referrals and introductions.

When you're trying to design a client-centered business, it's important to get differing points of view and to learn from the mistakes and successes of others. Your advisors will become your sounding board for your most ambitious plans. If your vision is inspiring, your business will take on a life of its own. Unexpected support will come from many different places.

Chapter at a Glance

Many people still think work means trading your time for money, doing something that isn't fun. I'm suggesting that you define your personal mission and then figure out how to make money fulfilling it. By doing that, you can have it all: a super-profitable business and a wonderful life. You'll have more fun and make more money with less effort.

Your business should be built solidly on your values, beliefs, and, yes, even dreams. Your goal should be to create a business that enables you to do the kind of work you love, associate with the types of people you most enjoy, and get paid extremely well for doing it.

By incorporating your values, beliefs, passions, mission, and purpose into an inspiring vision of your ideal life and ideal business, you'll create a solid foundation for a wonderful life experience.

Joseph Campbell, a philosopher and author of the book *The Power of Myth* (Anchor, 1991), wrote, "What we're looking for is a way to design a life experience on purpose so we experience the rapture of being alive."

You write your own script every day. No one's in charge of your life but you. Will you create an exquisite life that's a joy to live? Or will you allow yourself to get bogged down chasing dollars and grinding through meaningless activities simply because you haven't taken the time to use your creative imagination?

Real success is not *just* about money. Real success comes from doing the activities and achieving the results that charge your life with purpose, meaning, and joy. This will enable you to live every minute in *your* Endorphin Zone. And that's what life is all about.

Chapter 3 Action Steps

Exercise 1: Answer the questions in "Define Your Ideal Life Experience" on page 38. Using what you learned, write a clear description of your ideal life experience. Include specific details. Keep this summary somewhere handy so you can easily refer back to it. Make a practice of reading it and visualizing yourself experiencing it every day.

Exercise 2: Answer the questions in "Define Your Personal Mission" on page 40. Think about how you want to make a difference in the world.

Exercise 3: Answer the questions in "Define Your Business Purpose" on page 42. Your responses should help you find a way to fulfill your personal mission and generate an income.

Exercise 4: Answer the questions in "Design Your Ideal Business Model" on page 45 to help guide your thought process about your ideal business model. Write a clear and inspiring description of this business.

Exercise 5: Set some clear and specific goals to achieve on your way to creating your ideal life experience. Start by setting an income goal. Then calculate how many clients you'll need to meet this goal. Decide how long, realistically, you want to spend building your business. Determine how many new clients you'll need to add each month to reach your income goals. Make adjustments until you're satisfied with the equation. Review these goals every morning.

Exercise 6: Brainstorm to create a list of candidates for your informal board of advisors. Think about your clients, local centers of influence, and strategic alliances. Come up with ten names and tell these people about your vision, mission, purpose, and goals. Ask them if they would be willing to support you as you work to fulfill your mission and purpose.

Step 2

Target Profitable Market Niches

Pretend for a moment that you're a prospector looking for gold. You could try your luck panning in the nearest riverbed. Or you might try to improve your odds by prospecting in a riverbed where others have discovered gold. But most rivers have been panned for more than 150 years. All the "easy" gold has already been found. You would be lucky to get even a modest monetary return for your efforts.

Go straight to the mother lode.

A more sophisticated prospector would focus on discovering the *source* of gold. Once the veins of solid gold were located, gold nuggets could be mined efficiently all day long. Meanwhile, the other prospectors would be down in the riverbed panning for flakes.

Discovering your source—*rich niches*—is what Step 2 is all about. Packed with valuable research data, chapters 4, 5, 6, and 7 illustrate the power of niche marketing. Starting with a look at the big picture—the universe of everyone who could conceivably be a prospect—you'll learn how market segmentation can help you identify the specific community of individuals who will benefit most from your services.

Because these individuals are in the same niche, by definition they have similar hopes, concerns, and needs. So keeping them happy is simple. By focusing on a single niche—or even a couple of niches—you'll quickly become an expert at identifying, attracting, and helping people in that group. Focusing and narrowing the scope of your business this way will help you master the effort-less marketing process.

Section Preview

- Take advantage of the five benefits of targeting.
- Identify the top 20 market segments for financial advisors.
- Apply the 80/20 rule to your current clients.
- Uncover the two to three niches that you'll make the most money in and have the most fun with.
- Profile your ideal client.
- Use the Ideal Prospect Profile to find high payoff prospects.

Maximize
Your Productivity

Concentrate your energies,
your thoughts, and your capital.

—Andrew Carnegie, late 19th- and early 20th-century American
industrial leader, philanthropist, and founder of Carnegie Hall

When I was presenting a workshop on niche marketing, a financial professional asked me, "Why do we need to target niches? Why don't we just find people who have at least $250,000 to invest?"

"You target rich niches," I told her, "because that's where you find *groups* of wealthy prospects. Professional marketers know that you can't market to *everyone*. Instead, you must market to *someone*. But to whom?"

That's the million-dollar question. The answer is you want to market to people who have substantial net worth and investable assets. If you know where to look, you'll find them in very predictable occupations, life situations, and geographic areas.

Every town has identifiable communities of individuals (*niches*) with extremely high concentrations of wealthy prospects. There will also be many scattered or fragmented households that control wealth, but they aren't easily identified because they don't fit into any predictable patterns. I call these households "orphans."

Niches are easier to market to because people in established communities are already communicating with each other. You may be able to attract many orphan households through public seminars. But that would require a lot of cost and effort. And not everyone likes doing seminar marketing.

By targeting specific groups of people with the same needs you can streamline your business model and minimize your marketing effort.

I'm suggesting that you'll have a better bottom line if you are well-connected than if you are "well-seminared." Set your goal to identify the highest opportunity niches for you—and then build trusting relationships with the movers and shakers in them. Once these centers of influence trust you and know you're client-centered, they'll bury you in qualified referrals. The quality of your business will go through the roof.

Only by targeting niches can you reach deep into the pockets and networks of wealthy prospects. Endorsements, referrals, targeted group presentations, and plain old introductions are the keys to effort-less marketing. Targeting niches is simply the most cost- and time-effective way to identify and build relationships with large numbers of ideal wealthy clients.

Use the Scientific Method

The more successful you are, the more valuable your time becomes. Busy advisors have to make their marketing pay, or they can't afford to invest their time in it. You want to get the highest return possible on the time and money you invest in your marketing. And you'd like to invest the smallest amount of time, money, and effort to make it work.

Effort-less marketers can learn from the gold mining business. You can pan for gold, dredge for gold, or mine for gold. The panners are prospectors just eking out a living by randomly sifting through pans of gravel. The dredgers methodically move tons of gravel for a few ounces of gold. But the mining engineer who locates a vein of solid gold sets up a mine and continuously harvests the rich mother lode of solid gold.

Panning is similar to cold calling, mass mailing, or seeking random referrals. The dredging system is similar to publicly advertised seminars for financial products. The highly trained mining engineer is like the niche marketer. Once you've identified your rich niches (or veins of gold), the hard work is behind you.

A knowledgeable mining engineer would look for gold using a scientific method. He would look for rock formations that had a high probability of encasing a vein of solid gold. Once a promising location was found, the engineer would dig test holes at the base of the mountain to look for traces of gold in the dirt.

If he found gold traces, the engineer would dig a series of test holes in the direction that had the most gold in the soil. Eventually, he would find the source of the gold traces.

The mining engineer's process isn't based on random digging and luck. Rather, activities are based on an intimate knowledge of how gold was formed and where it's most likely to be found. If the engineer didn't find any gold on a certain mountain, he would simply move the search to the next promising mountain.

I see a direct parallel between this scientific approach in mining to niche marketing in financial services. Identifying opportunities is often the hardest part of the process. Once you zero in on them, you can mine them for years to come. But to effort-lessly identify opportunities, you need specialized knowledge and a strong information network.

The traditional prospectors are panning for gold down in the riverbed, just managing to make a meager living. The sophisticated gold mining engineers are getting rich by mining the mother lode. Who would you rather be like? You can work much smarter by basing your activities on detailed knowledge of wealth, its creation, and who controls it.

Segment Your Market

To find your groups of qualified prospects, you must divide the mass market into *segments*. Then further divide the segments into *subsegments* and finally into identifiable niches or groups of individuals.

You can segment the market for financial consumers three ways: by 1) occupation, 2) recreation, or 3) special interest/cause. Segmenting by occupation is most effective for financial advisors. Occupation is the primary indicator of an individual's social and economic status. You can get some economic clues from recreation or special interest affiliations, but occupation is the most telling.

Rather than finding opportunities in veins of solid gold, you'll find it in rich niches, where there are high concentrations of wealthy people. Most of the people who control investable assets in these niches are over 50 years of age. In fact, people over 50 control more than 70 percent of U.S. assets (this is true for most countries). However, because of the explosion of the stock market, business startups, entertainment and sports, many younger people are also becoming very wealthy.

Work With the Wealthiest Households

Most wealth is concentrated in small groups of people. So you should aim your marketing activities at the most lucrative niches. According to Chip Roame, managing principal of Tiburon Strategic Advisors—a market research and strategic consulting company in Tiburon, California serving investment brokerages and management firms—the top 3.1 percent of households in the United States control 52 percent of the nation's total investable assets. These are the people who can benefit most from the help of a competent advisor. (See "Focus Your Energy on the Affluent" on the next page for further details.)

Often these wealthy individuals are difficult to contact. They're busy and discerning with their time. But if you don't focus on top niches, you'll end up working with the bottom niches by default—those in the bottom 96.9 percent.

Focus Your Energy on the Wealthy

3 Million households
or 3.0% of
U.S. Households

91 Million households
or 96.9% of
U.S. Households

100,000 households
or 0.1% of
U.S. Households

$4.9 Trillion in investable assets
or 42% of
U.S. investable assets

$5.6 Trillion in investable assets
or 48% of
U.S. investable assets

$1.2 Trillion in investable assets
or 10% of
U.S. investable assets

The Wealthy

$1.6 million average
per household
•
Between
$500,000 and
$5 million each
•
You can't go wrong with this segment. Wealth is highly concentrated.

The Mass Market

$61,000 average per household
•
Maximum of
$500,000 each
•
Odds are you'll spend lots of time hunting for ideal clients in this segment.

The Super Wealthy

$11.6 million average per household
•
Minimum of
$5 million each
•
This segment is excellent, but mostly locked up.

Source: Tiburon Strategic Advisors

Target Incomes in the Top 20 Percent

Here are some 1997 numbers to give you an idea of income distribution in the United States. By targeting those with household incomes in the top five, ten, or 20 percent, you'll improve your odds of finding ideal clients. And frankly, if you don't go after the top 20 percent, you'll end up working with the bottom 80 percent by default.

INCOME	NUMBER OF HOUSEHOLDS	PERCENT OF HOUSEHOLDS
Up to $71,500	82,022,400	80%
$71,501 and up	20,505,600	20%

A Closer Look at the Top 20 Percent

INCOME	NUMBER OF HOUSEHOLDS	PERCENT OF HOUSEHOLDS
$71,501–82,499	5,292,200	5.2%
$82,500–97,499	4,924,000	4.8%
$97,500–126,549	5,163,000	5.0%
$126,550 and up	5,126,400	5.0%

Total Households: 102,528,000

Median Income All Households: $37,005

Average Income All Households: $49,692

Average Income Top 20% of Households: $122,764

Average Income Top 5% of Households: $215,436

Source: The Bureau of Labor Statistics and the Bureau of the Census, 1997.

How Wealth Is Created

To target the wealthiest households, you must first understand where wealth comes from. In our society, most wealth is created by business people who *combine existing ideas and technologies in new ways.* Others accumulate retirement capital over years of work and investing.

The original creators and accumulators of wealth are easiest found in specific occupations. There are three primary sources of income and wealth for the top households:

1. entrepreneurs, especially those who dominate niches;
2. self-employed professionals in such hot specialties as plastic surgery, computer consulting, and environmental geology; and
3. key corporate employees in successful companies, especially in manufacturing, high-tech, software, financial services, and health care.

Concentrate on marketing to these groups and you'll have a high probability of meeting many wealthy prospects. Once someone has started to create wealth, *pools of capital* form. These consist of personal investment portfolios, retirement accounts, or equity in a private business or in stock options.

Ultimately the wealth is transferred (as *money in motion*) to people who didn't earn it, usually through inheritance, gifts, endowments, and divorce.

Your goal is to build relationships with the people who originally created the wealth and the people who will receive, or have already received, someone else's wealth. You'll find high concentrations of both groups in specific niches. You'll learn more details about these rich niches in the next chapter.

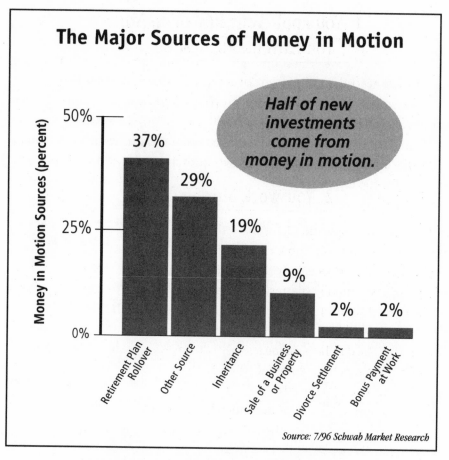

The Major Sources of Money in Motion

Half of new investments come from money in motion.

37% Retirement Plan Rollover
29% Other Source
19% Inheritance
9% Sale of a Business or Property
2% Divorce Settlement
2% Bonus Payment at Work

Source: 7/96 Schwab Market Research

The Benefits of Targeting

Most financial advisors who have built their business on massive marketing seem to think that if they target certain groups, they'll miss something. They're right: They'll miss those people who have no money, no interest, no need, or no desire for their services. They'll be "limited" to working in communities where there's plenty of money, interest, and opportunity. That's not a bad trade-off!

There are five main benefits of targeting profitable niches. And there are no legitimate reasons *not* to target. The five key benefits are as follows.

1. You Apply Your Resources Where You Earn the Highest Return

I once read that 80 percent of a typical salesperson's time is wasted talking to poorly qualified or completely unqualified prospects. By targeting rich niches, you can spend 100 percent of your time talking with highly qualified and highly motivated prospects. This one technique alone can dramatically increase your marketing productivity and your income.

2. You Work More Efficiently

People in a specific niche share the same hopes, fears, and financial concerns. You'll soon know every objection, problem, and concern that your targeted prospects have. By working with the same scenario over and over, you'll eventually master it. You can then design systems—including prepackaged solutions—to deliver your service more efficiently.

An advisor I know works out of his home. When I asked him what he did during the day, he gave me a one-word answer: research. He explained, "All of my clients have different problems, so I have to constantly keep on top of their changing needs."

That approach requires too much effort! When all of your clients are in the same niche, you do the research only once. Having a narrow focus creates a more efficient business model.

One of my good friends is a financial advisor who has penetrated a rich niche. He works exclusively with clients in the oil industry. He was earning more than $1 million a year, and I asked him what had made him so successful. I was surprised when he said the answer was service. I was expecting him to say it was specializing in a niche.

At the time, he had a part-time assistant and spent a good deal of time driving to meet with clients and prospects. I asked him how he could provide great service without a large support staff. He replied, "Steve, when all of your clients have the same goals and concerns, are in the same industry, and have the same investment and insurance products, service is a snap."

3. You Quickly Become an Expert

By specializing in *prospect groups* rather than in *products*, you quickly become an expert in specific niches. You and your organization become the highly desired value-added ingredient in the financial planning and investment management process.

When you start doing business with the first client in a niche, you'll be unaware of his or her unique concerns. By the time you get your second client, you'll know the basic issues, challenges, and solutions. By the time you land a third client, you'll have developed some specialized knowledge. From there on out, it just gets easier and easier.

Everyone would rather work with an expert in their needs. As your expertise increases, so will your attractiveness, confidence, and closing ratio. Your marketing will require less effort each year.

4. You Maximize Referrals

Targeting specific niches dramatically increases your number of quality referrals. When clients and centers of influence discover that you're an expert in solving their problems, they become much more willing to refer you to others who are like them. They know you really *do* add more value than a generic financial advisor.

It's easy for your clients to identify others in their niche who might need your help. And, of course, referred prospects are more receptive if you have helped a few of their friends solve a similar problem. There's nothing better than positive word of mouth to build your reputation and your client base.

I work with a financial planner who once had a dentist as a client. The dentist eventually contacted a firm that specializes in working with dentists. The dentist thought the specialist would provide more value, and it was absolutely true. One of the primary reasons people will leave their current advisors and decide to work with you instead is that you have specialized knowledge of their niche.

5. You Work With People Who Have a Natural Rapport With You

As you become more specialized and start to work with people you really enjoy, you and your clients will become friends. People will always want to work with friends rather than technicians. You'll recall that the transaction-oriented, product-centered phase of the marketplace is all about making transactions. In the client-centered phase you need to build long-term relationships.

I'm sure you've been exposed to sales training that divides people into four personality styles. Usually these personality styles fall into these categories: *drivers, analytics, expressives,* and *relators.* These sales courses are based on the premise that you should first determine the personality style of your prospects. Then you're supposed to adapt your personality and presentation to the personality of your prospect.

As a target marketer, I think this premise is ridiculous. My goal is to be the best Steve Moeller I can be—not to be someone I am not. Plus I won't have fun if I have to pretend to be something I'm not.

Your goal should be to work in specific niches where the general personality style is compatible with your own. Then you'll enjoy the people you work with, and they'll have a natural feeling of trust, rapport, and even affection for you. Working with them will be effort-less.

Even Accidental Targeting Works

One extremely successful interior designer discovered her rich niche only after she had left it. She became so successful that she and her husband were able to purchase a new house in the country. To move there, they had to take their kids out of private school and put them in a public school near their new home.

Much to her dismay, she realized later that most of her clients were parents of other children attending the private school. Unconsciously, she had been reaping the benefits of effort-less marketing. She was in a rich niche and didn't even know it. And, unfortunately, by leaving the circle of parents, her business lost momentum.

This shows you what a powerful impact targeting can have on your business—and how much it costs if you don't target. Once you begin to work with a group of individuals with similar interests and concerns, the referral process takes on a life of its own. The amount of time and energy you put into each client is far less than if all your clients raised unique issues and questions.

As you'll learn in the following chapters, one of your goals is to identify communities of people who share a common interest with you. Then simply by associating with them—by becoming familiar with their needs and earning their trust—new business will come your way.

Chapter at a Glance

I dentifying potential clients is like prospecting for gold. Cold calling is like random panning. Targeting profitable niches, on the other hand, is like mining veins of solid gold. These are your *rich niches.*

Targeting niches is mandatory if you want to increase your productivity in the fragmented and highly demanding client-centered marketplace. Five of the key benefits of targeting are that you

1. apply your resources where you earn the highest return,

2. work more efficiently,

3. quickly become an expert,

4. maximize referrals, and

5. work with people who have a natural rapport with you.

In the next chapter, you'll build on what you learned here and work your way toward selecting your target niches. Soon you'll look at all prospects in terms of market niches. By providing your expertise and products or services to niches that can benefit most, you'll generate the highest payoff on the time and money you invest.

Chapter 4 Action Steps

Exercise 1: Review the chart on page 61, "Focus Your Energy on the Affluent." Think about which group you would prefer to target. Remember that although the super-affluent group has the highest average dollars per household, it's a small market in terms of members and total value. Also keep in mind that, although the mass market controls the greatest total value, the average per household is low and it would take a great amount of time to identify ideal clients among such a large number of households.

Exercise 2: Review the sidebar on page 62, "Target Incomes in the Top 20 Percent." Using the income distribution data as a guide, begin to think about the minimum income requirements you would like to set for clients. Keep this dollar amount in mind as you review estimated income figures for selected professions in the next chapter.

Select the Best Segments and Niches for You

*A man may be so much of everything
that he is nothing of everything.*

—Samuel Johnson, 18th-century English author and literary critic

One Canadian financial advisor, who specializes in providing financial advice to surgeons in the Vancouver area, has seriously loyal clients. She once told me that two of them had so enthusiastically raved about the advisor's knowledge of their special needs that a third doctor switched financial advisors later that day. What's so amusing about this story is that the two had sung her praises not over coffee, but over a patient in the middle of an appendectomy!

By identifying and penetrating the right niche, you, too, can expect your clients will do this kind of word-of-mouth marketing for you—the kind that no direct mail, public seminars, or cold-calling will ever accomplish.

The research I've done will help you identify these markets. Some of this data is based on third-party research and some of it is based on my personal experience. Use this information to make decisions about which market segments and niches are best for you to target.

The Difference Between Affluence and Wealth

Newspapers often describe people who are financially successful as rich. I'm assuming you want to target the top ten percent of the richest households in your community. Yet the term *rich* is a meaningless designation for target marketers. Effort-less marketers need to separate these so-called rich people into two distinct markets: the affluent and the wealthy.

The English word *affluent* comes from the Latin *afflure* ("to flow freely"), so we could say affluent people spend their money freely. *Wealthy* comes from the Anglo-Saxon *weal* ("a great abundance of money, property, or real estate"), so we could say wealthy people are savers and investors.

Many people who appear wealthy are actually affluent. They seem to have money because they drive expensive cars and live in big houses. But the truth is they simply have big debts. People who are very wealthy rarely flaunt it. Some of the wealthiest people I know live in modest neighborhoods. I can't tell you how many times I have been to a blue-collar or middle-class home to pick up a $50,000 or $100,000 check.

Remember what Wal-Mart creator and discount store magnate Sam Walton used to drive in Bentonville, Arkansas? A beat-up, old pickup truck. And he was one of the wealthiest men in the world!

Affluent people can make great business-builder clients because they add more money to their investments each year. Wealthy clients, on the other hand, usually start with a large pool of capital and may or may not add to it depending on their unique circumstances. They want you to help them keep what they've got and make it grow.

Historically, most insurance agents have worked primarily with affluent clients. Investment advisors have worked mostly with wealthy clients. But today, there's a convergence between the services of insurance agents and investment professionals. The most successful ones, those at the top of their game, are typically offering asset management services and estate planning. When you're client-centered instead of product-centered, you tend to offer a complete package of services to help your clients meet their needs.

As a general rule, you'll find the biggest opportunities—regardless of your background—in the wealthy markets. But you must decide which one of these two major markets holds the greatest potential for you to effort-lessly build a super-profitable business and a wonderful life. For example, if you're selling variable life insurance as a non-qualified retirement plan, the affluent market is best. But if you're offering estate planning or asset management services, you need to focus on the wealthy market—especially households with $1.5 million or more in assets.

The Difference Between a Segment and a Niche

In addition to understanding the difference between affluence and wealth, it's important to understand the distinction between segments and niches.

The way I define the term, a *market* is made up of anyone who could benefit from the services of a financial advisor. That's almost everyone over age 21. A *segment* is a large group of people in certain occupations or life situations, such as professionals or widows. Within a segment there are many *subsegments*. For example, doctors form a subsegment of the professionals segment. In the same way, franchise owners are a subsegment of the business owners segment.

As explained in the previous chapter, a niche is an identifiable community of people with common wants, needs, concerns, problems, and communication channels. An example: Wealthy widows over the age of 50 who belong to the Big Bucks Country Club in Hartland, Michigan.

Each niche usually has a unique personality, income range, club or organization, and gathering spot at which you can find high concentrations of people in that niche.

Let's look at attorneys as an example. Within the legal profession there are dozens of specialties. Each specialty attracts a different personality type. Trial attorneys have different personality styles, opportunities, and challenges from estate planning attorneys. They also have completely different types of clients. A rich niche could be the clients of an estate planning attorney who is over 50 and belongs to the Estate Planning Council in your community.

You must first divide the affluent and wealthy markets into specific segments. Then you need to define the subsegments within those segments. And finally, you need to identify the rich niches in your community. What follows is a head start on your segmentation.

The Top 20 Market Segments

A couple of years ago, I did some research for a large insurance company. My task was to identify the best niches for financial advisors to target. I looked closely at more than 400 occupations. Ultimately, I identified 20 segments that offered the most promise.

This section outlines those 20 segments. These are the areas in which you'll find the highest concentration of opportunity. Start by focusing on these market segments. Then, as you read through this chapter, begin to think about which of these 20 segments definitely are not for you. Then identify which of the remaining segments are most interesting to you. This is the first step in arriving at your "short list" of target niches.

You don't have to read this entire chapter. If you like, just read the sections that discuss the segments and niches that most interest you. If you're interested in *self-employed professionals*, go to the self-employed professionals section of this chapter and cross off those subsegments you have no interest in pursuing. Those you don't cross off are the niches you'll want to research further. Future chapters will show you how to conduct this research.

As you scan the income figures in this chapter, resist the urge to focus on the specific numbers. Like everything else, these figures keep changing.

Instead, focus on the relative sizes of the markets and the incomes relative to each other. Income levels change, but the income differentials between groups remain relatively constant.

Also, keep this in mind as you look at the income figures: The numbers represent just one wage earner. Many households have two wage earners, so any particular household could be in a much higher income bracket than the one listed. Many individuals are also likely to inherit money, especially self-employed professionals. To add to the difficulty of determining true income levels, there are often other factors that determine total household income and net worth.

Many financial advisors say they're going to focus on widows, professionals, business owners, and retirees. That's not targeting. Targeting is selecting no more than three niches while deciding to ignore others. Targeting specific niches doesn't mean that you won't work with people in other niches. It means you'll focus your marketing efforts just on specific niches. The particular niche or niches you choose depends on what opportunities exist in your local community, as well as on your experience and interests.

The Top 5 Affluent Market Segments

Let's start with the affluent market. There are five primary affluent segments in which you can find concentrations of individuals who earn high incomes. I define high income households as those that generate more than $100,000 a year. If you're on either coast, add another $25,000 for the higher cost of living. Only about seven percent of America's households fit in this group. Roughly the top 12 percent of the nation's households earn more than $75,000 per year. Depending on where you live, you may consider this group affluent.

The top five occupational segments with concentrations of people who are affluent are

1. self-employed professionals (especially specialists),

2. salespeople (especially technical salespeople or salespeople who sell services),

3. key corporate employees (including executives, managers, professionals and highly skilled technicians),

4. artists and entertainers (the creative industries), and

5. professional athletes (a small but growing niche).

Clearly, not everyone in these occupations earns $100,000 a year. But these are the market segments with the highest concentrations of households earning high incomes. If you focus on these segments, you'll have a high probability of meeting people who are affluent. If they're over 55 years old, they might even be wealthy.

The Top 5 Wealthy Market Segments

Let's take a look at the five occupational segments that have the highest concentrations of people who are wealthy.

In 1990, the Congressional Budget Office estimated that only three percent of American households had a net worth of $600,000 or more. Today, roughly the top five percent of America's households control assets worth $500,000 or more. Remember, because of the exploding stock market, this figure is a moving target.

The top five segments with concentrations of people who are wealthy are

1. entrepreneurs (especially in niche markets),

2. retirees (especially those who worked for big corporations for many years),

3. divorced women (mostly those who were married to entrepreneurs, self-employed professionals, or key corporate employees),

4. widows (same as divorced women), and

5. inheritors (especially from self-employed professionals).

Again, not everyone in these segments is wealthy. But if you stray from these segments, the probability of finding wealthy people goes down dramatically. You may find gold in a lead mine, but it's extremely unlikely.

The Top 5 Institutional Market Segments

If you're offering asset management services, the five institutional market segments you should note are

1. small qualified retirement plans ($250,000 to $3 million),

2. charities and foundations (ones with endowments, such as Ronald McDonald House),

3. not-for-profit organizations (private schools, symphonies, zoos, etc.),

4. municipalities (cities, water districts, fire departments, etc.), and

5. large qualified retirement plans ($3 million and up).

Many financial professionals have a low tolerance for long sales cycles and long committee meetings. Most advisors I've worked with who targeted 401(k)s found the competition to be brutal, the fees to be low, and the effort to be high. The individual wealthy retail investor is a much faster growing market and requires much less effort. But for those readers who are comfortable with these processes, the above can be profitable niches. I recommend you stay in the smaller institutional segments, under $3 million in endowments, so you're not competing with the giant institutions.

The Top 5 Strategic Alliance Market Segments

If you're interested in creating strategic alliances with other professionals, there are five key segments you should know about and understand. Strategic alliances will be discussed in greater detail when we get to Step 5. The key strategic alliance segments are

1. accountants,

2. attorneys,

3. insurance agents (if you're an investment advisor),

4. management consultants, and

5. investment bankers.

Creating powerful strategic alliances with centers of influence who have many clients just like your ideal clients is one of the best effort-less marketing strategies you'll ever find.

A Closer Look at Affluent Segments

In the next sections, I'll outline each of the affluent and wealthy segments. We'll look at a sampling of rich niches within each segment. You'll use this information to focus on the niches of most interest to you.

These prospects control the vast majority of America's discretionary income. Older individuals in these segments often have accumulated substantial assets.

Self-Employed Professionals

When I mention self-employed professionals, most people first think of doctors. But there are more than a dozen types of professionals: doctors, attorneys, airline pilots, professors, engineers, consultants, dentists, optometrists, chiropractors, architects, counselors, chefs, cinematographers, golf pros, and so on. And each subsegment has many rich niches within it.

The best way to further divide the self-employed professionals segment is by professional accreditation, area of specialty, and geographic location. The bigger the local market, the more narrowly you can define your niche. In smaller communities, you have to focus on broader market niches. For instance, you may focus on doctors if you live in a smaller community and radiologists if you live in a big city.

A key challenge all professionals have in common is this: Their business has very little value when it's time for them to retire. This means

Relative Incomes of Selected Self-Employed Professionals

	APPROXIMATE NUMBER	AVERAGE INCOME	TOP 10%
MEDICAL PROFESSIONALS			
1. All Doctors	600,000	$210,000	$425,000
2. General Practice	60,000	$140,000	$345,000
3. Surgeons	90,000	$260,000	$300,000
4. Psychiatrists	30,000	$137,000	$230,000
HEALTH CARE PROFESSIONALS			
1. Chiropractors	48,000	$92,000	$175,000
2. Dentists	170,000	$140,000	$160,000
3. Optometrists	45,000	$90,000	$130,000
4. Podiatrists	16,000	$120,000	$175,000
MISCELLANEOUS PROFESSIONALS			
1. Attorneys	650,000	$75,000	$130,000
2. Race Car Drivers (Indy Class)	*	$458,000	$5,390,000

*Figures unavailable.

that all professionals must establish and aggressively fund retirement plans to ensure a financially secure retirement. This creates a great opportunity for financial advisors who specialize in these segments and niches.

Review the facts in "Relative Incomes of Selected Self-Employed Professionals" shown above. Figures are approximate. They have been adjusted for inflation and rounded. Don't focus too much on the actual data as this information is for relative value and background information only. The "high" figures are estimates of the average incomes of the top ten percent in each niche.

Salespeople

Salespeople make up one of my favorite groups because people who sell for a living are a lot like you and me. And as we move to a service- and information-based economy, the demand for professional salespeople who can sell intangible as well as technical products and services will continue to grow. This is also a group that is largely ignored by other financial advisors.

The best way to further divide the salespeople segment into identifiable niches is by specific industry. Some sales-oriented rich niches can be found in the medical equipment industry, high-level software companies (enterprise software), printing companies, mortgage brokerages, and real estate firms. The highest paid salespeople are those who combine technical knowledge with great people skills and solid follow-through.

See "Relative Incomes of Selected Salespeople" below for some of the niches with concentrations of high-income salespeople. (Numbers are approximate. Income figures have been adjusted for inflation. Use them for relative values only.)

Relative Incomes of Selected Salespeople

	APPROXIMATE NUMBER	AVERAGE INCOME	TOP 10%
1. Equipment Lessors	*3,000	$83,000	$110,000
2. Executive Recruiters	25,000	$70,000	$240,000
3. Mortgage Brokers	100,000	$65,000	$130,000
4. Real Estate Brokers	69,000	$65,000	$260,000
5. Stockbrokers	100,000	$95,000	$175,000
6. Wholesale Reps.	1.6 million	$40,000	$80,000

*Number of companies

Key Corporate Employees

Key corporate employees like executives, managers, professionals, and skilled technicians often earn high incomes—especially if they're exceptional at adding value for their shareholders. However, most of the financial services needs of this group are usually taken care of by their companies. In addition, the wealth of these key managers and specialists is often concentrated in their companies' stock or in stock options. Because of these two factors, the best times to attract these individuals are when they change jobs or right before they retire. You'll learn strategies for attracting key corporate employees when they roll over their pension funds in Step 5, "Communicate Your Benefits Effectively."

The best way to penetrate these markets is to target specific manufacturing plants or headquarters and develop relationships within the company and with influential retirees.

The biggest accounts in the corporate employee segment come from those people who, in addition to their retirement plans, own stock options

Relative Incomes of Selected Key Corporate Executives
(Top 20 percent of 3 million corporations)

	APPROXIMATE NUMBER	AVERAGE INCOME	TOP 10%
1. CEOs	600,000	$192,000	$448,000
2. Marketing VPs	600,000	$140,800	$224,000
3. Information Officers	600,000	$102,400	$256,000
4. Human Resources VPs	600,000	$115,200	$256,000
5. Airline Pilots	90,000	$110,000	$205,000
6. Hospital Administrators	*	$62,000	$195,000
7. Meteorologists	*	$61,000	$220,000

*Figures unavailable.

and/or have inherited assets. You'll find that fast-growth companies are great veins of solid gold because many key employees in those companies have valuable stock options. See "Relative Incomes of Selected Key Corporate Executives" on the previous page. (Numbers are approximate. Income figures have been adjusted for inflation.)

Artists and Entertainers

Musicians, artists, entertainers, writers, and photographers. Ah, the glamour industries! That's where I started out—as an advertising photographer. But I soon had to change careers. I have a low tolerance for poverty.

Obviously, some artists and entertainers make huge incomes. And some make very decent livings. But the typical individual in this segment is earning a below-average income. Also, this can be a very difficult niche to penetrate because most successful people in these careers have agents who act as gatekeepers. Many of these prospects are young and have flamboyant and unstable lifestyles. As a group they're extremely hard to work with.

If you live in Nashville, Los Angeles, or New York, you may be able to work in the entertainment niches. However, for the most part, unless you're wild and crazy and have an inside track with this market, I suggest you avoid it.

Relative Incomes of Selected Artists and Entertainers

	APPROXIMATE NUMBER	AVERAGE INCOME	TOP 10%
1. Symphony Conductors	*	$115,000	$720,000
2. Fashion Models	*	$85,000	$205,000
3. Musicians	*	$52,000	$124,000
4. Newscasters	*	$72,000	$205,000
5. Singers	*	$52,000	$103,000

*Figures unavailable.

Professional Athletes

There are more than 40,000 people employed in the fast-growing professional sports industry. This industry includes players, managers, referees, and support staff. Like the creative industries, the sports industry is a difficult market to penetrate.

Athletes are making more money than ever before. It's not unusual for an average baseball or football player to earn over $1 million a year. And an exceptional NBA basketball player can easily earn $5 million a year. But the serious money comes from product endorsements and movie deals. Don't get too excited about this market, though. It's one of the least likely markets for 99.9 percent of the readers of this book.

The biggest challenge advisors face is the youth and extremely short professional careers of these athletic prospects. Advisors also have to contend with the lawyers, accountants, and managers who act as gatekeepers to limit access to the players. Again, unless you have an inside track, there are easier markets to pursue. I recommend you avoid the professional athlete segment as well.

Relative Incomes of Selected Athletes

	APPROXIMATE NUMBER	AVERAGE INCOME	TOP 10%
1. Basketball Players (NBA)	*	$1,500,000	$5,000,000
2. Football Players (NFL)	*	$800,000	$4,800,000
3. NCAA Basketball Coaches	*	$55,000	$130,000
4. Major League Baseball Umpires	*	$140,000	$175,000

*Figures unavailable.

Keep these thoughts in mind as you consider targeting affluent markets: Not everyone in these careers is affluent. But these markets and their many niches have high concentrations of people making big incomes. If you look outside of these markets, your chances of finding high income prospects (rich niches) diminish dramatically.

The greatest opportunities in the affluent market are usually with professionals, sales and marketing executives, and key corporate employees with stock options and equity in publicly traded companies. Consider these segments first.

A Closer Look at Wealthy Segments

As you might suspect, the individuals in the wealthy segment are older than the people in the affluent segment. People over age 60 control most of America's assets. No income figures are available for these segments. These individuals may have huge net worths but may not earn big incomes. Where appropriate, I've included information to help you identify clues pointing to wealth.

You'll find high concentrations of people with more than $1 million of total net worth in the following segments.

Entrepreneurs

Entrepreneurs form the backbone of the free enterprise system. These individuals drive virtually all of the real growth in the economy. The income and net worth of business owners varies widely. In the same industry, one may earn $1 million a year and another may be losing as much or more. This makes it difficult to define incomes for specific niches.

Most business owners never achieve serious wealth. But, as in any industry, the top ten percent of the players dominate the market. Focus on the most successful entrepreneurs in any industry, and you hit the mother lode.

Here are a few points that will help you improve your odds of success when identifying opportunities in this segment. First, there's a big difference between a serious business builder (an entrepreneur) and a small business owner. Most small business owners really own a job. They get to a certain income comfort zone and flatten out because they don't have the drive (or skills) to grow a serious business.

Look for those entrepreneurs who have been successful in creating a growing business. Focus on businesses that are at least ten years old and owned and run by people who are 50 years old or older.

If you focus on business owners who work in unique niche markets, you'll have a higher probability of success. Here's an example: One day I was on a plane, and the lady next to me mentioned that her son was selling his home for $1.2 million. Curious, I asked her, "What business is he in?" She answered, "Weather stripping and caulking." Of course. Didn't a lot of your friends go to college to get into this lucrative field?

I also know of a painting contractor who earns more than $500,000 a year. His niche is sandblasting and painting large storage tanks for oil companies. Another successful blue-collar entrepreneur I ran across replaces existing gas tanks in gas stations with double-walled tanks. One of the advisors I work with has a client who manufactures animated animals for amusement parks. This entrepreneur is in his late fifties and employs more than 60 people. The common denominator of all these successful business builders is they dominate their niches.

Remember, there's far more money in blue-collar businesses than most people ever imagine. There's a huge difference between affluence and wealth, just as there's a big difference between status and net worth. Blue-collar entrepreneurs typically have lower status but very high net worth.

Another entrepreneurial subsegment that's often overlooked is the franchise industry. The niches are specific franchise companies. Often you'll find each franchise has a local association of owners, such as the Arizona Taco Bell Owners' Association.

When I lived in Phoenix, I used to walk with my wife, Brooke, for exercise. One afternoon we hiked up Camelback Mountain, which overlooks the city. The higher up the mountain we went, the more expensive the homes became.

I was curious about the family who lived in the house on the very top of the mountain. One day as Brooke and I passed the driveway of this incredible home, someone driving a new Cadillac pulled in and stopped to take some things out of her trunk. She seemed friendly, so I stopped to chat.

I introduced myself and at one point asked her what her husband did for a living. She answered, "He used to be one of the largest home builders in the Southwest. But a few years ago he sold that business and now owns a hundred and nine one-hour photo processing franchises."

Show me a franchise owner over 55 years old who has been in the business for more than ten years and owns three or more retail stores, and I'll show you an entrepreneur who has a high net worth and a healthy cash flow.

If the franchise owner is under 55 years old, he or she will probably be expanding the number of franchises. But as owners get older and wealthier, they usually start thinking of selling out.

Be sure to avoid the new crop of "clean carpets out of your home for a $5,000 investment" franchise

---

A Vein of Franchise Gold

One advisor I know bought an auto repair franchise in his town. The company required a $750,000 net worth to buy a franchise. The advisor hired a professional manager to run the business, so he spent little of his own time running the operation. In the first year, my advisor friend made a $50,000 profit. The bigger pay-off came, however, when he went to the company-spon-sored meetings and conven-tions. He was the only financial advisor in this huge communi-ty of wealthy franchise owners. All the other owners asked him for investment advice. He had found his vein of solid gold.

---

owners. Look for serious entrepreneurs with established national chains who have substantial capital invested in real estate and equipment. You can find publications that give detailed information about various franchises at the library or on the Internet. *Franchise 1* (www.franchise1.com) publishes an annual directory.

You can also find useful information on the *International Franchise Association* Website (www.franchise.org). These publications and

Websites will tell you the minimum investment and the minimum net worth a person needs to have to buy one of the franchises.

Retirees

There are now more than 30 million people over the age of 65. Another 33 million baby boomers will retire in the next few years. As I mentioned earlier, people over 50 years old control most of the country's assets. This is a very profitable segment for financial advisors. But many retirees are struggling financially. Here are a couple of things to look for to help you spot wealthy, retired niches.

First, look for upscale neighborhoods with custom-built homes. One clue is a high percentage of three-car garages. These homes should be at least 25 years old. Look for neighborhoods in which high concentrations of original homeowners still live. If they could afford these homes when they were in their thirties or forties, they were probably affluent then and have a high probability of being wealthy today.

I once worked with an advisor in Buffalo, New York, who wanted to market financial services to retired people. He quickly discovered that most of the people who had money left Buffalo when they retired. Because of the climate, the northern retiree market is limited.

The wealthier individuals are, the more likely they are to move to a new home in a warmer climate when they retire. There are entire communities in the United States' Sunbelt built to attract these wealthy retirees from the colder areas of the country. These neighborhoods are rich niches for the advisors in these communities.

I know some very successful advisors in California, Florida, Texas, Arizona, and New Mexico whose primary businesses are built around wealthy retirees moving from metropolitan areas in the eastern and northern U.S. Remember that when people move across the country, they're in a transitional time in their lives and they're open to meeting a new financial advisor. Publicly marketed estate planning and even investment seminars work well in these communities.

There are several ways you can identify communities of potential or current retirees. Some of the niches with high concentrations of people who either have retired or are about to retire include the following.

- **Individual company facilities**: Particularly those companies with strong retirement plans or stock options. Focus on individual sites like factories, refineries, corporate headquarters, etc.

- **Local associations and clubs**: These organizations provide you with a back door into a lucrative market niche. An example is the Retired Communications Workers of America.

- **Local union chapters:** Look for chapters interested in financial education for members. Telecom unions have been an especially lucrative niche for some financial professionals I advise.

- **Outplacement services**: Outplacement professionals perceive your financial advice as adding value in helping their clients assess their opportunities. They can make great strategic alliances. This is the side door into target niches.

- **Retired employee networks**: Both formal and informal networks are good places to meet likely prospects.

- **Neighborhoods**: Some neighborhoods are full of recent or future retirees from a specific company or industry. They can be one of your rich niches.

Divorced Women

There are more than 8 million divorced women in the United States. Approximately 1.2 million divorces occur each year. Most states attempt to split the property evenly between the husband and wife. One of the quickest ways to become poor is to become a divorced, single mother.

But in the top 5 to 10 percent of the most financially *successful* families, often one spouse (usually the husband in wealthy, more mature families) is running a business or professional practice or is a key corporate employee. In the divorce settlement, the husband typically keeps the income-generating job or asset. The wife typically gets all of the liquid assets and often the house.

This creates a unique opportunity for advisors. There's even a term for the person who has been given the liquid assets: Attorneys and accountants call these individuals the "out spouse." This means the person is out of the relationship with the accountant, the investment advisor, the attorney, and the insurance agent. These spouses have all of the money, but no one to provide them with competent financial advice.

An investment advisor in the San Francisco area captured more than $40 million in five years from referrals from one divorce attorney. Clearly, this can be a lucrative niche.

In this niche, events drive the business opportunity. In marketing terms, this is a *synchrographic event*. A synchrographic event is typically a transitional event that creates great opportunities for astute financial advisors. The best way to reach wealthy out spouses is through divorce attorneys and business evaluation accountants who specialize in these situations.

Widows

Consider this: A woman marries a Type-A personality man who's two years older than she is. He's smart, works extremely hard, and accumulates a substantial net worth. But he works himself to death at an early age. The woman lives an average of seven years longer than her husband does.

This is a common scenario. Wealthy widows control a large share of the money in any society. In America, four out of five surviving spouses are female. This market is comprised of more than 12 million women whose average age is 73 years old.

Over 650,000 women are widowed every year. These widows must take over all the brokerage accounts, real estate holdings, and business interests. Usually they just want to simplify everything and consolidate it into one manageable portfolio. They also want to get their own wills and estate plans in order.

Again, this is a transitional event that creates opportunities for financial advisors. The best way to get to this market is through introductions and by creating strategic alliances with estate planning attorneys.

Inheritors

The last group in the wealthy segment is inheritors. You've probably read the statistics. Over the next 20 years there will be the largest generational transfer of wealth the world has ever seen. In the United States, this will amount to $10 to $15 trillion in transferred assets.

But how do you identify inheritors? The easiest way is through their parents. If you're providing estate planning or investment management services, it's likely that most of your clients are 55 years old and over. Realistically, they won't live forever. If you don't establish a relationship with the children before their parents die, you're likely to lose those assets.

If you're an investment advisor, this is a classic opportunity for you to create a strategic alliance with estate planning professionals. I recommend you get the children involved in this process. By working together, you can help the parents plan for an efficient transfer of the estate to their heirs.

You'll provide a useful service for your clients. You'll also improve your chances of maintaining the relationship for at least two generations. If you don't have a strategy for maintaining a multigenerational relationship, the inheritors are likely to move the money to another financial advisor. They may even try to go it alone.

Wealthy Segments: Final Thoughts

Just as with the affluent segments, not everyone in these segments is wealthy. But if you stray from the market segments outlined here, you'll have to find wealthy prospects one at a time—expending too much effort and diminishing your marketing effectiveness.

Keep these facts in mind: A huge amount of money for advisors comes from retirement rollovers, inheritances, or sales of businesses. You'll undoubtedly find a greater amount of growth and opportunity working with wealthy retail clients than affluent individuals or the institutional segments. Wealthy individuals are the fastest growing segment.

A Closer Look at Institutional Segments

The institutional market segments include small qualified retirement plans, charities, not-for-profits, municipalities, and large qualified retirement plans, which are usually 401(k)s.

Financial planners, stockbrokers, and insurance agents should focus on the small institutional segment, so I haven't included a special section on the large plans. Let's look at the opportunities in each of these segments.

Small Qualified Retirement Plans

For investment professionals, I identify the best small-plan niches as organizations with $250,000 to $3 million in assets. This market has insurance needs, but the competition is fierce and the margins are low. The biggest opportunity in this market for most financial professionals is investment management or company-owned life insurance.

At this size, these plans are usually too small to attract the large institutional money managers. I think of these qualified retirement plans as part of the institutional segment because in this segment individuals make financial decisions for others. The pooling of capital and the fiduciary responsibilities essentially create an institutional situation. Financial professionals have the opportunity to provide both insurance and investment products and services to these organizations.

What's the most useful way to further segment this huge market? You can start by looking at the characteristics of various industries. My favorite way to identify niches is to divide the segment into two types of companies.

Knowledge-intense companies are often professional service firms, such as accounting firms or law firms. They have a small asset base and a high cash flow. In these educationally oriented businesses, the capital is locked in the minds of their highly learned workers. These workers are sometimes referred to as "gold collar employees."

Knowledge-intense companies have many highly paid employees who build equity in their companies. Key executives, as well as regular employees, often have stock options and stock grants. These companies are usually in the industries of the future, such as software, the Internet, biotechnology, and high-tech manufacturing.

Financial advisors can leverage their marketing costs if they target the company retirement plan and also pick up plan participants as individual clients. This makes it a two-for-one niche for investment advisors. Here are some of the types of companies in this knowledge-intense segment.

- Accounting firms
- Advertising agencies
- Consulting firms
- Employee leasing firms
- Entertainment firms
- Executive search services (headhunters)
- Film/TV production and support services companies
- Investment bankers
- Law firms
- Market research companies
- Public relations agencies
- Software development companies, and
- Temporary staffing agencies

In contrast to the knowledge-intense companies are the *capital-intense companies*. They have a large capital base and low cash flow. They're typically found in the manufacturing sectors and in industries that are equipment-based or real-estate-based. These industries are characterized by two tiers of employees: The first tier includes a team of key managers and technicians. The second tier includes low-skilled, low-paid workers. These are usually mature, industrial-age companies, as opposed to the newer, information-age or service-era organizations.

Most of these companies' value is in their real estate, equipment, raw materials, and finished goods. The owners of these companies are good prospects for estate planning. But because most of the employees don't make very high incomes, you may not want to provide pension plans to theses low-payoff industries. These capital-intense industries include the following.

- Car dealerships
- Dry cleaning plants
- Farming companies

- Traditional manufacturing companies
- Mining companies
- Plating companies
- Real estate development firms

Within these two broad segments—capital-intense and knowledge-intense organizations—are millions of businesses and niches. Select the type of organization that works best for your business model.

A Word about Small Communities

Often when I speak, advisors tell me they live in small towns. They don't see how they can target niches in such small communities. These advisors are right! If you live in a small town, the whole town or county will probably be your niche. Remember, your goal is to find an identifiable community of people with common interests, concerns, opportunities, problems, and communication channels. Focus on the most successful people in your market area who are over 55 years old. Chances are they all know each other.

Charities

The charitable marketplace is large and growing. However, you should proceed with caution in this segment. Most charities don't have much money. They run from month to month. The first thing you must do in this market is make sure your targeted organizations have endowments you can manage or charitable programs that will support your business goals.

One major problem with targeting charities is the personality type attracted to this field. Most of the people who run charities are volunteers. They have the best intentions but aren't always great at implementation. Their decision-making is often slow and can frustrate you.

You need a fair amount of patience to work with this type of committee approach to money management. Stick with organizations with under $3 million in endowments, and you won't have much competition from the large institutional money managers. You can add value by developing investment policy statements and minimizing fiduciary liabilities for the trustees.

This is a viable market. I have seen investment advisors pick up many multimillion-dollar accounts from Buddhist temples, various church organizations, a Catholic diocese, and a Ronald McDonald House. I've also known some very successful insurance professionals who created strategic alliances with charities. That's a way to sell life insurance to the charity's supporters. The main opportunity with most charities, however, is managing their endowment funds.

You should also look at local foundations. Most libraries have lists of the charities and foundations that are active in their cities. You'll have to develop your own list of the actual assets that each charity or foundation controls.

Approach this market selectively, and you'll be rewarded with large accounts. In addition, you'll get to work with people who are committed to making a positive difference in the world. You'll be more successful in this market if you target charities that are in alignment with your personal mission.

Not-for-Profit Organizations

What's the difference between a charity and a not-for-profit organization? Each has a different purpose. Charities and foundations aren't operating businesses. They usually have a minimal cash flow from operations. Their cash flow comes from investment returns or contributions from supporters.

Not-for-profit organizations—such as hospitals, schools, associations, symphonies, zoos, and clubs—may have a huge income from operations. But since their primary purpose is not to make a profit, they get special tax treatment. The more established institutions in this segment often have enormous cash flows and many large endowments for specific projects or favorite causes.

These larger organizations usually hire professional management firms and outside consultants. They are much more businesslike than most charities. If you approach these larger organizations, you'll probably be subjected to intense screening. Stick with the smaller, financially stable not-for-profit organizations that are run by a small team of professionals. These individuals will value your advice and help.

Once again, target organizations that are in alignment with your personal mission. You'll make many new friends and associate with some of the best and brightest people in your community.

Municipalities

When I was an investment wholesaler, Don, one of the top stockbrokers in my territory, did a huge amount of business with city treasuries throughout the state. Don had spent years building relationships by attending city council meetings in many of the small towns. He pointed out to me that even a small city has huge tax revenues and many different financial services needs. He found the municipal market very rewarding.

Since meeting Don, I've seen a number of investment advisors capture significant assets from fire departments. One advisor in the southern U.S. has more than $65 million invested for fire department disability funds.

Many financial advisors never get involved in institutional markets. Other advisors thrive there. If you do well with committees and fairly long decision cycles, this market may be great for you. The dollars are bigger and the needs are greater than in the individual market. But you don't have as much opportunity to add value with your personal relationships and coaching. This is more of a bottom-line market than the individual affluent and wealthy segments.

Strategic Alliances Segments

This is my favorite segment: strategic alliances. You can create mutually beneficial business partnerships with accountants, attorneys, associations, investment bankers, consultants, and a whole host of other centers of influence.

If you live in a small town or focus on narrow subsegments, your rich niches may be the client base of your strategic alliance partners. By working with these gatekeepers, you can often identify communities of ideal clients who already have a trusting relationship with another non-competitive professional.

I've devoted chapters 16 and 17 to creating strategic alliances. All you need to know at this point is creating only two or three strategic alliances is the surest road to securing great clients and achieving financial success. You'll effort-lessly build a super-profitable business in just a couple of years if you build solid strategic alliances.

Chapter at a Glance

You now know the 20 most profitable market segments. And you looked at the specific subsegments and niches within some of the segments. As you move through the next few chapters, you'll continue to narrow your focus, ultimately picking one to three target niches.

The first step to penetrating profitable niches is to identify those in which you want to work. Evaluate segments, then subsegments, then the niches within those segments. There are four main markets and 20 main segments in which you'll find the biggest opportunities for financial advisors. These four main markets are as follows.

1. **The affluent market:** People who are affluent make a lot of money, spend a lot of money, and look great.

2. **The wealthy market:** People who are wealthy often live in modest homes and don't outwardly display their wealth.

3. **The small institutional market:** These organizations are beneath the radar of large institutional money managers.

4. **The strategic alliance:** This market contains powerful centers of influence.

If you live in a small town or rural community, the town or county may be your niche.

Even in these targeted markets and niches, not everyone is a good prospect for a financial services professional. Look for clues in your prospects that indicate a very high income or high net worth. If you focus on people over 55 years old, your chances of success will go up dramatically. You'll learn more about identifying qualified, motivated prospects in the next two chapters.

Chapter 5 Action Steps

Exercise 1: If you haven't already done so, go back and cross off the segments and subsegments that don't interest you. Put asterisks by the ones that do interest you, regardless of whether you have many current clients in these segments. Consider which of these groups you have a natural affinity for and would like to study in greater detail.

Exercise 2: Decide which groups need the types of services you prefer to provide. This process will help you focus on the markets you want to research in greater depth. You'll learn how to do this in future chapters.

Learn What Motivates Wealthy Individuals

You can get anything you want,
as long as you give enough other
people what they want.

—Zig Ziglar, American motivational speaker
and author, *See You at the Top*

A couple of years ago, my wife and I moved across town to a new home and changed veterinarians in the process. One day, Brooke came back from taking the dog in for a check-up and was extremely upset. She said, "I don't like our new vet. I'm going back to Dr. Richards." Dr. Richards' office was 20 minutes across town, so I asked why. She said, "The new vet doesn't have a good rapport with Roxie."

I thought this was a little silly because I figured a vet's a vet and a dog's a dog. Why worry? But Brooke explained that Dr. Richards was always very loving with the animals and told her how sweet and attractive they were. Apparently Dr. Richards' "petside manner" made Brooke feel good about the relationship and about her role as the caregiver for our pets. The new vet, on the other hand, didn't say nice things about the animals and didn't even seem to like touching them.

So Brooke made the decision to drive across town to work with our previous vet. Not long after we switched back to Dr. Richards, Roxie developed a lump and needed surgery. We arranged for the X-rays and the surgery, and we were hopeful we'd done the right thing to improve our dog's quality of life.

But a few weeks after her operation, Roxie started stumbling and falling down. We took her back to Dr. Richards and were horrified to learn she had an advanced stage of lung cancer and was having trouble breathing. Ten days later, Roxie died.

We had taken Roxie to Dr. Richards for a check-up every six months. She'd had an X-ray before the surgery. Yet the vet hadn't found the lung cancer. Roxie died almost without warning. I asked Brooke if this changed her opinion of Dr. Richards. Brooke looked at me sincerely and said, "I know Roxie died unexpectedly, but Dr. Richards was so nice about it."

Now that's a clear example of valuing style over substance! We'll really never know which vet was the better technician. All we know is Dr. Richards sure seemed to care about us and our pets.

What Clients Want

When a client is working with any professional, there's so much more involved than technical competency. There's also the relationship. Most financial advisors think clients only want good investment performance or cheap rates on their insurance policies. But clients also want empathy, caring, concern, great service, and even fun. Most important, clients want a trusting relationship with their advisor.

Your clients want these *emotional payoffs* just as much as they want the economic benefits. After all, financial instruments have no value in themselves. Their value is tied directly to what they can do for your clients.

Mostly, your clients just want to feel good. To make your clients feel good you need to be more than a financial advisor; you need to be an *endorphin creator* or *lifestyle enhancer* for your clients. Make sure they experience both the financial and emotional benefits they want and need.

To get a grasp on how to help them experience both kinds of benefits, you need to thoroughly understand the *psychographics* of your target niche. You need to study their emotional motivations. Market researchers define psychographics as the "opinions, attitudes, interests, and lifestyles of a defined group of people."

You're probably a financial product and strategy expert. But the most profitable new knowledge you can acquire is an understanding of what motivates your ideal clients. To talk their language, you need to know their hopes and fears about life and death, money, and investing.

If you understand the thoughts and feelings that go into your clients' decision-making processes, you'll be more effective in attracting and keeping ideal clients. You'll also be better at helping your clients arrive at the best decisions to meet their unique needs. This is what being a client-centered advisor is all about.

Think about this: Salespeople want to sell products to make commissions. But most people don't want to buy financial products and services so the salesperson can make a commission. They want the benefits and emotional payoffs that financial products and services can provide them.

Once you have a handle on what motivates wealthy individuals, you can use this information to develop a compelling marketing message. You'll use this message in all your marketing presentations, sales interviews, and literature. Having a clear understanding of your prospects' motivations and thought processes will enable you to say the right thing at the right time to start hugely profitable, long-term relationships.

This knowledge of your prospects' and clients' deep emotional needs will also enable you to provide value-added services that make your clients extremely happy that they're working with you.

The Three Investor Personality Styles

There's a strong connection between people's emotional motivations and the way they think about investing. Understanding this phenomenon will help you identify the highest-payoff clients to build a super-profitable business.

Over the years, I've discovered investors almost always fall into one of three psychographic categories. I call them "Thrill Seekers," "Guru Groupies," and "Prudent Investors."

Take a look at each group's characteristics on the next page. You'll probably recognize that all of your clients fit one of these profiles. Note: These concepts apply to insurance clients as well, but the profiles are slightly different.

Prudent Investors
Make the Best Clients

By combining your knowledge of demographics (the information you reviewed in the last chapter) with psychographics, you can identify the people who have the most money and who you'll enjoy working with the most.

Think about the clients you have in each of these three psychographic profiles. Which ones are best suited for building long-term recurring revenue? Which ones appreciate your advice and services the most? Which group has the highest concentration of wealthy investors? Clearly, it's the Prudent Investors in all cases.

This is the mother lode for retail financial services professionals. Prudent Investors are the most appreciative and profitable clients, by far. They are also your lowest-maintenance clients. They don't expect you to take complete financial responsibility for them. They just want you to guide, advise, and implement strategies for them.

The key distinction is that Prudent Investors think managing their money is a burden. Thrill Seekers and Guru Groupies think managing their money is fun.

Prudent Investors probably control 70 to 80 percent of the assets in most countries. People who have a lot of money usually don't want to risk losing it. They want you to help them protect their money and achieve their goals. The best way to work with Prudent Investors is to partner with them. You can achieve your goals by helping Prudent Investors achieve their goals. You become a very important part of their lives.

Three Types of Investors/Clients

THRILL SEEKERS	GURU GROUPIES	PRUDENT INVESTORS
• Sophisticated • High interest in money and financial products	• Confused • High interest in money and financial products	• Uninterested • Low interest in money and financial products
• Think money is *exciting* • Aggressive investors • Seek hot performance	• Think money is *confusing* • Gullible investors • Seek magic bullet	• Think money is a *burden* • Conservative investors • Seek to preserve capital and quality of life
• Want information	• Want "wealth without risk"	• Want "total solution"
• Medium maintenance • Want lowest cost	• High maintenance • Whine about paying	• Low maintenance • Happy to pay fairly for your advice and service
• Strategy-oriented • Motivated by greed	• Product-oriented • Motivated by hype	• Relationship-oriented • Motivated by fear
• Seek hottest financial trick of the week	• Constantly changing products and services	• Simple and stable service/product mix
• Work with multiple brokers	• Move sequentially from broker to broker	• Same advisor over three generations
• Mostly young professionals	• All ages and careers	• Mostly over age 55
• Love "playing the market"	• Always chasing the hottest products and gurus	• Consistent need for core investments and services over life of client or longer
• Believe they can beat the market	• Believe a guru can beat the market	• Believe the market can beat them
CONCLUSION	CONCLUSION	CONCLUSION
• Avoid these low payoff "brain pickers." • They don't usually become serious clients.	• You have to over-promise to attract them. • They make unappreciative clients.	• They are the ideal client for fee-based asset management and estate planning services. • They make very appreciative clients.

Wealthy Prudent Investors are probably the only clients you really want. They form the economic foundations of today's retail financial services business. They are especially appropriate if you want to build a fee-based asset management business.

If you identify what these Prudent Investors want and give it to them, you'll be flooded with more business than you'll ever be able to handle. And since Prudent Investors are relationship-oriented, they're more likely to ride out a bad market with you. And they make great referral sources.

They have legitimate needs for core long-term investment products and services. They aren't usually getting the level of service and professionalism they want or need. That's a huge hole to fill. What an opportunity! You can form a partnership with these people to provide much wanted and needed financial services. And if you help them achieve their goals, they will be happy to help you achieve yours.

Avoid Thrill Seekers and Guru Groupies

People who don't have many assets will often take excessive risks with their money to try to gain more. This is often the case with Thrill Seekers. They're essentially gamblers at heart, and they want the adrenaline rush of playing the market. They're the archetypal day traders on the Internet.

Thrill Seekers generally won't become clients, because they like to play with their money themselves. They may open small accounts with you to get your investment ideas and some service. But they'll conduct the bulk of their business with discount brokers or over the Internet. Some retail brokers open accounts with Thrill Seekers by convincing them that their brokerages are good sources of "profitable information" or "hot tips."

A typical Guru Groupie is a retired engineer or teacher. Guru Groupies would like to manage their money themselves, but they don't have enough self-confidence. They typically worked their entire lives for a big organization. When they were working, Guru Groupies traded opportunity for security. They trusted their financial security and personal finances to their employers. Once they retired, they started looking for a guru to take the role of the employer to take care of their investments and financial affairs for them.

Usually they aren't affluent or wealthy. Guru Groupies are mostly in the great middle market. They may have saved a couple hundred thousand dollars. These people never made much money, but they never spent much either. They often subscribe to *Money* magazine and follow the investment media.

Guru Groupies are always looking for the next hot guru. They're nervous, so they aren't very loyal. They seem to think there's someone or something better that they don't know about yet. They're very receptive to hype. They love Charles Givens' book, *More Wealth Without Risk* (Pocket Books, 1995).

Guru Groupies sincerely believe there is a magic bullet—the investment or insurance product with all of the benefits and none of the risks. They're easily swayed by short-term performance numbers and tax gimmicks. And, of course, they don't want to pay commissions. Right now these people are buying variable annuities. These insurance products perfectly meet the Guru Groupies' definition of the ideal product.

Both Thrill Seekers and Guru Groupies are product- and performance-driven. They are not relationship-driven. They want to consistently beat the market. Because they move their money around so much, they're usually beaten by the market.

If you deliver 20 percent performance for five years in a row and then drop 10 percent in the sixth year, Guru Groupies will move their money to the new hot guru of the hour. Prudent Investors, by contrast, will call you to see if you're OK.

To build a super-profitable business and a wonderful life, I suggest you avoid both Thrill Seekers and Guru Groupies.

Mass Marketing Attracts the Wrong Types of Prospects

Here's an important marketing question: Which of these three investor types is most likely to respond to the traditional mass marketing techniques used in the financial services industry?

Generally, it's the Thrill Seekers and Guru Groupies who are most likely to respond. Thrill Seekers actively seek out free information they think might help them beat the market. Guru Groupies want to find out if you have any magic bullets they haven't heard of yet. Guru Groupies also want to find out if you're the hottest new investment guru.

Prudent Investors generally have such a low interest in their money and investment management and place such a premium on their time that they won't come to you. They almost never respond to mass mail, newspaper ads, cold calls, or any other attempt to get their attention.

Prudent Investors almost never attend investment seminars (although they do occasionally show up). It's like trying to coax me to a seminar about keeping my lawn green. I don't want to know how it's done. I just want to pay someone else to take care of it for me.

If you want to start relationships with Prudent Investors, you'll most likely have to go to them or be introduced to them. You'll learn how to do this in Step 3. Specifically, you'll learn how to use research interviews to start relationships with people in your targeted segments and niches.

Do you have Thrill Seekers, Guru Groupies, and Prudent Investors in your client base? I'll bet you do. If you have been using traditional prospecting and marketing techniques, you probably have a few Thrill Seekers, mostly Guru Groupies, and a few Prudent Investors. I'll bet most of your Prudent Investors—your best clients—came from passive referrals, not from your marketing activities.

Of these three types of investors, which ones do you want to build your business around? If you want to market effort-lessly, you'll want to work with the Prudent Investors. To attract them, you'll have to build relationships in target niches. Forget about mass marketing.

If you set up systems to attract these low-maintenance, highly appreciative, wealthy clients, you'll build a super-profitable business that's a valuable asset. And you'll have clients who are a joy to work with. Many of them will become clients and friends for life.

What Prudent Investors Want Most

As Chapter 5 explained, wealthy clients have substantial amounts of money. Affluent clients have high cash flow. Generally speaking, you'll want to focus on attracting *wealthy* clients. Let's look at what wealthy

Prudent Investors want from their lives, money, investments, and financial advisors.

I won't spend time describing Thrill Seekers or Guru Groupies. They're generally unappreciative clients who expect you to always have them in the hottest investments or sectors. They're often "C" and "D" clients. You should transfer them to another advisor as soon as you attract enough Prudent Investors, your "A" and "B-plus" clients.

Prudent Investors Want to Be in Charge

Self-made, wealthy investors are usually smart, independent thinkers. One of their success traits is the ability to gather and evaluate information. They believe strongly in their own decision-making abilities.

Sales techniques that work for the middle market will backfire when you're working with wealthier clients. Self-made individuals have a tremendous need to be in charge. Don't try to sell to these prospects in the traditional way.

Rather than telling them what to do, help them gather and analyze information. You can advise them on what you would do. But don't strong-arm them into a final decision. Let them adopt your recommendations as their own ideas. In other words, be an advisor and not a salesperson.

You can say something like the following:

> *"I've gathered all the information and evaluated the possible outcomes. If I were in your situation, this is what I would do. But you're the only one who can make the final decision about what's right for you."*

Since Prudent Investors want control and power, show them how your recommendations will give them more control and more power.

Alternatively, people who received their money from someone else—widows, those who are divorced, inheritors, and winners of legal settlements—often want to be told what to do. These people want a top-notch professional to take over the responsibility of managing their wealth for them.

Prudent Investors Are
Willing to Defer Gratification

Famed feminist and astute social commentator Gloria Steinem once said, "Rich people plan for three generations. Poor people plan for Saturday night." One of the primary traits that separates self-made investors from unsuccessful individuals is the ability to defer gratification.

People who have accumulated a substantial net worth almost always have a high degree of self-discipline. They're willing to make sacrifices today to ensure a brighter tomorrow. For these people, you want to minimize emphasis on current taxable income and stress long-term tax advantaged growth strategies. With people who are retired or financially independent, you should stress total return, not just income.

Prudent Investors Are
Politically Conservative

Most self-made, wealthy individuals are politically conservative. The old adage, "Your politics change with your position," holds true. As people accumulate more assets, they usually become more politically conservative. One of my clients once told me, "A liberal is someone who doesn't have anything to conserve." Not surprisingly, Prudent Investors are usually Republicans.

The major exceptions to this conservative bent are people who have inherited a large amount of money and highly successful people in the artistic and entertainment industries. These people are usually more altruistic and politically liberal than the typical self-made millionaire.

Approach philanthropy cautiously. For most wealthy people, their favorite charity is themselves. In fact, researchers have found that poor people actually give a larger percentage of their incomes to charities than wealthy people do.

The main reason most wealthy individuals give to charity is to keep more for themselves and their families. Stress the tax savings and the "maintaining control" benefits, not the philanthropic aspects, and you'll usually find more interest in planned giving strategies.

Prudent Investors' Attitudes Toward Money

When it comes to money, the self-made wealthy are different from everyone else. Many of them actually believe that money *can* buy love, approval, security, power, status, and happiness. They may be on to something. Money does allow you to pursue emotional payoffs because your physical needs are already met.

What's more, no matter how much money they have, most wealthy clients don't think of themselves as rich. In fact, many of the super-rich don't feel financially secure at all. And when it comes to spending their money, they want every penny to count.

Money Offers Emotional Payoffs

Subconsciously, these wealthy individuals feel that if they get enough money, they can get the emotional payoffs they want and heal their *psychic wounds*. This is a fancy term for deep psychological scars from an emotionally painful experience in their past.

Many wealthy people grew up in poverty and will do almost anything to avoid the pain they associate with the humiliation of being poor. Often their self-esteem is tied closely to their financial position.

Prudent Investors aren't very interested in the financial products or the process. They're interested in the payoffs. Find out what emotional payoffs your ideal prospects and favorite clients want from their money. Then link yourself and your products and services to the things and feelings these individuals want most in life.

Emotional payoffs include peace of mind, a feeling of security, love, appreciation, status, the happiness they experience by sending their grandchildren to a great college, a sense of control over their lives, and being free from financial worry. They also include fun and toys, such as skiing, travel, golf, great vacations, fine dining, and a better home. Money allows Prudent Investors to pursue and fulfill their dreams.

Charles Revlon, founder of the Revlon empire, had this emotional connection figured out. He once said, "In the factory, we manufacture lipstick. But in the stores, we sell hope."

Money Provides for
Their Families

Second only to their sense of self-esteem is the desire to be good providers for their families. Most wealthy Prudent Investors would do almost anything to protect the financial security of their families. This is why estate planning is such a big issue with wealthy couples. These couples often believe their children will be well provided for, but they want to ensure the financial security of their grandchildren.

Prudent Investors Believe
They Can Never Be Too Rich

After Henry Ford had become one of the world's first billionaires, a reporter asked him, "Mr. Ford, now that you've made your fortune, can you tell me how much money it takes for the average man to feel financially secure?" Ford put his thumb and forefinger about a half-inch apart and replied, "Just about this much more."

Because of this persistent need for more money, many self-made Prudent Investors prefer money over material goods. That's why most wealthy people don't show their wealth. They often drive older domestic cars and live in blue-collar or middle-class neighborhoods. This propensity to downplay their success often confuses financial advisors who equate high net worth with yachts, big houses, and flashy imported automobiles.

The emotional need for financial security often makes wealthy people act and spend like they're impoverished. A client I worked with when I was a financial advisor had a net worth of more than $2 million. He told me that whenever he needed to open a new bar of soap for the shower, he insisted on sticking the old sliver of soap onto the new bar. Apparently, he was never able to get over the poverty of his youth.

Prudent Investors Are
Discerning Shoppers

One of the biggest challenges advisors face when dealing with wealthy clients is that they're smart shoppers and frugal bargain hunters. Sometimes these people tend to be penny-wise and pound-foolish. They may let small fees prevent them from enjoying big financial benefits. This isn't a logical decision; it's an emotional reaction.

To be more successful with these types of clients, don't focus on the features of your products. Make sure you're appealing to deeper, subconscious needs. Even frugal people spend money on the things they value. That's what money is for—to buy positive feelings and experiences.

To create these emotional experiences, you'll need to understand your ideal client's deepest values, fears, and hot buttons. Your clients are probably motivated by values that are very different from yours. You'll learn how to discover what your clients really value through the research process in Step 3.

Prudent Investors'
Attitudes Toward Investments

Money (dollars) and investments (financial instruments) are not exactly the same. Here are some insights into the attitudes many Prudent Investors have about investments.

Almost all financially successful people have become wealthy through direct ownership of equity investments—usually in their own businesses, real estate, or stocks. They have a tendency to favor these types of equity ownership situations over debt instruments.

Because of their strong preference for control, they're often resistant to packaged products like mutual funds. That's why separately managed accounts are popular with many of these people. When you combine the control factor with the tax benefits and lower cost, you can clearly see why wealthy individuals like these investment products.

To meet this need for control, consider recommending investments in areas about which these clients have special knowledge or expertise. If you're dealing with a wealthy clothing manufacturer, you might recommend stocks in the apparel sector. If you're working with a doctor, consider recommending investments in biotech, pharmaceuticals, or medical devices. This will make your clients feel they have more control over their assets.

In the case of your doctor clients, this strategy may also give them "bragging rights." They love to impress their friends with their brilliant investment ideas. It makes them feel smart.

Since this investment approach often works against your clients' best interests, here's a strategy for giving them what they want *and* what they need. This is critical if you're going to keep your clients for life. Allocate their investment portfolio to meet their risk tolerance and time horizon. Invest 95 percent of their money in that prudent portfolio. Then let them play with the other 5 percent in investments that meet their emotional needs.

When a wealthy business owner tells you, "My best investment is to plow my money back into my business," he's expressing an emotional need for power, control, and direct ownership. In many cases this is a good strategy. Often there's no better investment vehicle for business owners than their own businesses.

Don't try to convince your potential new clients that they're wrong. Instead, look for unmet investment needs, such as pension plans. Try to discover and meet their unmet emotional needs with value-added services that competing advisors don't offer.

Business owners are often more open to diversifying outside their businesses as they grow older. A business owner who is 40 years old will want to grow the business. But this same business owner at 57 years old may want to cash out or start investing seriously in a retirement plan.

A small minority of the wealthy—typically the super-wealthy, inheritors, or very mature senior citizens—favor defensive, fixed-income investments. Find out about the past experiences of these individuals and their current hopes and fears. Be sure your recommendations match their risk tolerances and their emotional needs.

A Lesson from Saturn

Now that you have a sense of what your ideal clients and prospects want from their money and investments, let's look at what they want from their relationship with you. It turns out that most Prudent Investors are looking for the same thing Saturn automobile buyers are seeking.

Recent surveys by J. D. Powers & Associates show Saturn getting much higher initial consumer satisfaction ratings than its competitors. Although many had fewer initial defects, Saturn was better liked.

According to a friend of mine who works with one of those competitors, his company conducted focus groups with Saturn owners to find out what was going on. The research process went like this: The Saturn owners were asked to talk about their new cars. The owners usually complimented the car they'd just bought. The interviewer would then ask what owners liked most. They would enthuse, "The service is incredible!"

The interviewer would then request, "Tell me about the service." The owners would typically respond, "Whenever I take my car in for repairs, everyone is extremely enthusiastic about seeing me. They know my name, and they know the names of my kids. They treat me like royalty."

Then the interviewer would ask, "How many times have you had your car in for repairs?" Owners would answer, "Oh, a few times." When the interviewer asked how long they'd had the car, the usual answer was about six months.

With the competitor's cars, it would be unusual if the car needed repairs *even once* in the first six months! But the employees in Saturn's service department were so nice that the Saturn owners didn't even think about the repairs as a problem. In fact, some looked forward to taking their cars in for service.

Even though Saturn had an inferior product, the manufacturer had a superior relationship with clients. That *relationship* generated a more positive feeling about the car than the quality of the car itself.

Most Prudent Investors want the same thing: a great relationship. Above all else, Prudent Investors desire a long-term relationship with a knowledgeable, trustworthy advisor who understands their problems, has empathy for their goals, and has the knowledge, skills and processes to help them get what they want.

Results Prudent Investors Want From Financial Advisors

There are six key results-oriented benefits that wealthy individuals expect to receive from their financial advisors.

1. Solid investment performance: Prudent Investors want good returns but not necessarily great returns. They would rather sleep comfortably at night than have to worry about their aggressive investments. If you educate them about the realities of the markets, this group will be perfectly satisfied with index funds and prudent asset allocation. Stress capital preservation and maintaining quality of life, not performance.

2. Minimal taxes: Most wealthy individuals are self-employed, so they must make quarterly estimated tax payments to the IRS. This is significantly different from an employee who gets money back at the end of the year. Many wealthy clients believe they have a moral duty to avoid taxes because each dollar they send to the government is money they can't reinvest in their businesses. They believe taxes are a confiscation of their hard-earned money.

Index funds and tax managed accounts are very attractive to this group. Minimizing taxes is also one of the easiest ways to maximize real investment performance.

3. Control and simplicity: The more you can simplify and "bottom-line" your clients' investments and personal finances, the more they'll value your relationship. Information is power and helps them feel in control. The more money they have, the more complicated, time consuming, and stressful it is for them.

By taking over the burden of management and giving them the right amount of information, you can help your clients control and simplify their financial lives. Be sure not to overload them with information they don't really need. Less is more.

4. Appropriate products and strategies: Prudent Investors don't want to become experts in investments, insurance products, and financial strategies. They want you to help them choose the right investments and insurance products for their risk tolerances and their unique situations.

This doesn't mean recommending the hottest performing products. It does mean recommending the products and strategies that they'll feel the most comfortable owning.

5. Help in planning or maintaining a secure retirement: Wealthy clients want your help in planning for retirement so they can maintain their lifestyles when they stop working. Although most wealthy individuals truly enjoy their occupations, they're still looking forward to the time when they can retire and have time for other things. They recognize the need for a relationship with a financial advisor who can help them create a better future.

6. Guidance in helping them avoid mistakes: Wealthy clients want you to help them avoid mistakes. They've probably already made plenty of mistakes on their own. They're looking for a professional to help them avoid losing money. There's often a big difference between investment performance and investor performance. Many investors in the best performing mutual funds actually lose money. That's because they invest at the peak and pull their money out in the troughs.

Teach and coach your clients to be successful long-term investors. Protect them from their fears when markets bounce around. You can dramatically improve their returns by managing their fears so they stay in the markets for the long run.

Each Niche Has Its Own Personality

In the past, if you've sold financial products and services to anyone who could fog a mirror—without targeting specific segments or niches—you undoubtedly have a wide variety of personality styles among your clients. Some of your clients are just like you. You feel a natural connection. Establishing rapport with many of your other clients, however, may require tremendous effort.

Trying to be all things to all people requires a great deal of effort. But it's effort-less to attract and work with clients who you have a natural rapport with and like. You have common values, interests, and personality styles. People with whom you have this easy rapport are usually your favorite clients.

My friend Hal says his favorite client is a truck driver who had worked in the oil industry for 30 years. Surprised? Hal's not. His dad was a truck driver.

Get to Know Your Clients

You should now have some excellent insights into the general psychographics of wealthy individuals and Prudent Investors. But how well do you know your existing favorite clients? See if you can answer the following questions with confidence. As we proceed, you'll start to use the information in this and previous chapters to profile your ideal clients and prospects.

1. Are my clients mostly Guru Groupies, Thrill Seekers, or Prudent Investors?
2. Which group do I most enjoy working with and helping?
3. What is the biggest concern or problem I can solve for my favorite clients?
4. What other financial concerns motivate them?
5. How do they prioritize their concerns?
6. What benefits are most compelling to them?
7. What deep-seated emotions (psychic wounds) motivate them?
8. What do my clients want to avoid?
9. What are my clients' risk tolerances?
10. What do my clients want their money to do for them? That is, what payoffs are they seeking?
11. What's the most compelling thing I could say to my clients that would lead them to work with me?

As you evaluate specific segments and niches, ask yourself, *Are the people in those segments compatible with me?* If you have the same values and the same belief system as your clients, you're going to naturally like them and connect with them. If you don't share these attributes, it won't be a good match. To have a wonderful life, you must enjoy every one of your clients.

Chapter at a Glance

Not all investors think alike. This primer on the motivations and attitudes of wealthy clients should help you mentally segment your market to target and attract ideal prospects more effectively. It should get you thinking about the types of clients you want in the future.

You can combine the information presented here with your own knowledge of your targeted prospects to develop brochures, sales letters, introduction scripts, and other communication tools. But this is only the beginning. You'll to want to continually learn how to better serve your clients' wants and needs.

Remember to harness Prudent Investors' motivations to drive the success of your business. As you learn more about the motivations of this group, you'll be able to satisfy their emotional needs more effectively.

One of the strongest relationship-building processes with any client is to let them know that you clearly understand their wants, needs, and motivations. If you use psychographic research successfully, wealthy individuals will want to work with you because they feel you understand them. And once they become clients you'll know better than anyone else how to satisfy them.

Meeting your clients' needs should come naturally to you. People naturally like people who are like them and dislike people who are not like them. If you want to market effort-lessly, make sure you're attracting people who are effort-less to be with and help.

Chapter 6 Action Steps

Exercise 1: Name an existing top client—or someone you know— who is a Thrill Seeker. Name one who is a Guru Groupie. And name one who is a Prudent Investor.

Exercise 2: Which type of individual makes up the largest portion of your current client base? Which group do you want to attract in the future?

Exercise 3: Answer the questions in the sidebar "Get to Know Your Clients" on page 116.

Profile Your Ideal Prospects

Beware of dissipating your powers:
Strive constantly to concentrate them.

—**Goethe,** late 18th-century and early 19th-century German author,
a major influence on European literature

My dad was an orthodontist for more than 20 years, as I shared with you earlier in this book. What I haven't told you yet is that toward the end of his career, he confided to me that his practice was doing incredibly well. He explained he was making five times as much money as he had made when he started.

I knew he was working only three- and four-day weeks, so I wondered how he made so much money in so little time. I said to him, "Dad, you must be a lot faster than when you started."

"No," he said, "I was pretty fast when I left dental school, and I'm not any faster now."

I thought I knew the answer. "You must be charging a lot more money."

"No," my Dad responded, "there are so many orthodontists now that I have to charge less for my services."

For a moment I was stumped. Five times the money with only 60 to 80 percent of the effort. How did he do it? "Ahhh. The technology has changed," I blurted out.

"No," my father said patiently, "the procedures for straightening teeth haven't changed much over the past 20 years."

Then I was stuck. I wanted to know the secret. I listened intently as my father explained. "Steve," he said, "I simply choose my patients much more carefully now."

Selectivity Maximizes Your Effectiveness

Let me repeat that. My father increased his income more than 500 percent by simply selecting his clients more carefully.

My dad explained the 80/20 rule to me. He had learned a long time ago that 80 percent of his profit came from 20 percent of his patients. He decided to maximize his income by working only with new patients who were like those in the top 20 percent.

Once he recognized the distinction between high- and low-payoff patients, he simply developed a detailed profile of his ideal patient. He called his "A" prospects "people who can benefit most from my services." He described their problems in detail to dentists and other referral sources. When they ran across a patient who matched my dad's client profile, they knew he could help them.

When he interviewed a potential new patient, he would probe for clues to determine how good a client they would be. If he didn't have enough "A" patients, he would accept "B" patients. These were satisfactory, but less desirable than those in the "A" category. His "B" patients were steady but not really profitable relationships.

Near the bottom of his list were the "C" patients. These were the patients who were uncooperative with their treatment, missed appointments, and paid slowly. Finally, the "D" prospects had all the problems of the "C"s but were also just plain rude and unpleasant.

When my dad met with prospective patients, he poured on the charm to convince the "A"s to hire him. He wouldn't accept the "C"s or

"D"s under any circumstances. He simply referred them to another orthodontist who was newer in town.

That is the secret. To dramatically increase your income and the quality of your life, simply be more selective about the people with whom you do business.

To build a super-profitable business *and* a wonderful life you must learn to turn away low-payoff, high-maintenance clients. I know this goes against conventional wisdom in our industry. If you're serious about reaching the top of this profession, you'll have to learn to say no to certain people who want to work with you. Just because they have money doesn't mean they'll add to the quality of your life.

Effective marketing gives you options. In future chapters you'll learn how to generate so many high-quality leads that you'll never have to take on a "C" or "D" client again.

Spot the Worst Clients From a Distance

One day, an advisor I was coaching called to relate a horror story about a client. I mentioned my dad's "C" prospect concept, and we started discussing the worst clients we'd ever known. Soon we developed a profile of the worst clients for financial advisors.

Whenever you're profiling a prospect or a client, it's important to include both demographic and psychographic descriptors. The demographic description focuses on the facts about the person and includes such things as age, occupation, location, and family situation. The psychographic description focuses on the individual's personality type, risk tolerance, and general attitude toward money and life.

As we worked on the profile, my friend grew less and less amused. He recognized that many of his clients fit this description. He said, "Steve, a lot of my clients are retired engineers, and they're exactly like what we have described." And here's the worst part. This advisor is very right-brained, but he was working with left-brained analytical types. It was a total mismatch. Without a clear vision of what he wanted, he took any client who came along. He was paying dearly for his decision to take the "easy" route.

In my experience, many financial advisors work with grade "C" and "D" clients and don't even know it. If you take on prospects just because they want to work with you—even those who are "C"s and "D"s—you'll regret it. These marginal clients will drive you nuts. You'll be working with clients you don't want to serve. In the end, you'll dread going to work.

Review the demographics and psychographics of the worst clients on the next page for more information. Then let's take a look at the flip side of this dreary picture.

Know Who You Want to Attract

Ideal clients are those people you earn good money from and enjoy helping. They're usually Prudent Investors who value your advice, service, and relationship. Think of the clients you have now. Which ones do you look forward to seeing? Visualize one of them. The thought of this endorphin-creating client should make you smile.

These clients will help you build a more profitable business. There are plenty of great prospects out there who want and need your services. Writing an "Ideal Prospect Profile" will help you recognize people fitting your ideal description when you meet them.

To do this, review the general profile of universally ideal prospects. (See "How to Recognize Ideal Clients" on page 125.) No matter what part of the retail financial services industry you're in, this profile is a great place to start. We'll narrow the focus later in this chapter.

I think $250,000 to $500,000 of investable assets is a good starting point for your ideal prospect (or family unit). Prudent Investors in this category will have many things they would rather do than manage their money. They believe managing their money is a job for an expert like you.

My mom is an ideal client for her financial advisor. (I gave up my license ten years ago when I started my consulting business.) She's a retired widow who inherited money from her father. Since she didn't make the money, she feels detached from it. She's very healthy and leads an active lifestyle, traveling to the four corners of the earth. She'd much

How to Avoid the Worst Clients

Any of the following characteristics are red flags that a prospect would become a poor client.

DEMOGRAPHICS

- Are so young they know it all—or so old they can't make decisions
- Have just enough money to entice you to work with them but barely qualify for your minimum investment or premium
- Are in an occupation or niche that doesn't interest you
- Have few social or business contacts they can refer to you
- Don't expect to make any additional investments or future insurance purchases
- Are spending more than they're making and don't have a bright financial future

PSYCHOGRAPHICS

- Have plenty of spare time, so they don't value your time
- Want information, not advice
- Are performance-focused and want to earn above-market returns consistently
- Are concerned about paying your fees
- Are financial hobbyists with plenty of time on their hands to "play with their money" and "check out your competition"
- Don't have even a basic understanding of insurance, investments, or the markets
- Are overly analytical and constantly compare your recommendations and performance to your competitors
- Have a short-term perspective
- Demand a high level of service and seem to enjoy getting attention
- Worry about their investments and insurance policies, so they require constant reassurance and reinforcement
- Become easily confused, so they frequently need your help reading statements, order confirmations, and correspondence
- Are extremely frugal and whine about your compensation
- Are Guru Groupies or Thrill Seekers

rather be having fun in Mexico than watching the stock markets. This makes her a low-maintenance client for her advisor.

She likes her fee-based, independent investment advisor much more than her former commission-based broker. But she never compares the performance or the fees to her old broker. She once told me, "Since I've started working with Scott, I've been around the world twice, put a new roof on my house, and have more money than when I started. As far as I'm concerned, he's doing a wonderful job for me."

What a great client! She likes her financial advisor, trusts him, and believes he's competent. That's all that matters to her.

Build Your Business Around Your Ideal Clients

In Chapter 1, I mentioned that earlier in my career I was in charge of marketing for a financial advisory firm in Phoenix. When I joined the firm, the first thing I did was evaluate all the business we had done with our 200 active clients. I discovered that 65 percent of our business in the previous year had come from just six clients.

Let's say I wanted to increase our company's income by 65 percent in the next year. How many new clients would I need? The answer, of course, is only six—the number of clients who generated 65 percent of our business in the past year. But they would have to be exact duplicates of the six best clients we already had.

I developed a detailed profile of each of these ideal clients. The profiles consisted of both a demographic description and a psychographic one. A prospect must have both the financial need (demographics) and the desire for help (psychographics) to become an ideal client.

Once I had outlined clear profiles of the exact types of people who were the best clients for our business, I could begin to determine the most effective ways to identify and attract a steady stream of people just like them. I evaluated the results of our current marketing tactics against this profile. Then I tweaked our marketing strategies until we were consistently attracting ideal prospects.

How to Recognize Ideal Clients

Seek out prospects who have the following characteristics.

DEMOGRAPHICS

- Are Prudent Investors in one of your target niches
- Were referred to you by happy clients or by one of your centers of influence
- Are so busy they don't have time to research and manage their finances themselves nor the interest to do so
- Are old enough (generally 45 to 80) to accept your advice, but still young enough to benefit from it
- Have substantial discretionary cash flow (more than $25,000 a year to invest or apply to insurance premiums)
- Meet your investment minimums ($250,000 to $500,000)
- Have a financially bright future and will be making ongoing contributions to their accounts (or will need more insurance in the future)
- Are respected centers of influence who know many people who can benefit from your services
- Are likely to inherit a fair amount of money

PSYCHOGRAPHICS

- Know they have a financial problem or opportunity
- Are highly motivated to act now
- Want to work with a professional financial advisor
- Like you, trust you, and believe you're an expert
- Are decisive and inclined to implement your advice
- Have a long-term perspective and want a long-term relationship
- Have realistic expectations
- Are open-minded and curious—eager to learn new things
- Understand your strategies and products, but have a low level of interest in doing the work themselves
- Are honest with you and fully disclose their assets, values, goals, and concerns
- Value your service, advice, and professional relationship
- Are willing to pay fairly for your time and expertise
- Are helpful and friendly
- Are willing to help you by becoming a member of your informal board of advisors

Using this strategy, I generated a consistent flow of qualified, motivated clients who had an average of $200,000 to invest with us. It cost us $250 per appointment in hard marketing costs. We closed one out of three prospects and earned an average of $10,000 per new client in the first year. We spent $750 to generate three prospect meetings and closed one client with an average commission of $10,000. That's an efficient marketing machine.

And this is exactly the way you're going to do it.

Evaluate Your Current Client Base

In keeping with the 80/20 rule, it's entirely possible that nearly 80 percent of your business comes from just 20 percent of your clients. The easiest way to increase your income by 80 percent is not to double your client base—but to clone the top 20 percent of your clients.

Identify All of Your Current Ideal Clients

Use the following format to list *all* of your "A" clients by net worth, income, and fees or commissions. (Don't stop at five.)

Name	Net Worth	Annual Income	Your Fees/ Commissions
1. _____	$ _____	$_____	$ _____
2. _____	$ _____	$_____	$ _____
3. _____	$ _____	$_____	$ _____
4. _____	$ _____	$_____	$ _____
5. _____	$ _____	$_____	$ _____

Total annual income from these clients: $_____

Percent of annual income from these clients: _____ %

Your future successes will most likely follow predictable patterns based on your past successes. What you want to do is identify the best clients you've attracted through massive random activity and then develop systematic processes for attracting exactly those types of clients in the future. Only from now on you're going to do it effort-lessly. We're looking for a natural pattern in this process. Once we find it, we'll want to replicate it.

First, identify which clients are on your "A" list. As a general guide, they're the ones who made up 50 to 80 percent of your revenue over the last two years. You should also enjoy working with them. To begin, rank all of your "A" clients according to the income you earned from them over the past 12 months. (If you don't have any "A" clients you want to clone, don't worry. You'll learn how to attract them in later chapters.)

Next, take that same list and look for patterns that will help you target two to five subsegments or rich niches that you have had success with in the past. Use "Classify Your Top Clients by Niche" on the next page to assist you.

Select Your Top Segments

You should see some patterns in your past successes. In which segments, subsegments, and niches are most of your ideal clients classified? Also consider your answers to Exercise 1 in Chapter 5 in which you identified the markets and segments that most interest you.

Now select between two and five niches that you'd like to study in depth. You'll be investigating whether or not your community has opportunities in one or more of these niches and how to do the research in Step 3.

The Power of Written Profiles

Before I met the love of my life, Brooke, I wrote a profile of the perfect mate for me. (Brooke fits all of my criteria except one: She doesn't downhill ski. But I found she does like to be in the mountains with her friends.) Developing the profile helped me focus on what I wanted. It also

Classify Your Top Clients by Niche

Now take the same list of clients you just identified and break it down by market segment, subsegment, and niche. (Don't stop at five.)

Name	Segment	Subsegment	Niche
1.			
2.			
3.			
4.			
5.			

gave me criteria for making decisions most likely to meet my wants and needs. Brooke was the best fit and an easy choice.

To focus your mind, you need to develop different profiles of ideal prospects in each market subsegment or niche that interests you. You'll need two versions of the Ideal Prospect Profile for each segment or subsegment—one profile that you show others for referrals and one profile that's more detailed to help you qualify the referred person.

You'll start by turning an intangible idea into a real person by writing down who this person is (demographics) and how he or she thinks (psychographics). You'll paint a verbal picture when you can clearly describe this ideal prospect, and other people will say, "I know someone just like that."

In the next few pages you'll find seven sample profiles for some profitable subsegments. Note that they mostly describe the prospects' demographics.

Anyone who fits these profiles is highly likely to be wealthy. We use 50 years old as the starting point because people in this age group control over 70 percent of America's assets. Why did I put "happily married to first spouse"? This indicates they are relationship oriented and have not had to split assets in a divorce. If someone is working on a third spouse, he or she is probably on the tenth advisor.

There's a fine balance between making profiles too vague and making them too specific. If your profiles are too vague, no one will be able to visualize the person you're describing. If your profiles are too detailed, they'll screen too many people out because your clients and centers of influence won't be sure the prospects they're thinking of fit your criteria.

You'll notice I haven't included any income or net worth figures in these profiles. I've found these qualifiers work against your goal of getting referrals. If you're describing a person who can benefit from your services, and you say, "and earns over $200,000 a year," or "and has more than $1 million in investable assets," your referral sources may be stumped. They most likely won't know how much their friends and colleagues earn. So they won't include them on their lists.

The Ideal Prospect Profile is designed to help you and your clients recognize qualified prospects. It does this by describing their age ranges, occupations, or life situations. For example, your profile could include the description, "franchise owners over 50 years old who own three McDonald's restaurants and have been in the business for more than ten years." You wouldn't need to describe their net worths. We already know these individuals will have net worths of several million dollars and close to $1 million in annual income.

Construct your profiles so all referred prospects have an extremely high probability of meeting your minimum requirements. You can do your financial qualifying over the phone when you call to set the appointment. You'll have to wait for your in-person interview to determine if you want to work with them. I'll explain how to do this in Chapter 19 ("Make Your Clients Ecstatic").

Keep an open mind as you work through these written profiles. You may discover a new interest you hadn't been aware of in the past. One advisor I worked with was a financial planner in her late twenties. Most of her clients were in her age group. But when she developed a profile of the types of people she liked to work with most, she realized her favorite activity was estate planning for people over 50.

When she showed her revised profile to existing clients, they eagerly referred her to their parents and aunts and uncles. Simply by knowing exactly what she wanted—and then asking for it—she got it.

Define Your Ideal Prospects

Now it's your turn. Take the segments you're thinking about specializing in and write two Ideal Prospect Profiles for each niche. The first one is for public use and should omit dollar amounts. You'll use this profile to give referral sources, centers of influence, and potential strategic alliance partners a concrete idea of who they should be referring to you.

The second, more detailed version is for your eyes only. You and your staff will use it for qualifying purposes, so it should specify an ideal income, net worth, assets, geographic area, and psychographics. Make it as detailed as necessary. You'll use this profile to screen and prioritize prospects quickly and easily.

If you profile people in the right segments and the right age groups, you'll end up with clear descriptions of the types of new clients you're seeking: Prospects who meet your minimum qualifications and want, need, and value your services.

Define Your
Acceptable Prospects

Having finished your Ideal Prospect Profiles, you now have written profiles of your "A" prospects in each of the two to five niches you're interested in pursuing. Next, follow the same process to describe those clients who aren't ideal but who are *acceptable*—your "B" prospects. These were like the "B" patients for my dad. If you don't have enough "A" prospects you can accept some "B"s.

You'll never show others profiles of your minimally acceptable prospect. But be prepared to verbally describe this minimally acceptable client when appropriate.

Sample Ideal Prospect Profiles for Selected Affluent Segments

MEDICAL PROFESSIONALS

- Physician or surgeon
- Established, highly successful, and respected by peers
- 50 years old or older
- Good businessperson
- Happily married to first spouse
- Friendly, helpful, and influential

AIRLINE PILOTS

- Worked for one of the top airlines, such as Delta, United, or American
- Started flying commercial airlines in the 1960s
- 50 years old or older
- Spouse works or runs own business
- Highly successful and respected by peers
- Happily married to first spouse
- Helpful, friendly, open-minded, and influential

KEY EMPLOYEES OF LARGE OR FAST GROWING COMPANIES

- Established and successful executive, manager, professional, or technician
- Outgoing and respected in their community
- Worked for major company 20-plus years (or five years at a fast-growing company with stock options)
- 50 years old or older (or 40 or over if at a fast growing company with stock options)
- Happily married to first spouse
- Friendly, helpful, open-minded, and influential

ATTORNEYS

- Established, highly successful estate planning practice
- Respected by peers
- 50 years old or older
- Outgoing and social
- Happily married to first spouse
- Friendly, helpful, and influential

Sample Ideal Prospect Profiles for Selected Wealthy Segments

FINANCIALLY INDEPENDENT, SINGLE, OLDER WOMEN

- Lives in an older, established upscale neighborhood or a new, upscale retirement community in the Sunbelt
- Family-oriented
- Outgoing and social
- 55–80 years old
- Young at heart
- Friendly, helpful, open-minded
- Open to learning

SUCCESSFUL ENTREPRENEURS

- Owns an established, highly successful business
- Respected in the community
- In business for more than ten years
- 50 years old or older
- Happily married to first spouse
- Friendly, helpful, and influential

RETIRED COUPLES AND PRE-RETIREES

- Highly successful and respected professional, key executive, or entrepreneur (retired or soon-to-be retired)
- Lives in an older, established neighborhood or a new, upscale retirement community in the Sunbelt
- 55 years old or older
- Likes to socialize
- Worked for major company for more than 20 years
- Happily married to first spouse
- Friendly, helpful, and open-minded

The most important aspects of the Acceptable Prospect Profile are your minimum account requirements and the psychographic descriptions. Your ideal and your acceptable clients should have a minimum investment or annual premium amount, and there should be a minimum commission or annual fee you'll earn from each transaction or new account.

For Advisors Only

You should also create a second version of each Ideal Prospect Profile. These profiles are more detailed and for internal use only. Include everything from the public version plus a list of descriptors that will help you qualify your prospects. A list of common clues that you may be talking with a wealthy prospect follows. Consider including any of these in your advisor-only profiles.

- Travels and entertains frequently
- Home(s) is well kept
- Belongs to a prestigious club
- Active in organizations or associations
- Has multiple brokers
- Is paying for grandchildren's education
- Attends cultural events
- Pays for friends' and family's expenses on vacation
- Holds leadership positions in national or local organizations
- Has hobbies or other strong interests
- Worked for a targeted company with known great benefit program

When prospects don't meet your minimally acceptable profile, don't accept them as clients.

An advisor in Atlanta I worked with developed a profile with a $50,000 minimum for his managed accounts. He had a good client who wanted him to work with her son. But her son had only $30,000 to invest. He said,

> *"I'd love to work with your son, but it wouldn't be cost-effective because my minimum fee is based on a $50,000 account."*

The lady perked right up and said, "That's no problem. I'll just give him $20,000 so he meets your minimum." When you're clear on what you want, you usually get it. I don't claim to understand this phenomenon but I've seen it work over and over again. Ask and you will receive—larger accounts. Maybe it's the power of positive thinking.

Screen Your New Prospects

The best time to get rid of bad clients is before you ever work with them. Remember, the two primary functions of marketing are to *identify* and to *attract* ideal prospects. Good marketing will attract ideal prospects and screen out unqualified ones.

Your objective is to clone your "A" clients, upgrade your "B" clients, minimize service to your "C" clients, and transfer your "D" clients to someone who will look after them. As soon as you develop a consistent flow of "A" prospects, start transferring your "C" clients to the advisor you sent your "D" clients to.

You should compare each new prospect to your Ideal Prospect Profile. Refer those who don't fit your criteria to someone else who will appreciate them. Don't ignore the cost of missed opportunity. The time you spend with a "C" prospect is time you can't invest attracting or helping an "A" prospect.

Make Space for More "A" Clients

When I was in charge of marketing for the advisory firm in Phoenix, we developed a consistent system for bringing in quality prospects with at least $200,000 to invest. One day we picked up a new client with over $800,000 worth of investable assets.

The owner of the firm came to me and said he had a client he'd sold an IRA to a number of years ago who required high maintenance and yielded low payoff. To be blunt, she was a whiner.

He had always wanted to transfer her to another advisor, but he thought maybe she would get an inheritance or refer him to somebody. None of that had happened and probably never would. Since we had developed a consistent flow of high-quality new clients, he told me he now felt comfortable transferring this client.

The point is you don't have to transfer your "C" clients right away. Just transfer your "D" clients now. Begin using the techniques in this book to help you develop a more effective marketing process and to cultivate a consistent flow of new clients. You'll gradually upgrade your client base painlessly and gracefully.

Here's a good strategy: For every new "A" client you get, transfer three "C" clients. And for every new "B" client you get, transfer one "C" client. At this point, you should begin to accept only those new clients who meet your acceptable requirements. When you're ready, transfer all of your "C" clients to another advisor who will take good care of them. You'll free up space for more "A" clients.

Also, as your business evolves and grows, it's normal to discover that clients who were acceptable or even ideal in the past are no longer acceptable or ideal today. In fact, after a year or two, people who use my techniques usually dramatically upgrade their perceptions of what it takes to be an "A" client.

In later chapters you'll learn how to adjust your message and your communication channels to attract exactly the right types of clients. Net worth, income, age, niche, and personality style can all be carefully identified and attracted—as long as you know what you want. And now you do.

Chapter at a Glance

If you want to increase your income effort-lessly, be more selective about the people with whom you do business. Develop written profiles of your ideal prospects. Once you have determined what types of clients will create your ideal business, you'll be able to develop marketing systems to attract those people.

The good news is that there's plenty of room at the top. As you move up the food chain and become more selective and effective, there will be fewer and fewer advisors who will be able to compete with you.

Each year, your business will become easier and easier, and each year you'll receive more and more referrals from happy, helpful, influential clients and centers of influence. You'll be working at serving your niche. You'll be working *with* the market forces, not *against* them.

After completing the exercises in this chapter, turn to Step 3 to learn how to identify rich niches, money in motion, and pools of capital in the segments that interest you the most. You'll be one step closer to implementing your new marketing campaign and finding yourself buried in ideal new clients.

Chapter 7 Action Steps

Exercise 1: Identify your "A" clients. These clients should have been responsible for 50 percent to 80 percent of your revenue over the last two years. Follow the format in "Identify All of Your Current Ideal Clients" on page 126. List all your "A" clients according to the income you earned from them over the past 24 months.

Exercise 2: Using the same list of clients you just identified in Exercise 1—current clients who generate a fair amount of income for you—look for common or related segments you've had success with in the past. Note the segment, subsegment, and niche to which each client belongs. (Follow the format of "Classify Your Top Clients by Niche" on page 128.)

Exercise 3: Taking your personal interests (see Exercise 1 in Chapter 5) and your current client list (see Exercise 2 above) into consideration, list two to five niches in which you think you may want to specialize. Refer back to the information in this chapter and the previous one to help you choose.

Exercise 4: Write Ideal Prospect Profiles for each of the segments you listed in Exercise 3. At the top of each page, write, "Person Who Can Benefit Most From My Services." The first is for public use. The second includes more details and is for your eyes only.

One easy way to identify key characteristics for your Ideal Prospect Profile is to describe your existing ideal clients. Visualize your favorite clients from exercises 1 and 2 above. Then make up a fictional, ideal person with all the best qualities of your favorite clients.

Describe your *ideal* prospect, not one you think of as *realistic*. In marketing, as in life, you get what you pursue. Feel free to refer to the samples in the sidebars in this chapter and modify them for your needs. Look back at the information in Chapters 6 and 7 to help you get started.

Exercise 5: Describe your "B" prospects in an Acceptable Prospect Profile. Follow the steps in Exercise 4 above, developing an Acceptable Prospect Profile for each of your niches. Be sure to clearly describe your minimum account and psychographic requirements.

Step 3

Research to Discover New Opportunities

My friend, Jon, who manages a brokerage branch office, drew this analogy to explain the haphazard way most financial advisors market their businesses. *After studying guns and ammunition intensively, a duck hunter goes into the middle of a field. Using a 12-gauge, pump-action shotgun, he*

Study prospects, not just products.

points his weapon into the air and starts shooting wildly—hoping a duck will fly by.

If you're interested in hunting ducks, knowing about guns and ammunition is helpful, but it's the ducks you really need to understand. The first thing you should do is study where they are at different times of the year, what types of food they like, and what kinds of sounds attract them. Becoming an expert in the habits and patterns of ducks would make you a much more successful duck hunter.

Similarly, understanding the habits and patterns of ideal prospects is the missing link in our industry. Product sponsors make sure you're well-informed about products and strategies. But to be a client-centered marketer, you also need to have an intimate understanding of the hopes, dreams, motivations, fears, and concerns of your ideal prospects and clients. You need to know where to find them and how to attract them. That's how you create a quantum leap in your productivity and your marketing effectiveness.

Thorough and systematic research will help you uncover the best niches and most profitable opportunities. The chapters in this section will show you how to find out what you need to know.

Section Preview

- Achieve *market resonance,* a powerful competitive advantage.

- Discover rich niches, money in motion, and pools of capital.

- Use research interviews to discover hidden opportunities, demonstrate your client-centered approach to business, and win easy referrals.

- Take advantage of third-party research.

- Organize and keep track of your new contacts.

Interview Your Key Clients and Niche Experts

A single conversation across the table
with a wise man is better than
ten years' study of books.
—Chinese proverb

n the 1980s, Mazda was desperate for a new car design that would turn the company around. Management needed to identify new customers and design a new car that would generate the most profit. Senior executives knew the automobile market was saturated, but they were hoping to discover a niche to keep their company afloat. They decided on a radical course of action.

To identify their most profitable opportunities, they sent a team of market researchers to southern California to interview car owners. By conducting face-to-face interviews with hundreds of car owners, they eventually identified a market no other manufacturer was serving.

They discovered a small group of people who still harbored a passion for the old MGB. These potential customers wanted the fun and excitement of the classic, frisky English sports car combined with the reliability and handling of a modern Japanese car. Armed with this information, the marketing team flew back to Japan and convinced management to design and build a totally new car: the Mazda Miata.

When these cars hit the showroom in the mid-1980s, they sold so fast dealers couldn't keep them in stock. In a market saturated with cars, the demand for the Miata was so great that dealers routinely charged thousands of dollars more than the suggested retail price.

What Mazda had achieved was the magical state of *market resonance*. When your products or services are perfectly in sync with your prospects' wants, your offerings literally sell themselves. And if your customers truly value what you're offering, cost is not an important factor.

Remember that selling is trying to get people to want what you have, but marketing is having what people want. With market research, you can learn exactly what it will take to attract and satisfy your ideal clients. You'll discover how to unlock the awesome power of market resonance.

But first, like Mazda, you have to identify a viable market segment or niche. Then you need to develop specialized products and services that perfectly match the wants and needs of the people you want to serve. Face-to-face research with key clients and niche experts is the easiest way to accomplish this.

The Miata was so successful because Mazda used research to give its ideal prospects exactly what they wanted. In a saturated car market, people happily paid a premium for the privilege of owning this cool little car. One way to determine what people value is to watch what they buy. If they're not willing to write you checks, you simply haven't achieved that state of market resonance—yet.

What You'll Learn From Interviewing

In Step 2, you used profiling to help you determine a short list of segments or subsegments you're interested in targeting. This chapter will help you evaluate those segments and discover rich niches in them. You may also discover new subsegments and niches during this stage of the research process.

By the time you complete the exercises in this chapter, you'll have identified the subsegments and niches that will form the basis of your super-profitable business. You'll also have a good idea of the right mix of products and services that will perfectly match your ideal prospects' and clients' wants and needs. And you'll start to learn how to add value beyond your core products.

These niches aren't a final decision. You're never really finished evaluating opportunities, because markets change. This research process gives you constant feedback from the market, alerting you to changes and keeping you in tune with the desires of the marketplace.

Don't view the subsegment selection process as limiting. Instead, the process should teach you how to expand your thinking beyond your current client base. One goal is to identify overlooked opportunities in your community.

There are four primary subjects for research interviews. Each type of interviewee requires a different set of questions and can generate different outcomes. The four groups are

1. current key clients,

2. centers of influence (local and segment experts),

3. potential ideal new clients, and

4. potential strategic alliance partners.

This chapter will get you started with the first two, which we'll call "round one": interviewing key clients and centers of influence in the subsegments and niches you've selected. You'll learn more about interviewing potential new clients in the next chapter. Later, two chapters in Step 5 are devoted to developing strategic alliances.

Most financial advisors know all about their products and financial strategies, but they know very little about their clients, prospects, or local economy. But in a client-centered market, you must become more niche-oriented because different people define *total solution* and *value* differently. Once you know what your prospects value and how to deliver it, you can dominate your target niches and subsegments. It will be very difficult for generic advisors to compete against you.

You'll be rewarded handsomely if you get to know your clients on a deeper and more meaningful level. Individual interviews are the best way to do this. In fact, conducting research is a core competency of all effortless marketers.

The Four Key Benefits of Client Interviews

There are four direct benefits of conducting face-to-face research interviews.

1. Gain knowledge. Research interviews will help you identify the types of clients you want to work with and discover specific opportunities, such as money in motion and pools of capital. You'll learn what products, value-added services, and strategies will attract and satisfy your ideal clients. In addition, research interviews will help you determine the most compelling message for attracting your ideal new clients.

2. Gather referrals. During the interviews, you'll be referred to potentially ideal clients and excellent information sources. By interviewing centers of influence and potential strategic alliances, you'll penetrate lucrative niches simply by making new friends—on purpose.

3. Build relationships. These interviews strengthen existing relationships and enable you to establish new relationships with people who can help you build your business. Once your clients and new friends know what you stand for and who can benefit most from your services, some of them will become your marketing apostles. (Remember the two doctors in the operating room?) Others will become members of your informal board of advisors. And many of the people you meet will become great clients.

4. Generate new business. Don't be surprised if these interviews generate additional business from your existing clients. That's very common. One of the advisors I work with picked up $1.5 million just from interviewing ten of her favorite clients.

There's also at least one critical indirect benefit: Conducting interviews is a fundamental way to help you become client-centered. After listening to ten or 15 of your favorite people describe in intimate detail their hopes, dreams, and concerns, you can't help but understand them on a deeper level.

One Successful Interview
Pays Big Dividends

In 1992, Jim was conducting a research interview. His goal was simply to understand his clients' wants and needs better. But on this day, the market forces were with him.

Jim had gone through the normal interview process. He'd asked the client about motivations, challenges and concerns, and any areas in which the client thought the advisor could help. Then Jim asked a key question:

> *"Knowing what you know, if you were me, how would you market to people like you?"*

Much to Jim's surprise, his client said, "I would ask your best clients for referrals."

Jim said, "That's a great idea. I only wish I had thought of it. Who do you know who could benefit from my services?"

The client responded, "I belong to one of the finest country clubs in this city. I know many of the members personally. I have a list of their phone numbers and addresses. What if I went through the list and told you who I thought could benefit most from your services?"

About three months later, Jim called me. He was ecstatic. He said, "Steve, I just had the best month in my life. I made more than one hundred thousand dollars from the referrals of a single interview!"

Jim's success was extremely exciting. I knew that study after study indicated the best way to build your business is through referrals. But I also knew that many financial advisors were reluctant to ask for them. Here was a way to get clients to offer referrals *on their own*. Jim had begun harnessing the market forces.

Then Jim revealed another interesting point. He told me he had worked with this client for eight years. He'd gone to graduate school with the client's son. Jim was almost part of the family. Yet he'd never received one referral before this. He had asked, but the client had always been reluctant.

I asked Jim, "Why, after all these years, did this key client finally decide to give you referrals?" Jim said he believed it was because the interview process itself changed his client's perception of him. He said that as he went through the questions, he started to understand the client on a deeper level. He felt the questions repositioned him as a competent, caring advisor who understood his clients and had empathy for their problems.

In short, when Jim proved himself to be client-centered by listening to and involving the client in what he was trying to do, the client responded by offering to help Jim build his business.

In my experience, these interviews not only change clients' perceptions of their advisors, they also reposition the advisors' perception of themselves. The foundation for a new type of partnership is created. This is probably the biggest payoff from client research interviews.

Once both you and your clients start to see your relationship as a valuable partnership, you *both* begin to think and behave differently. You truly become client-centered—and your clients become *advisor-centered*. You look for ways to help each other achieve your respective goals.

Look for Money in Motion

When an advisor and I were conducting an interview with the business development officer for Long Beach, California, we discovered that the Port Authority of Long Beach had more than $1 billion to purchase land around the port so it could expand. That meant money in motion.

We learned more about the expansion plan and discovered other people we could talk to about it. If $1 billion was going to business owners, we wanted to see if we could help them as they went through this important life transition.

As you conduct research interviews with clients and centers of influence, realize that timing is critical. If you can get the right message to the right people at the right time, your chances of starting a profitable new relationship go up astronomically. In fact, getting the timing right is one of the biggest marketing challenges.

One of your key interview objectives should be to discover whether the interviewee has—or is likely to have—money in motion. You also want to find out if your interviewee *knows anyone* who has, or is about to have, money in motion.

In marketing, the study of timing is *synchrographics*. The concept of synchrographics evolved when market researchers realized you could get the right message to the right people and they still wouldn't buy. Something was missing from the equation. The missing factor was *timing*.

People are more receptive to your offerings at certain times than at others. You know this from watching for needs events and money in motion. Synchrographics is the term used to describe times of major transition: life events such as having a baby, retiring, selling a business, the death of a spouse, and relocating.

To get the really big sales, you must catch your wealthy prospects at the height of their liquidity. I would rather have a prospect with $100,000 of ready cash than a prospect with $1 million in illiquid business assets.

Just like you or me, wealthy individuals are more receptive to spending or investing when they have money in hand or are about to receive it. Liquidity events create a problem financial advisors are happy to solve.

Some key indicators of impending needs events are the sale of a business, house, investment, real estate, stocks, a boat, a luxury car, or a private plane. Whenever these expensive items change hands, money will be in motion. This indicates not only liquidity for the seller, but also a wealthy buyer. And don't ignore the salespeople. Investment bankers, real estate brokers, yacht brokers, and auctioneers often are rewarded handsomely when they close a sale.

Also Look for Pools of Capital

An advisor in Texas interviewed some of her clients who worked at a major company and learned that the company had more than $600 million in its pension plan. The company's managers were planning to disband the fund and distribute the money to the participants. Of course, this advisor's currently developing a list of as many employees as possible. Where is she getting the names? From interviews with clients and their friends who work at the company.

She's discovered a huge pool of capital that's about to become money in motion. She's already an expert on the company's pension plan. Now she's getting ready to capture her share of the $600 million bonanza. A little research has helped her identify the opportunity of a lifetime.

Interview Your Key Clients

Start your research by interviewing clients with whom you are the most comfortable. I call this "practicing on your friends." Once you have mastered the interview process with people you know, you can start interviewing people you've just met.

Don't delegate the interviews, or you'll miss out on one of the best client interactions you may ever have. If you become so busy that you can't conduct them yourself and so proficient with them that you can teach someone else to do them, then you can train a competent marketing person to assist you.

Use what you learned from the exercises in the previous chapter to help you identify your first group of interviewees. Choose ten to 15 key "A" or "B" clients in the subsegments you have selected. These people might be, but aren't necessarily, your wealthiest or favorite clients. Your goal is to select people who can lead you to new opportunities.

In the beginning, limit your research to people in two to five different niches. Don't fall into the trap of trying to target everyone. You want to go narrow and deep, not broad and shallow.

Transitional Events for Specific Market Segments

I t's profitable to anticipate the kinds of needs events that are specific to your target segments and subsegments. Here are a few examples to help stimulate your thinking. Recognize that many of these needs events overlap a few different market segments.

ALL MARKETS

- Divorce
- Funding of qualified retirement plans
- Bonus
- Retirement
- Death of spouse, parent, or close family member
- Inheritance

BUSINESS OWNERS

- Sale of the business (which often represents your biggest opportunity)
- Public stock offering
- Sale of a capital asset
- Mergers

SELF-EMPLOYED PROFESSIONALS

- Sale of practice

LAWYERS

- Winning a lawsuit or settlement

SENIOR EXECUTIVES

- Exercise of stock options
- New job
- Promotion
- Bonus
- Big commission check

RETIREES

- Receipt of IRA rollover assets
- CD matures
- Bonds called
- CD rates drop

INHERITORS

- Receipt of inheritance

WIDOWS

- Death of spouse

You don't have to wait for money to be put in motion. In fact, you can actively encourage it to happen. Here's a classic example: A San Francisco advisor helps dentists package and sell their practices and then helps them invest the proceeds. This active involvement in creating business by facilitating needs events is a growing trend in the financial services industry.

Remember that this is an ongoing process. There are probably many opportunities you haven't discovered yet, so be open to revising your list of target segments, subsegments, and niches. Always be on the lookout for new and better opportunities as markets evolve and as you learn and grow personally.

If you follow my process, you'll be referred to additional qualified people to interview in the segments you want to work in. This process is self-sustaining and will continue as long as you want it to continue.

How to Set Interview Appointments

Once you have developed your profiles and selected your interview subjects, you're ready to set up some client interviews. Use the following scripts to do this. Contact your key clients and briefly tell them about your goals for the meeting. This is easier than you think. Simply say something like this:

> *"I need your help. I'm developing a more focused approach to my marketing. I've created a profile of my favorite clients, and you're exactly the kind of person I most enjoy helping. Could we get together for ninety minutes or so? I'd like to get your ideas and opinions about how I could be more effective at helping people like you achieve their financial goals."*

When you get together, you need to frame the conversation so your interview subject will understand what you're trying to accomplish. You can say,

> *"I'm not here to try to sell you anything. My goal for today's meeting is to better understand the wants and needs of people like you. I also want to discover how I can provide the most value for people in your situation. I also want to learn how to be more effective at attracting high quality people like you to work with my firm."*

It takes time to learn how to do these types of interviews well. In market research, only the most experienced researchers conduct these *depth* interviews. Tell your interviewees you're new to the process and they'll help you. For your first couple of interviews, you might want to say something like this:

"I really want to become more client-centered. But I'm new to this interview process, so please help me if I'm a little rough."

Client Research
Interview Questions

Here are some sample questions to use during client interviews. Use these questions as a guide only. Your goal is to better understand your clients' motivations and to discover specific opportunities—not just to ask the questions on the interview form.

Before each interview, decide what you want to learn from your interview subject. Write down specific goals, then select relevant questions. Adapt the questions on the following pages as you discover new areas you want to explore.

Learn More About Your Clients

MOTIVATIONS

These questions set the stage for your interview and help you understand your clients' emotional motivations and concerns. You'll recognize some from previous chapters.

1. "What's important about money to you?" *

2. "What would have to happen for you to feel you were accomplishing —————?" *(Name each of the values you discovered in the previous question.)*   *(continued next page)*

---

*This powerful question is part of consultant Bill Bachrach's "values conversation," an interview for high-level sales situations. I recommend Bill's book, *Values-Based Selling: The Art of Building High-Trust Client Relationships for Financial Advisors, Insurance Agents and Investment Reps* (Aim High Publishing, 1996), and his coaching program.

3. "What are the biggest financial challenges people like you face today? Please explain."

4. "What are your thoughts and feelings about having a relationship with a financial advisor?"

5. "What has to happen for you to feel that our relationship is working for you?"

6. "Would you be comfortable sharing with me some of your hopes and dreams for the future?"

BACKGROUNDS

This section gives you some background on your client and a better understanding of your client's lifestyle.

1. "What clubs or organizations do you or your friends belong to? Which one do you suggest I join?"

2. "What sports, hobbies, or other leisure activities do you enjoy?"

3. "What publications do you read? What radio programs do you listen to? Which publications should I have my articles published in? Which radio program should I be interviewed for?"

4. "Who is your accountant? Are you happy with him or her? May I open the lines of communication with him or her?" *(Get the name and address of the accountant.)*

5. "Tell me about your previous investment experiences."

Conduct an Effective Interview

DISCOVER WHAT YOUR CLIENTS THINK OF YOU

This section will give you insights about your perceived strengths and competitive positioning.

1. "How did you first hear about me?"

2. "What do you see as my strongest points?"

3. "Who do you see as my major competitors?"

4. "Why did you select me?"

5. "What personal benefits have you received from our relationship?" *(This describes the emotional payoff.)*

6. "If they asked, what would you tell your friends about me?"

ASK FOR ADVICE

Get your clients to help you design the ideal business to fit their wants and needs.

1. "What additional products or value-added services could I offer to help people like you solve their financial problems and achieve their life goals?"

2. "What other ideas do you have for me to more closely match my business or services to the wants and needs of people like you?"

3. "What's the most compelling thing I could say to people like you to interest them in doing business with me?"

4. "If you were me, knowing what you know, how would you market to people like yourself?"

5. "I'm thinking about offering a new service. How would you feel about paying an all-inclusive annual fee for comprehensive financial advice and investment services?" *(Discuss your plans or thoughts on new products and services you're thinking of offering.)*

(continued next page)

DISCUSS THE PROFILE OF YOUR IDEAL PROSPECT

This section will help you refine your Ideal Prospect Profile and usually prompts your clients to think of specific people who fit your profile.

1. "I've developed a profile of the type of person who can benefit most from my services. What insights can you give me about this profile or person?" (*Show the client your profile.*)

2. "How could I improve this profile?"

3. "Where can I find high concentrations of people like this?"

4. "Who do you know who fits this profile? What do you know about this person that would be helpful for me to know to refine my profile?"

5. (*Optional*) "I have a list of people in your —————." (*Insert occupation, club, industry, neighborhood, and so on*). "Would you be willing to go over the list and give me your insights on the people you know?"

6. (*Optional*) "Which of these people do you think could benefit most from my services? Why?"

ASK FOR OTHER PEOPLE TO INTERVIEW

Your clients should be able to refer you to their peers and other centers of influence to interview. This is an important outcome of each research discussion. You'll learn what to do with these leads in the next chapter.

1. "Who do you know who I should interview for additional information? They should either fit one of my profiles or be a center of influence in your circle." (*Ask about specific groups of people like church members, neighbors, co-workers, family, friends, and so on.*)

2. (*Optional*) "I'm also thinking about working with people in another niche." (*Show them another profile.*) "Do you know anyone in this niche who I should interview?" (*continued next page*)

3. "Would you be willing to introduce me to them?"
    (Or) "May I use your name when I contact them?"

4. "Would you help me prioritize the 'A,' 'B,' and 'C' people to interview?"

5. "What key points would you make to each of your 'A' referrals to open their minds to meeting with me?"

FINAL THOUGHTS AS YOU CLOSE THE INTERVIEW

These questions give you an opportunity to explore additional areas that interest you.

1. "What other ideas do you have to help me improve the value of my services and the effectiveness of my marketing?"

2. *(Optional)* "I'm thinking about adding value beyond my core products and services. What to you think about . . . ?" *(Share your ideas with them.)*

3. "What is the biggest business opportunity you would pursue if you were me? Why choose that one?"

4. *(Optional)* If you're considering a new product, service, company name, or company mission statement, share these with your interview subjects. Ask for their feedback and first impressions.

5. "Are there any personal financial questions you have that I can answer for you?"

6. "If you have any additional thoughts later, please call me."

7. *(If appropriate)* "I'm creating an informal board of advisors. Would it be OK to call you from time to time to get your opinions and ideas on my plans?"

Tips for Client Interviews

Most salespeople tend to be better at talking than listening. But the most effective salespeople listen more than they talk. As you listen to your clients talk about their hopes and dreams—the things they want and the things they value—a bond forms between the two of you. This is important because, without exception, people want to work with others who truly understand them.

As my friend Jim learned, there was more selling going on during the 90 minutes when he was listening than in the previous eight years when he was talking and advising. That one experience of active listening fundamentally changed his relationship with his client.

Listening may also change some of your long-held perceptions of your clients. Many advisors make assumptions about their clients. Some of these advisors have told me, "I know what my clients want." I ask, "How?" They say, "I just do." But when they go out and talk to their clients, they learn they had been assuming their clients think the way they do. Misunderstandings like this keep advisors from achieving market resonance.

As you conduct these interviews, encourage your clients to talk freely. Ask many open-ended questions that your clients can't answer with simple one-word responses. Let them do 90 percent of the talking. Practice active listening. Don't ask questions your clients have already answered. And don't answer questions for them. If they take a little time to answer, it's because they're thinking. Give them time to think and process their responses. It's likely nobody has ever asked them these questions before.

Open your mind, and pretend you don't know anything about these market segments and niches. Be investigative, like Columbo. Use inferential thinking to read between the lines. This is where your sincere curiosity about how to serve your clients better is critical.

Try tape-recording the interviews. You'll gain additional insights when you listen to the tapes. Simply tell your interviewees that you value their ideas and opinions, and you want to record the conversation so you can review it later. Most everyone will be flattered.

Stay focused through the conversation by jotting down the answers to your questions on a legal pad. Put asterisks in front of the points you want to learn more about later. Come back to these questions after your subject has run out of steam on the current question.

Look for patterns and new opportunities. One interview won't reveal any patterns, but ten interviews will. Often the most useful information your clients give you will be unsolicited. Here's why: When you start the interviewing process, you don't know what you don't know. As you discover new opportunities, you can explore them more deeply in subsequent interviews with others.

Plan on each interview lasting 90 minutes or so. And don't worry if the interviews run a little long. Think of these interviews as your clients making an investment in your success.

Interview Centers of Influence

If you've been in this business for a while, you probably have some great clients. But you may not have many clients you want to clone. Or your top clients may not be in the niches that you're most interested in pursuing.

To expand your thinking and to identify hidden opportunities in your community, you should interview *centers of influence*—niche or segment experts and experts on your local economy. Your clients should be able to refer you to these individuals, and you can identify others through the Internet or library research.

Every area of the country has a unique economic foundation. In central California, your best market might be farmers. In Seattle, a tremendous amount of wealth comes from the software industry. In a retirement area, your target market may be retirees. It's critical to understand the engines of wealth creation, capital formation, and income generation in your community.

But what's the easiest way to find these opportunities?

Ask Local Experts These Questions

Practice on your key clients first. When you get to centers of influence and experts, you'll be comfortable with the interview process. Here are some basic questions to help you identify opportunities with local experts.

1. "Could you give me an overview on the local economy with respect to _____ niche?"

2. "What has been the economic foundation for this area?"

3. "What are the major industries?"

4. "What types of companies do we have the most of?"

5. "What major changes or challenges are those industries experiencing?"

6. "What are some of the major companies?"

7. "Which companies are growing most quickly?"

8. "Which companies or industries are declining?"

9. "What companies are the most numerous?"

10. "What neighborhoods have the highest concentrations of wealthy homeowners?"

11. "What local conferences, associations, or organizations might be helpful to me?"

12. "Do you know of any publications or reports that might help me understand the local economy and markets better?"

13. "Who else can I talk to for more information?"

14. "I'm particularly interested in these market segments and niches: ————, ————, and ————. Do you know of any resources? Or anyone I could talk to who might give me insights into those specific areas?"

15. "If you were me, knowing what you know, what opportunities would you target? Why?"

Business Development Officers

My grandfather was the business development officer for Anaheim, California in the 1950s. He helped bring Disneyland to that city. As the business development officer, he coordinated the sale of 160 acres in 22 parcels to WED, Inc., the organization Walt Disney created to design and build Disneyland. My grandfather was a wealth of knowledge about the economic inner workings of that burgeoning city simply by virtue of his position in the local government.

Almost every city, county, and state today has a business development officer. These individuals are excellent sources of information about your local economy, and they can introduce you to the key centers of influence in your community. It's the responsibility of these individuals to bring new businesses to their municipality, keep businesses from leaving, and encourage growth and profitable relationships among the existing businesses.

The people holding these positions are important centers of influence and excellent sources of information about the untapped opportunities in your community. They also can be great referral sources because they're matchmakers by nature and know all the local movers and shakers.

Local Experts

In addition, you can interview reporters, editors, and publishers of local business publications. They're often extremely knowledgeable and well known to influential people in the community. These people can steer you to the major economic drivers of your local economy.

Once you have identified specific opportunities in your community, interview the industry experts and niche insiders in the segments and subsegments that interest you. Association officers, trade reporters, and consultants can often give you valuable insights into key issues and opportunities in specific niches.

Contact the chapter presidents of local associations that have high concentrations of the prospects you want to target. Tell these centers of influence that you're conducting market research to determine how you can make the biggest contribution to their industry. Ask them to lunch. If they won't meet with you, ask for an interview over the phone.

College professors who study your local economy are also excellent sources of information. Call the dean of a business school and ask which individuals on staff study and track the local economy. Then contact these people and arrange to interview them.

These interviews are usually more open-ended than client interviews. Keep your antennae up and dig deep when a specific opportunity presents itself in your discussions.

Since you've done your client interviews first, you'll have had some practice discovering hidden opportunities. You'll be able to focus on your subject's information rather than the interview process.

Schedule Expert Interview Appointments

Setting interview meetings with experts is slightly different from arranging meetings with existing clients. Simply call your expert, and phrase your request like this:

> *"I'm a local business owner. I'm doing some market research on ———— [your community or your target industry]. I'd greatly appreciate meeting with you and getting your insights about how I can provide the greatest value to people in your field [niche, industry, etc.]."*

Conduct Secondary Research

Once you have identified the segments, niches, and opportunities that you want to explore more deeply, you can conduct some secondary research. This means reading material and data someone else has compiled. I suggest you send your assistant or marketing director to the library for a half-day to start.

Library Research

Have your researcher ask the reference librarian for two current directories: *The National Trade and Professional Associations* (NTPA) directory (Columbia Books) and the *Encyclopedia of Associations* (Gale Research). These two resources list most of the major associations in North America. Many local libraries also have directories of local clubs and associations. The librarian will know what resources are available.

Have your marketing person jot down the descriptions of the organizations that serve the niches you're interested in pursuing. Contact the groups and ask for a new member kit and a media kit for their magazines, if they publish them. Review this material.

Dun & Bradstreet is a resource for learning more about companies that interest you, but most smaller companies aren't profiled. I highly recommend that you read key articles and subscribe to the magazines and newsletters people in your target niches read. It's one good way to become an expert. The reference librarian at your local library can help you find the library's list of periodicals. Copy and keep a file of key articles for future reference.

Audiotapes

A painless way to gather up-to-the-minute information on issues affecting your target segments is to listen to audiotapes recorded at conventions and workshops. Find out which company records the conventions and regional workshops sponsored by your target groups. Call the company and ask for a list of tapes from the most recent meetings. Order those tapes that seem interesting or relevant.

Online Research

You can also use online databases to search publications for interesting articles. *Lexis-Nexis* (www.lexis-nexis.com/lncc/) and *Dialog* (www.dialog.com/au) are two of the largest and most popular. These services are normally expensive for individuals, but they are free at most libraries.

Avoid the pay-per-view cost of some databases by signing up for an annual subscription to an online database such as *Hoovers* (www.hoovers.com), *The Wall Street Journal Interactive Edition* (www.wsj.com) or *The Electric Library* (www.elibrary.com).

Yellow Pages

A low-tech research source is your local yellow pages directory. You can simply count the number of companies in the target markets that interest you. The ads will give you insight into companies' services, position, size, longevity, and personality.

One advisor I worked with decided he was going to target scuba diving companies in San Diego. I asked him to get the phone book and look them up; he found four. I told him it was going to be one of the shortest marketing campaigns in history!

To expand his niche, we identified what he liked about the scuba industry, which was its outdoor-sports connection. He broadened his niche to include the action sports market subsegments in southern California, which includes yachting, car racing, rock climbing, hiking, mountain biking, and so on—and is a growing, multibillion dollar industry.

Local Publications

Finally, for a wealth of knowledge about local businesses and business owners, search your local business journal. Often these publications will do special issues on specific industries or types of business. In Orange County, California, the local business journal comes out once a week. It profiles a major industry at least once a month and publishes a detailed list of the top companies, complete with phone numbers, numbers of employees, areas of specialization, years in business, and sometimes even annual revenue figures.

As you start to target specific industries and niches, be on the lookout for information that can help you understand the segments, subsegments, and niches, as well as their opportunities, problems, and players. You'll be amazed at how information materializes out of thin air once you've selected some target niches. *Focus* is the key to identifying profitable opportunities.

Chapter at a Glance

The choice is yours. You can either cold call until you burn out, send mass mail until you go broke, or you can conduct a little research. The knowledge you gain will allow you to identify new niche opportunities you never knew existed. Remember, we're now in the information economy. Specific information on your ideal prospects and their niches is your "unfair" competitive advantage.

Understanding your prospects' perceptions and motivations will put you miles ahead of your competitors. Just like Mazda, you need to do something radical: Get out into the market and ask focused questions. Research and focus are critical keys to effort-less marketing. Discovering profitable new market subsegments and niches is an important step in creating a super-profitable financial services business.

Chapter 8 Action Steps

Exercise 1: Prepare for your client interviews. Make sure you have an Ideal Prospect Profile for each subsegment you're planning to target. You wrote some of these for Exercise 4 in Chapter 7. If you discover new niches you want to pursue, you'll need to write profiles for them.

Limit your initial research to two to five subsegments. Once you've selected the subsegments, identify ten to 15 key "A" or "B" clients in those markets. Draft a set of interview questions. Use the sample lists found on pages 153–157 to guide you. Finally, schedule your client interviews. Adapt the scripts included in this chapter.

Exercise 2: Conduct your client interviews. Bring your Ideal Prospect Profile, a tape recorder, and a notebook. Listen intently, and ask follow-up questions when you sense the client is implying opportunities such as money in motion or pools of capital.

Exercise 3: Prepare for your interviews with centers of influence. Identify a list of five to ten industry or local experts who are likely to lead you to new opportunities. Prepare your interview questions. Schedule interviews with centers of influence. Follow the suggested script in this chapter.

Exercise 4: Conduct interviews with centers of influence.

Exercise 5: Have an associate gather secondary research from the library or electronic sources. Request new member kits from associations and media kits from industry trade magazines. Listen to audiotapes from industry conferences. Gather articles and background material about your target niches and your prospects within those markets.

Interview Selected Referrals

*The more of himself a customer leaves
with your company, the greater
the hold you have on him.*

—Patricia Seybold, business strategy analyst and
author, *Customers.com*

Alan, a Canadian advisor, called me after purchasing a list of franchise owners and asked me for advice about creating a direct-mail letter to send them. To his dismay, I told him, "Alan, throw the list away."

We talked about how important it is to work through the referral process, rather than through a cold-calling campaign or mass-mail process. While we talked, he identified ten individuals he knew who either owned franchises or were closely aligned with the franchise industry. I suggested he start there, building new relationships based on existing ones.

Then I asked him how his client research interviews were going. He confessed he hadn't done any of them. I coached him a bit and sent him out to interview his favorite client.

Although it was his first interview, it went extremely well. The client referred Alan to 65 key executives and business owners the client knew personally. Many of them were former IBM executives. Both Alan and his client were also ex-IBMers. What a coincidence!

Alan asked his client if any of the people on the list were currently experiencing a transitional event that might indicate they needed his help right now. The client said one of his friends had recently sold a business and had $6 million in cash he needed to invest.

Alan asked the client if he would be willing to introduce him to this friend. The client told him, "Sure, but I'm going out of town for the next few weeks. Then, when I get back, my friend will be out of town." Since an introduction was too difficult, Alan decided to send the potential new client a referral letter.

Alan showed his client a sample referral letter. (You'll learn how to use these in Step 5.) He told the client,

> *"Normally, if I'm referred to someone who needs my help right away, I like to arrange an introduction. If an introduction is not appropriate, I send a letter like this one. Would you be willing to review this letter and share any ideas you have for improving it?"*

Then Alan asked his client to help him customize the letter for this particular referral. He took detailed notes about the potential new client's situation, concerns, and interests. Then he had his assistant personalize the letter and send it to his client's friend.

He called the prospect one week later to set up a face-to-face meeting. During the meeting, the retired entrepreneur told him he had talked to the referral source. He said, "Stan said he wouldn't be in the comfortable financial situation he's in today if he hadn't started working with you six years ago."

There's nothing any advisor could say that would be more powerful than an enthusiastic endorsement from a happy client. Basically, Alan's client did the selling for him. The client was his *marketing apostle*. That's the power of the research interview.

In the previous chapter, you learned how to interview your favorite clients and centers of influence. The goal of those interviews is to help you understand why your clients are working with you, to show you what they want from you, and to discover some specific opportunities in your marketplace.

Interviews Help You Eliminate Unprofitable Niches

One advisor used this interview process to talk with people in the stock car racing industry. Since I believe strongly in combining personal and business interests, I encouraged him to conduct the first round of interviews. Over a period of four weeks he interviewed 15 experts in the stock car racing sphere.

From each interview subject, he received a number of referrals. He asked for help prioritizing the list of referrals. One interview led to the next. He ultimately worked his way up the food chain to Johnny Rutherford, a famous race car driver and the most successful local businessman in the stock car industry.

Unfortunately, after 15 interviews, Greg found there was little opportunity for a financial advisor in the stock car industry. Although they spent an average of $25,000 a year on their cars, none of them had any real net worth. They were affluent, not wealthy. But he realized this after only four weeks and was able to cross this market niche off his list. Just like the mining engineer who drills test holes and finds no gold, Greg went on to the next mountain.

Prioritize Your Market Segments

If you've done enough round-one interviews, you should have a substantial list of great prospects. Now you need to prioritize your market segments. Your best prospects are the ones you have the greatest rapport with and who have financial problems you can get paid to solve.

Until this point, you have had a list of two to five potential target niches. Narrow that list to between one and three. These are the niches you'll concentrate on as you work through steps 4 and 5. (Choose more than three, and your focus will be too fragmented as you learn this process.) Use these five criteria to prioritize your niches.

1. Easily identifiable: How easy is it to identify individuals in this segment or subsegment? Are there local niches or groups of these people in your community? I'm constantly asked how to find hot lists of rich prospects eager to buy. So far, I haven't found such a list. The ideal niche is a community of people you can get to know. And with the help of those contacts, you can build a list of names of the best prospects. You'd then qualify these prospects individually.

2. Fun and profit: You can identify your prospects, but can you make any money working with them? Will they be fun, too? Make sure your targeted prospects are worth pursuing. Normally this means you can identify many prospects in your targeted wealthy niches who are over 50 years old and who you'll enjoy getting to know.

3. Growth trends: Are your targeted market segments growing or declining? Usually a growing market is better. However, you can make big bucks in rollovers when employees leave declining industries and companies.

4. Accessibility: If your subsegments are big, prosperous, and easily identifiable, can you attract ideal prospects in them to face-to-face meetings? Doctors are a classic example of a market segment that's easy to identify. But because they work such long hours and are inundated with product pushers, doctors are extremely hard to access.

5. Receptivity: I like prospects who need and want what I have, don't you? Even if you can handle rejection, it's more profitable to market to people who are genuinely interested in your services.

After prioritizing your market segments and seeking the assistance of your clients in prioritizing referrals, you're ready to conduct interviews with these prequalified and, you hope, motivated prospects. The questions you ask will be similar to those in the previous chapter. See "Also Ask Referrals About These 12 Subjects" below for guidelines. By interviewing your clients' referrals, you'll learn exactly what it takes to attract prospects in your target niches, and you'll win new clients. Some of them will ask for your help during the interview.

Also Ask Referrals About These 12 Subjects

In this second round of interviewing, you'll be using many of the same questions you used in round one, and you'll be seeking similar information. Simply modify the list of questions you use for clients and experts, being sure to touch on these 12 subjects. One sample question is listed for each category.

1. **Motivations:** "What's important about money to you?"

2. **Vision of the future** (from Nick Murray's wonderful book, *The Excellent Investment Advisor*): "You are —— years old now. Take a moment, if you will, to picture yourself 20 years from now. You are —— years old, and well into a comfortable retirement. Tell me: What are you doing? And where is the money coming from?"

3. **Concerns:** "What are some of the major challenges or issues that people in your situation *[industry, etc.]* face today?"

4. **Financial advisor criteria:** "What is (or would be) important about a relationship with a financial advisor to you?"

5. **Current advisor:** "Where are you currently getting your personal financial advice?"

6. **Perceptions about fee-based money management:** "What do you think about a fee-based investment management process that provides ongoing monitoring, quarterly performance reports, and periodic meetings to review your investment results and strategies?"

7. **Advice:** "What's the most compelling thing I could say to individuals in your situation that would interest them in doing business with me?"

8. **The best channels of communication:** "Do you belong to any organizations? Which ones? What are some of the biggest organizations in your niche? If you were in my situation, which ones would you join?"

(continued next page)

9. **Refine your Ideal Prospect Profile:** "How could I improve this profile?"

10. **Refine referral letter:** "When I get a referral, I usually send the person a letter like this one and then call. How would you react if you got a letter like this?" (*Let interviewee read the letter.*)

11. **Other people to meet:** "Who do you know, who fits my profile, who could either benefit from my services or should be interviewed for additional information?"

12. **Final thoughts** (*if appropriate*): "I'm creating an informal board of advisors. Would you mind if I called you, from time to time, to get your opinions and ideas on my marketing plans?"

Bury Yourself in Ideal Referrals

Over the years, I have refined the research interview process and the questions I use during an interview. As a result, it's very unusual for an advisor following my method to interview a client, potential client, or center of influence and come away without referrals. In fact, it's not unusual to get *too many* referrals. Here's an example of what can happen and how to handle it.

An advisor in California interviewed one of his favorite clients. He called me, practically hysterical, after the interview. The advisor had taken an Ideal Prospect Profile that matched his client to the interview with him. At the end of the interview, he'd asked the client for feedback on the profile and insights about the person described in it. Then he'd asked the magic question:

> *"Who do you know who fits this profile who might be able to help me understand this niche better?"*

Much to his surprise, the client gave him a list of 88 people who fit the profile almost exactly. This concerned the advisor. He was buried in referrals. He didn't know what to do. The solution was easy: Call the client and ask a simple question.

The dialogue started like this.

> *"Normally when I'm referred to people who fit my profile, I simply do research interviews to gather additional information about how I should design my business to meet my ideal clients' wants and needs.*
>
> *"However, occasionally I'm referred to people who are actively looking for a financial advisor. In that case, it would be inappropriate to do a research interview.*
>
> *"So I need your help. Would you help me determine which of the people you referred might need my help right now, and which others would be most helpful in giving me insights on how to create a successful business?"*

The client, a retired teacher, was happy to oblige. He said the referrals were close friends or business associates. He wasn't sure which ones needed help right now. He suggested the advisor sponsor a workshop for his friends to explain how the advisor could assist them. With the cooperation of the client, Ken prepared a workshop invitation letter and sent it to his client's associates.

Thirty-five people showed up at the informal presentation to learn how this advisor could help them manage their retirement assets more prudently. Because these potential new clients closely fit Ken's Ideal Client Profile, many of them had substantial portfolios.

This one client interview led the advisor to discover a rich niche. Strangely enough, retired teachers who are wealthy is a viable subsegment. Their two-income households, propensity to save, investments in real estate, and likelihood to inherit all contribute to their wealth. Ken now has many new clients from his original client's list of referrals.

Likewise, Jeff is an advisor in Ohio who had a number of physicians as clients and successfully used the interview process to expand his business. During the first round of his research process, he contacted these physicians to schedule client interviews. They all expressed interest in meeting with Jeff, but because of their busy schedules, continued to delay their appointments. After 60 days, Jeff called to say, "Steve, none of my doctor clients have been able to meet with me. I'm getting frustrated."

Two of the primary things we look for in marketing are *receptivity* and *responsiveness to the message*. The doctors were receptive, but because of their busy schedules, they were unresponsive. This created a roadblock for Jeff and indicated it might not be an ideal market for him.

I asked Jeff what he thought of the franchise industry. He said he hadn't considered it. I asked him if he knew any franchise owners he could interview. He said, "I know one person who owns a McDonald's, but he's not a client of mine." I told him, "That's okay. In the beginning, it's important to interview anyone who can help you identify new opportunities and target markets."

Since Jeff didn't have the franchise owner's phone number or address, he simply walked into the restaurant one day. The owner, Dave, was standing behind the counter taking orders. He said, "Hey, Jeff, I'm glad to see you. In fact, I've been meaning to call you."

Jeff said, "Great! What's up?"

To his surprise, Dave told him, "I'm selling one of my franchises. My wife and I are making some changes in our personal finances and we need to talk to someone. We were thinking about contacting you, but we weren't sure how to get in touch with you."

Jeff said, "What a coincidence! I came in to find out how to contact you! I'm doing some research right now to determine if franchise owners could benefit from my specialized knowledge and, if so, how I could design a business that would perfectly match their needs. I'm interested in getting your ideas and opinions."

The owner said, "Great. I'll buy you a cup of coffee, and we'll sit down and talk. I've got some spare time right now."

During the interview, Jeff learned this individual owned three McDonald's restaurants. He planned to sell one of them. He was also inheriting some money. He didn't have an immediate need for Jeff's services but would need his help in the near future.

Jeff learned a good deal about the local McDonald's franchise marketplace. And Dave was impressed that Jeff was interested in specializing in the franchise industry. He knew Jeff could add more value if he understood the franchise business.

He told Jeff that 24 of the local McDonald's owners would be meeting in a few months and asked Jeff if he would be willing to make a presentation to them on investing and personal finances. Jeff said, "Sure. I'd love to do that. But before I can make an intelligent presentation, I need to do some more research so I can gear my presentation to the actual situations and needs of McDonald's owners."

He asked Dave for introductions to McDonald's owners who fit his profile of an ideal client. He left that meeting with a qualified, motivated prospect, additional insights into the needs of McDonald's owners, and a clear understanding that there was a definite need for help in that marketplace. He also had an invitation to speak to 24 McDonald's owners in the near future and received referrals to three of Dave's peers.

Jeff Contacts Referral No. 1

Jeff called the first referral and told him that Dave had referred him. (I don't recommend sending referral letters for research interviews.) Jeff said,

> *"A mutual associate, Dave, said you were very knowledge-able and suggested I call you. He said you may be willing to help me. I've been asked to speak at an upcoming McDonald's owners meeting about investments and personal finance. Although I have been a financial advisor for more than fifteen years, I'm conducting some research so I can customize my talk to the unique needs of McDonald's owners."*

This franchise owner said, "Sure, Jeff, come on over. In fact, I've got a couple of questions I'd like to ask you."

During this interview, the owner mentioned he had $330,000 in his pension plan and was contributing $25,000 a year. He told Jeff it was a 401(k), and he was paying more than $4,000 in annual administrative fees. He asked Jeff, "Is that high?"

Jeff said, "It sure is. In fact, we can set up a SEP (Simplified Employee Plan), and the administrative fees would be only about twenty-five dollars a year."

The franchise owner asked him, "What would I have to do to arrange it?"

"Give me your current statements," Jeff said, "and I'll develop an investment policy statement to show you how we would manage the money."

Then Jeff asked for referrals to other franchise owners or industry experts to interview. The owner told him he worked with an attorney who specialized in the franchise marketplace. Jeff called the attorney on the spot and set an appointment for an interview.

Jeff left this second interview with a new client in the local McDonald's niche, additional knowledge about the needs of that segment, and a referral to a high-level center of influence with many clients in the franchise industry.

Jeff Meets With Referral No. 2

The attorney expressed surprise. He said, "Jeff, you mean you're interested in specializing in meeting the needs of franchise owners?"

"Yes," Jeff told him. "I'm not sure, but it seems like there's an opportunity for me to help these people. What I'm trying to do now is identify the issues, problems, and concerns they have so I can become more effective at helping them solve their problems and achieve their goals."

The attorney told Jeff he represented a large ice cream franchise organization. One hundred of their top owners would be meeting in Phoenix in two months. They were looking for a financial professional to speak to the group. He asked Jeff if he would be willing to make a presentation. Jeff said he probably would be interested.

The attorney called his contact at the organization and told her he had a person in his office who would be ideal for their Phoenix conference. Jeff got on the phone, and she asked him if he would be willing to speak. He said he would—if two conditions were met.

"First, your group pays all my expenses. Second, I need to talk to five or six of your successful franchise owners here in my city so I can get a better understanding of their challenges and concerns. That way, I can customize my talk for your group. I'll need you to set up the interviews so the owners will be willing to speak with me." She agreed. Jeff left the attorney's office with additional relationships, a marketing opportunity, the chance to interview other franchise owners, and further understanding about the franchise marketplace.

Soon Jeff was managing $2.5 million for the local Ronald McDonald House and serving on its board of directors. He had also been asked by other Ronald McDonald Houses to make presentations to their boards about how to manage their endowment money more effectively.

This is a classic example of using research interviews to build relationships and penetrate markets. Jeff discovered that the average McDonald's owner with just one store nets about twice as much money as the average physician. He also learned that McDonald's owners have something physicians never will have: free time. As an added bonus, Jeff enjoys the personality style of McDonald's owners, which makes his work more fun.

Jeff Adapts His
Questions Over Time

Consumers don't evaluate professional service providers on their technical competency because there's really no objective way to define it. Consumers subconsciously base their evaluations on the quality of the questions professional service providers ask. As you become more knowledgeable in a specific field, you should modify your questions to demonstrate your keen understanding of the particular segment or niche.

For instance, as Jeff interviewed McDonald's owners, he learned they have something known as a "weasel clause" in their contracts. This clause dictates that if they die, their heirs can run their franchises for up to a year.

Then, if they don't hit acceptable numbers, the company can take the franchise back and pay the heirs nothing.

Initially, Jeff didn't know anything about this clause. But later, when he interviewed McDonald's owners, he asked them if they were concerned about that clause. Then he asked, were there some way to minimize or eliminate that problem, if they would they be interested. They always said yes. Now he had a compelling message that made people want to work with him.

Why Complete Strangers Are Willing to Help You

Many advisors wonder why successful people would be willing to meet with a financial professional they don't know. Not everyone will be willing to meet with you. But those who say yes will be helpful, friendly, open-minded, and curious about what you do. These are individuals who will become your marketing apostles if you do a great job for them.

Pretend you drive a Volvo. I call you up to say I own a Volvo dealership, and I'd like to come out and take you to lunch to talk with you about using our organization for servicing your car. You'd probably think, *Oh, he's trying to sell me something.*

What if, on the other hand, I told you, "I'm committed to creating a phenomenal service department to perfectly match the needs of busy people just like you. A mutual friend, Jeff, recommended you as an insightful person who could help me design this ideal service center. Would you be willing to share your ideas with me?"

When I say something like that, I clearly won't be perceived as a salesperson. Your curiosity might even have you saying, "Wow, I'd be interested in finding out more about that."

A New Way to Start Relationships With Prudent Investors

This represents an entirely different way of meeting potential new clients, especially Prudent Investors who normally won't respond to traditional marketing tactics. And it's not a bait and switch by any means. It's not a sneaky way to try to get in front of people and sell them something. Instead, it's a fair exchange of information. In many cases, prospects have a hidden agenda themselves.

They may want a second opinion on their current financial situations or advisors but don't know who to ask. Consumers have no strategy for identifying and qualifying client-centered financial advisors. A research interview is a low-risk way for them to get to know you better and determine if you're the type of advisor who may be able to help them.

An advisor and I once interviewed a lady in Tucson, Arizona. At the end of the interview she asked if he did estate planning. He told her he did. She stood up and pointed across a private airport landing strip to a 6,000-square-foot house on the other side and said, "My husband's mom and dad live over there. They need some estate planning. Can you help us?" It turned out that was the primary reason she had let us come out and talk with her.

Remember that your ideal clients, your Prudent Investor types, have a low level of interest in their money. They're not likely to come to you. If you offer to go to them, they're often willing to sit down and talk. Complete strangers are willing to talk with you if you've been referred to them by someone they respect and if they're curious about what you do.

Prudent Investors Want and Need Your Help

There's a huge demand for client-centered financial professionals today. In fact, one of my money manager clients conducted an interesting research project. He had college students interview 600 heads of households in a wealthy area of northern California. The students asked this question: "Would you like to have a relationship with a knowledge-able, trustworthy financial advisor?"

Eighty-five percent of the people interviewed said yes. They then asked these wealthy individuals whether they currently had a relationship with such an advisor. Surprisingly, only five percent said they did. This indicates a huge demand for competent, professional, client-centered advisors. If you can approach these people in the right way, about four out of five Prudent Investors should be interested in establishing a relationship with you.

The demand is there; the money is there; the wants and the needs are established. But how do you approach these people? What do you say to them to open their minds? How will they know you're competent and trustworthy when they meet you? And how will you determine which options will provide the greatest opportunity for you? The answer to all these questions is simple: You have to call them and ask for help.

The goal is to identify clients and centers of influence who will become your marketing apostles and help you build your business. Those people who aren't helpful, friendly, and curious save you time by not meeting with you. The basic concept is to knock on many doors. Those that open, you go through. Those that don't open, don't sell too hard because you don't want to waste your time. It's a simple screening and qualifying process.

Many of the people you would like to work with are busy and have many things they would rather do than try to find a new financial professional. They also, as a group, believe most financial advisors are generic. But anyone specializing in their marketplace has additional appeal for them.

Imagine what would happen if you simply interviewed two people a week for a year. You'd have 100 new friends and associates in the target segments that most interest you. And they would all be ideal potential clients or important centers of influence.

You'd have the beginnings of real relationships that could easily be converted to business relationships if you nurture them and keep in touch. When they have a need or know of someone who has a need for financial services, you'll be the one they call. So there's a high probability that these people will soon become consumers of the financial services you provide.

Why Interviews Are Better Than Mass Marketing

Mass marketing is for advisors who don't know where the money is or where the opportunities reside. But our goal, like the mining engineers', is to know exactly which segments and niches offer the greatest opportunity. Then you can concentrate your efforts on building relationships in those niches rather than diffusing your efforts with massive, random marketing.

Many advisors become impatient with this process in the beginning. But my clients and I have found that it's the fastest and quickest way to penetrate wealthy niches and establish relationships in new segments. This process isn't as immediately gratifying as a good response to a direct mail campaign, but it bears a greater amount of fruit over time. The quality of the relationships and the size of the accounts are on a much larger scale.

What normally happens with mass marketing is the people who need your help *right now* will respond. You do generate some hot leads, but they're often "C" and "D" prospects. With a client-centered, relationship-building approach, you're creating relationships with "A" and "B" prospects. This approach accrues cumulative benefits over time. It requires less and less effort each year.

The people you establish relationships with may not need your help right away. That's why it's critical to have a follow-up system to keep in touch with these individuals. Interviewing them is just the first step in building a long-term, mutually beneficial relationship.

A big part of client-centered marketing is serving, educating, and adding value for people in your market *before* they become clients. In traditional product-centered marketing, you always start the relationship with a product. With my approach, you start the relationship with a meaningful conversation about your prospects' favorite subject: themselves. Then you build trust over time until they eventually become ideal clients.

You're no longer picking the low hanging fruit, which is what mass marketers end up doing. Instead, you're cultivating your own garden.

When all the low hanging fruit has been picked, you're still going to have abundant opportunities because you've planted deep roots in fertile soil. Niche marketing gets easier and easier over time. But mass marketers will spend more and more time and money for less and less payoff.

Manage Your Contacts with a Marketing Database

You've interviewed your key clients, and they have referred you to their friends, business associates, and centers of influence. You've identified some huge opportunities and gathered reams of information. You've met with your referrals, and some of them have become your clients. Now what do you do?

You've met many great people you would like to have as clients, friends, and advisors. Now you need to keep in touch in a friendly way. This is the key to establishing trust. And trust is the key reason that wealthy prospects will want to become your clients. You need a marketing database to help you nurture your new relationships.

Don't use your portfolio management system for prospect communication unless it's truly user friendly. It's probably cumbersome with few features.

Instead, purchase contact management software. This is a specialized database application for helping you keep your prospects organized and to remind you when to follow up with them. It's inexpensive (under $200) and extremely easy to use. And having a system designed specifically for handling contacts will make it easy for you to generate and track correspondence with the people important to your business.

Set Up 4 Databases

I recommend you set up four unique contact files:

1. prospects,

2. clients,

3. vendors, and

4. public relations/media.

Many experts suggest having only one database and simply "tagging" the records to identify different contact types. We handle our contacts a little differently. The reason I use different databases for each contact group is that it allows me to use different data fields to describe each person in more detail.

For instance, in my database for speaking prospects, we have fields describing "event location." For coaching prospects we use the same data field to define "dollars under management." By setting up two different databases, we can use different titles for the same fields. It's pretty awkward trying to do that in one database.

Nurture Your Relationships

Once you have your contact management system installed, you need to decide what information you'll collect about each prospect. The basics are name, address, phone number, fax, and e-mail. One of the information fields should identify the contact's segment or niche. You should also profile contacts as "A," "B," or "C" prospects.

You may want to add notes about personal interests, concerns, or other useful information. You should also set callback dates if you have agreed to get together in the future.

Now that you're set up, what do you send to your contacts? Immediately after the interview, send them a personal thank-you note. Then keep in touch with some "warm fuzzies." Obviously, product pitches are out. You want to build a trusting relationship, not sell products.

Try One of These Systems to Manage Contacts

To make friends of your new prospects and then turn your new friends into clients, you need an easy-to-use contact management system. Contact the following software providers to learn more about their products.

- ACT! (877) 469-7467, www.symantec.com/act
- GoldMine (800) 654-3526, www.goldminesw.com

Ask yourself this question: *If I wanted to make these people my friends, what would I do?* You'd probably send them notes and cards mentioning the things that are most important to them in their lives. You'd occasionally invite them to lunch, a party, or a recreational event. You'd probably also send them referrals when possible and call them with ideas or contacts.

For the "A" prospects, send personal notes occasionally. A great technique is to send articles or inspirational quotes with a note saying that you thought they'd find it interesting. The idea is to let them know you're thinking about them. This will keep them thinking about you. In Step 5, I'll explain in more detail how you can keep in touch with these people by inviting them to events you host for your existing clients.

The game you want to play is called "making friends on purpose." That's really what high-level financial advising is all about—making friends and then helping them define what they want from their money and their lives. Then you help them get what they want. It's a wonderful way to make a living.

Your goal is to meet lots of people in your target segments and niches who are in the right age group and have a high probability of being wealthy. You'll start a meaningful conversation with them and then cultivate the relationship by simply keeping in touch with them in the same manner you would all of your existing clients.

Chapter at a Glance

If you were a mining engineer, you would identify rock formations where there's a high probability of finding gold. As a financial advisor, you need to identify segments (mountains), subsegments (promising locations on the mountains), and niches (veins of solid gold) in which there are a high probability of finding great opportunities. Like drilling test holes, you conduct research interviews.

If you discover opportunities, continue drilling until you identify the veins of gold, such as the group of 24 McDonald's franchise owners. If you don't strike gold, simply move on to the next targeted segment. Cultivate relationships with your best research subjects. Don't bother including contacts in your database who aren't well-connected, knowledgeable, or qualified prospects themselves.

With perseverance, you can build a super-profitable financial services business just by conducting research interviews with your most influential clients, centers of influence, and prospects. I call this process relationship-based niche marketing. It's the simplest and lowest cost way to bury yourself in qualified referrals to ideal new clients.

Chapter 9 Action Steps

Exercise 1: Prioritize your market segments and niches. Consider everything you learned from the first round of the interview process and in previous chapters. Eliminate those segments and niches you've learned won't be profitable. Rank the others. Select between one and three to concentrate on as you work through the rest of this book.

Exercise 2: Prepare for interviews with referrals. Make sure you have an Ideal Prospect Profile for each niche you plan to pursue. Compiling a list of referral prospects to interview should be an ongoing process. Determine your interview goal. Draft a set of interview questions. Use the sample list in this and the previous chapters to guide you. Schedule interviews with referrals. Follow the appointment-setting scripts suggested in this chapter.

Exercise 3: Conduct interviews with referrals. Remember that these interviews are less about choosing a segment or niche and more about becoming entrenched in one.

Exercise 4: Use a contact management database to keep in touch with the people you've met. They don't always need you right away, but they may need you at some point down the road. Cultivate your new relationships. Many of them will become clients in the future.

Step 4

Position Yourself to Attract Ideal New Clients

You're about to open a lemonade stand. You have a magic wand so you can create any marketing advantage you want. What is the one thing that will guarantee the success of your new business?

Get your ice-cold lemonade here!

Most people would guess that it's a great recipe, low prices, or an excellent location. But by this point, surely you know the one thing that will absolutely guarantee the success of a lemonade stand: *a thirsty crowd*. Once you find people *who already want what you have to sell,* you need only position yourself so they'll know what you have to offer—and they'll come to you.

You'll read how to use your research results to position yourself to attract your "thirsty crowd" in chapters 10 and 11.

Section Preview

- Position yourself on the *ladder of the mind.*
- Stand out as different from and better than your competition.
- Take the five actions to establish your position.
- Evaluate your current position and reposition yourself, if necessary.
- Package your services so you can communicate your benefits effectively to your targeted prospects.
- Attract ideal wealthy prospects like a powerful magnet.

10

Stand Out in an Overcrowded Market

*Positioning occurs in the mind of the prospect,
not in the product.*

—Al Ries and Jack Trout, marketing experts and authors,
Positioning: The Battle for Your Mind

When I was in college, I ran a summer business designing and installing redwood hot tubs. One client was a real estate developer who wanted a hot tub for his residence. Since he had other employees, he put me and my carpenters on his payroll.

When I received my first paycheck, I was dismayed with the net amount after all the deductions. My client promptly informed me I should be pleased because $8 per hour was as much as he paid his top journeymen carpenters. A little voice told me, "As long as they perceive you as just another *carpenter*, you'll never be able to charge more money."

So on my next job I presented myself differently. I explained I was a *builder* and charged my client $15 an hour. After that, I became a *designer/builder* and charged $20 an hour. Eventually, I called myself a *designer*. I charged $25 an hour for myself and $15 an hour for my carpenters.

By changing my clients' perceptions and expectations of me, I was able to triple my income in just one summer. The most interesting thing was that my skills were exactly the same at $25 an hour as they had been at $8 an hour.

Use Positioning to Break Through the Clutter

Positioning is the art of controlling your clients' perceptions. It's also a promise of benefits. Projecting a positive position—that you have what people want—increases your perceived value in the marketplace, helps you quickly make it easy to turn wealthy prospects into clients, and allows you to charge top dollar for your services. Positioning is the secret to *attracting* ideal clients.

Why? Each week, the average person is exposed to more than 2,000 ads and commercial messages. The wealthy, in particular, are bombarded with come-ons by financial services purveyors. In the last ten years, there has been an explosion of financial products and services. In fact, there are now more mutual funds than there are stocks on the New York Stock Exchange. And there are more financial salespeople and advisors every day.

After a barrage of conflicting messages—commonly referred to as "information overload"—people turn a deaf ear to new information. Only the information that will help these people solve a current pressing problem or satisfy a burning desire gets through the clutter. If you don't have a clear and strong position identifying the need or desire you can help satisfy, you'll be lost in the crowd.

Move Up the Ladder of the Mind

Decisions about who's the best advisor aren't made on an entirely logical basis. Like most people, wealthy prospects subconsciously assign relative positions or rankings to different individuals, products, and services. Relying on perceptions, they place competitors at different levels on what is called "the ladder of the mind." They use the ladder subconsciously to compare your market position to your competitors' positions.

Positioning occurs in prospects' *minds*—not in the product or service. If you want to be an advisor to the wealthy, you have to choose the right ladder (your position) and shoot for the top rung on that ladder. You do this by creating the *perception* that you are different and somehow better than your competitors. But you must be able to deliver, or your position is just a false promise.

The default position for financial professionals in most consumers' minds is that of product pushers. Your understanding and empathy for your prospect's situation, wants, and needs position you on a different and better ladder than your competitors.

One reason interviews are such a powerful way to build relationships and generate new clients is that they position you as a good listener and a client-centered advisor. By letting people talk about their favorite subject (themselves) for 90 minutes or so, they *perceive* you as trustworthy and caring.

How to Establish a Profitable Position

A word of warning: If you aren't careful about positioning, it can work against you. When a friend of mine and I were vacationing in Yosemite National Park, by sheer coincidence, we ran into his old girlfriend from college. The woman was overjoyed at their chance meeting.

When she asked him what he was doing for a living, he beamed, "I'm a stockbroker." Her joyful demeanor turned to ice. Obviously, she didn't feel the same way as he did about his new profession.

If he had called himself a financial advisor, her perception of him probably would have been more positive. Many people seem to believe that a financial advisor or account executive is a superior and more ethical person than a stockbroker. What you call yourself influences people's perceptions about you.

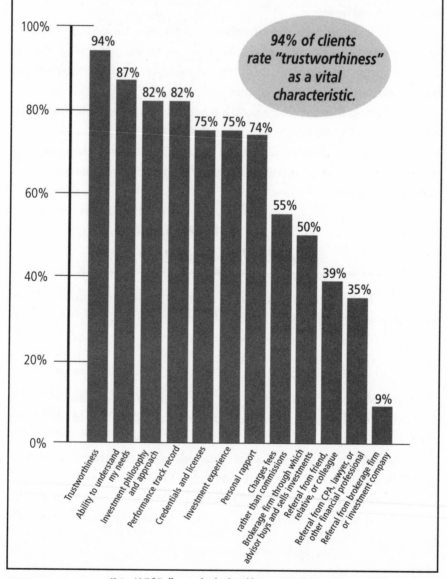

What Clients Want From Their Advisors

Clients' Key Selection Criteria for Advisors

Percent rating on a ten-point scale, where "10" means extremely important and "1" means not at all important

94% of clients rate "trustworthiness" as a vital characteristic.

- 94% — Trustworthiness
- 87% — Ability to understand my needs
- 82% — Investment philosophy and approach
- 82% — Performance track record
- 75% — Credentials and licenses
- 75% — Investment experience
- 74% — Personal rapport
- 55% — Charges fees rather than commissions
- 50% — Brokerage firm through which advisor buys and sells investments
- 39% — Referral from friend, relative, or colleague
- 35% — Referral from CPA, lawyer, or other financial professional
- 9% — Referral from brokerage firm or investment company

Note: 10/96 Dalbar study also listed honesty as a key criterion sought by investors.
Source: 10/96 Dalbar study; 7/96 Schwab Market Research

You can now see how critical it is to position yourself correctly. Stop a moment and consider your current position. What does your company name or tagline say about you now? What about the introduction you use when you network? Are you getting the right message out? Does what you say accurately reflect the benefits you provide? Do you make it instantly clear to people which problems you can help them solve?

Should You Reposition Yourself?

A money management company was communicating that it specialized in aggressive growth, but its track record didn't support this message. When they sought my advice, I told them they needed to change either the message or the products and services to improve their positioning in the marketplace.

So we changed the message. First, we raised the minimum investment from $250,000 to $500,000. Next, we repositioned the company. Our new message communicated that this company wasn't the money manager for people who wanted to make a lot of money. It was the investment manager for people who already had plenty of money and didn't want to lose any.

This new message was more in line with the benefits the company was actually delivering. After they changed it, they started to attract many more Prudent Investors who were perfectly content with their less aggressive performance.

A financial planner in Oklahoma named his company Innovative Financial Planning. He specialized in working with retired people. When he did his research interviews, he found out that most retired people had negative ideas about the word *innovative*, particularly when it had to do with their money. He renamed his company Retirement Investment Advisors.

Since he was on a main thoroughfare, he put a new sign out. Shortly after he changed his company name, people started stopping by to find out more about what he did. That had never happened with the old name. His new name created a stronger promise of benefits. And he started attracting more wealthy, retired clients effort-lessly.

So remember: Walk your talk or change your talk. Credibility with your targeted prospects is one of your greatest business assets. Your position must be compelling to your ideal clients—not just to you.

If you want to attract Prudent Investors you must position yourself as a prudent, conservative financial advisor. Positioning yourself as an aggressive, performance-oriented advisor will attract Thrill Seekers and Guru Groupies.

The good news is if you have a position that isn't quite right, it's simple to change it. For example, many stockbrokers are now called financial consultants. Many financial planners are now repositioning to become investment advisors, and many insurance agents are getting licensed to become full-fledged financial advisors.

Whether you determine your present position could use a minor adjustment or a complete overhaul, not to worry. Developing your position and locking it in people's minds isn't as difficult as you may think.

To craft your position, there are seven key tactics.

1. Become an expert problem solver.
2. Capitalize on trends.
3. Match your products and services to your targeted prospects.
4. Develop a unique selling proposition.
5. Create a perception of limited availability.
6. Develop a written positioning statement.
7. Prepare a verbal benefits statement.

1. Become an Expert Problem Solver

Traditional motivation theory states that people either move toward pleasure or away from pain. From a marketing perspective, it's generally much easier to attract consumers by helping them relieve pain than it is to help them gain pleasure. The pain or concern will prompt them to gather information and then take action to stop the pain. In marketing, you must often attract people by talking about the things they want (solutions to problems, in our case) to provide them with what they need.

You need to become an expert at solving the problems that financial success creates. Then you need to become an expert at attracting the people who want to solve those problems. If you position yourself correctly, they'll come to you. And they'll be interested in your services when they meet you.

Smart and sophisticated clients always seek the specialist in the field. One of my best clients runs an investment management company. The company pays its securities attorney more than $450 an hour. She's one of the most expensive—and definitely one of the best in the field. With professional services, you expect to pay for brainpower.

My hot tub clients were willing to pay more because they thought they were buying more *expertise*. This was my position. Positioning yourself as an expert is one way to set yourself apart in the overcrowded financial services market.

So, to improve your position as an expert, raise your hourly rate. One of my goals is to become the highest paid consultant in the financial services industry—and to have everyone know I'm worth it.

As you become client-centered, you'll learn the concerns, issues, and needs of your clients as well as their perceptions of what it would take to solve their problems. Your powerful message is that you have specialized knowledge in a specific niche. Expert problem solvers attract motivated prospects who run away from product pushers.

2. Capitalize on Trends

Wayne Gretzky, the world's greatest hockey player, was once asked how he was able to be so successful as a hockey player. He replied: "Everyone else skates to where the puck is. I skate to where the puck is going."

The Explosion of Wealth

It's important to anticipate trends as they develop. Clearly, one of the emerging trends in industrialized countries is the *explosion of wealth*. Because of the rapid changes in technology, the world is experiencing unprecedented growth of new businesses and personal wealth. In the United States, for example, a new millionaire is created every four minutes.

Contrary to what some politicians would like us to believe, the middle market is shrinking, primarily because more and more people are moving up into the higher income and higher net worth brackets. This is because of dual-income families, higher levels of education, and the overall explosion of wealth throughout the world.

The financial services industry has traditionally focused on the vast middle market. But now there are more people than ever in the higher income and net worth brackets and fewer people than ever in the middle market. It's time for you to make a choice. Do you want to stay in a declining market? Or do you want to move to the fastest growing marketplace?

Advisory Fees vs. Commissions

Another trend is the move away from *commissions* toward *advisory fees*, both in the securities industry and soon in the insurance industry. The more sophisticated, highly educated, and experienced clients prefer to pay for their financial advice with fees rather than commissions.

These investors have often lost money more than once and didn't like it. They know that when a commission is involved, the advisor is paid for making the transaction rather than for helping clients achieve their goals.

If you position yourself as a fee-based advisor who earns the majority of your income by providing advice and ongoing management services, you'll be very attractive. If you position yourself as a commission-based salesperson, you'll be fighting the trends.

These two major trends—the explosion of wealth and the move to advisory fees—will continue to grow because they're indicative of an industry in the client-centered phase of its life cycle.

3. Match Your Products and Services to Your Targeted Prospects

In mature markets, different segments and niches value different products, services, and value-added extras. One of the worst marketing mistakes you can make is to generate qualified leads but fail to convert them to clients because you don't offer the products and services your ideal prospects value.

According to research conducted by financial services trend expert Russ Prince, the most popular financial products and services for wealthy clients are

- asset allocation and fee-based money management,

- financial and estate planning,

- tax planning,

- asset protection, and

- philanthropic advisory services.

These should constitute your core offerings.

During your research interviews, you asked your targeted clients what services and products they value. You may have run this question by your informal board of advisors, too. Taking this information into consideration, you'll need to make sure you're prepared to deliver the products and services that will be in the highest demand by your ideal clients. Otherwise, your position will be unsuccessful.

If your target segments include younger professionals who are making good money, an ideal product choice might be variable annuities. For older retired people who have already accumulated money, you may want to focus on fee-based asset management services or estate planning. The target segments you choose determine your position and the products and services you offer.

Select Value-Added Services Your Ideal Clients Want

The same thing applies to your value-added services. Retirees love education meetings and client appreciation dinners. They value the information, attention, and socializing. These meetings make retirees feel important, connected, and well informed.

But what about successful entrepreneurs? If you target this lucrative niche, forget client appreciation meetings. These individuals are too busy and value their time too much. What about quarterly meetings? Many busy business owners would rather get a quick voice mail message:

> *"Hi, it's Steve. I reviewed your portfolio this quarter. We're down three percent for the quarter but up eight percent so far for the year. I'm recommending no changes at this time. Call me if you have questions. And say hi to Chris for me."*

Business consulting or an introduction to an investment banker are services entrepreneurs may value more than quarterly meetings. Will every business owner appreciate these services? Of course not. How do you determine what package of services will be most valued by your ideal clients? Just ask them. That's why you conduct the research interviews.

4. Develop a Unique Selling Proposition

A unique selling proposition answers this question: What's different and better about you that would make someone want to work with you rather than anyone else?

The interesting thing is you don't actually have to be unique. You simply have to claim a *unique position*. For instance, in the old beer commercials for Hamm's, the company used to say, "It's the water." Well, the reality is all beers use highly filtered and purified water. But Hamm's was the first beer to take that position, and then it owned that position for many years.

Own the Position of Specialization

There are three strong selling propositions: specialization, limited availability, and being the first in a niche.

The most powerful, unique selling proposition you can create is one of *specialization*. When doctors ask you, "Why should I work with you rather than anyone else?" you simply tell them: "The reason you should consider working with me is I specialize in working with doctors and have a number of clients with exactly the same problems you have. Because of this, I can offer tremendous value for you that you just can't get from a generic financial advisor."

Be First, Biggest, or Best

A classic way to achieve the top position is to be the first in a specific market. You have quite a jump on being successful when you're *first*, *biggest*, or *best* at something. These are positions people find hard to forget. For instance, name the first person on the moon. Now name the second person on the moon.

One of the ways to be first in the field is to start your own industry. If you develop a specialty and name it, you can literally own an entire industry. The early financial planners were good examples of this strategy. Be the first to specialize in a particular niche in your local area, and you can capitalize on being *first* in the same way.

5. Create a Perception of Limited Availability

When anything is in limited supply, it's typically in high demand and sells for a premium. To capture this position, you need to create the perception that you're available only to very few lucky clients who fit a specific profile. There are two ways to accomplish this: One is based on dollars, and the other is based on time.

Set Minimum Account Sizes

One way to create the perception of limited availability is to set minimum account sizes. An investment advisor I work with has created a number of strategic alliances with CPAs. He tells them the people who can benefit most from his services are medical professionals earning more than $150,000 a year. He actually had doctors call him explaining they're making only $135,000 this year, but their CPAs say they're on track to make $150,000 next year. Could they qualify for his services?

Here's another example. A financial planner in St. Louis had a prospect who sold a business, cashing out with over $5 million. The advisor recommended a specific investment strategy. After his presentation, the advisor asked, "So what do you think?" The client said, "It sounds pretty good, but let me ask you a question. What's the minimum?"

The advisor knew the prospect was also considering another money management firm. So rather than answering the question immediately, he said: "I'll be glad to answer that, but I'm curious. What's the minimum account size at the other firm you're considering?" The client said, "Oh, their minimum is half a million dollars."

Since I had coached the advisor on how to handle this situation, he was prepared. He drew in a deep breath, gulped, and said, "Well, our minimum is a million." The prospect said, "I think we can do that. In fact, I think we can probably do a little bit more."

The funny thing is the advisor had never opened a million-dollar account in his life. But look at this from the prospect's perspective. If one firm requires a half-million dollar minimum, and the other has a million-dollar minimum, which firm is better? Clearly it's the one with the higher minimum. This is merely a shortcut consumers use to determine which product, service, or advisor is better.

No wealthy client wants to work with an advisor who takes any and all comers. He or she wants to work with advisors who specialize in solving problems and achieving goals for people in their income or net worth bracket.

Explain You're Too Busy to Help Everyone

Another type of limited availability is the perception that you're extremely busy and don't really need the additional business. But of course you would be delighted to work with these individuals, if they asked for your help and fit your profile. Advisors who appear too hungry chase away ideal new clients. But advisors who appear to have all the business they need always seem to attract the best clients.

One way to communicate that you're extremely successful and don't need the prospect's business is to say,

"I'd be happy to help you if you want me to. Frankly, I don't need your business right now, but I think I'd enjoy working with you and can see how I can make a big difference for you."

This helps put your time in perspective and indicates the prospect will benefit more than you from your relationship. When they sense you don't need their business it makes your more attractive.

6. Develop a Written Positioning Statement

The centerpiece of positioning is the *positioning statement*—typically a name, slogan, or theme that describes a benefit, payoff, or solution to a problem. It articulates, in a simple and memorable manner, your unique selling proposition. Think of it as a promise you make to your potential new clients.

Some companies attach their positions to their company names. Consider U.S. Trust's tagline, "Uncommon Expertise Managing Money," and FNN's slogan, "It Pays To Watch." Products and individuals can also be positioned. You'll see products with names such as "High Income Fund," "Tax Free Trust," and so on.

Most of the major financial service firms have established corporate positions. If you work for one of them, you need to consider the corporate position as you devise your personal positioning statement. Ideally, the two should be complementary. At the very least, they must not conflict.

Classic Positioning Statements

Let's take a look at some well-known positioning statements used by a few of the larger financial services companies. Many of these statements have changed, and some of the firms are no longer with us. But I refer to them because they clearly illustrate the concept. I consider these strong.

- Dow Jones/News Retrieval: The Information that Powers Today's Business

- Merrill Lynch: A Tradition of Trust
- Van Kampen Merritt: Investing With a Sense of Direction
- The New England: Your Financial Partner
- Hutton: When E. F. Hutton Talks, People Listen
- PruBache: Rock Solid, Market Wise
- Mass Mutual: We Insure Success
- Dun & Bradstreet: The Fine Art of Managing Risks
- Bear Stearns: Sharing Opportunities

Notice that the stronger positioning statements promise benefits in a clear, direct manner. One of my all-time favorites is *Forbes* magazine's "Capitalist Tool."

These next three statements are not so strong. Can you figure out why?

- The U.S. Postal Service: We Deliver
- Xerox Financial Services: The Financial Machine
- Pacific Financial Companies: The Power of the Pacific

The weaker statements are vague or promise something the consumer takes for granted. For instance, the U.S. Postal Service says they deliver. But the question is when? The FedEx slogan, "When it absolutely, positively has to be there overnight," effectively out-positions the U.S. Postal Service. As in the martial arts, the battle is won before the first blow is struck.

Positioning Statements for Financial Advisors

Here are several slogans that have worked well for my financial advisor clients.

- Guiding Investors to Financial Security
- Charting Your Course to Financial Independence
- Securing Your Retirement Lifestyle
- Simplifying Your Investment Decisions
- Preserving, Protecting, and Transferring Family Wealth

Evaluate Your Current Positioning Statement

Here are ten questions to ask yourself to determine if your positioning statement is effective. Put a check mark by the questions you can answer with a yes. If the positioning statement you have now comes up short, consider repositioning yourself. It's well worth the effort. If you decide you need to establish a new positioning statement, you can also use this list to test your options.

1. *Does my positioning statement promise strong benefits and build expectations?*
2. *Does it create immediate positive interest and curiosity?*
3. *Does it relate to something already in my prospects' minds?*
4. *Does it solve a high priority problem for my clients?*
5. *Is it short, simple, and dramatic?*
6. *Is it believable, intriguing, and compelling?*
7. *Does it differentiate me from my competitors?*
8. *Does it reposition my competition and turn their strengths into weaknesses?* (As in the mouthwash Scope's attack on Listerine's "medicine breath.")
9. *Does it screen out non-prospects?*
10. *Does it generate a strong emotional response?* (People should either love it or hate it.)

A strong positioning statement will attract qualified prospects and repel unqualified prospects. Notice how much definition these businesses gain from a few well-chosen words.

- An insurance agent who wanted to upgrade her market and specialize in business insurance changed her company name from Hill & Associates to Key Executive Insurance. Her tagline became "Insuring Your Company's Most Valuable Assets."

- A group of financial planners decided to reposition themselves by offering fee-based asset management services to wealthy individuals. They changed their name from Midwest Financial Group to Midwest Wealth Advisors.

- A financial planner in southern California chose to call himself "The Money Doctor."
- A stockbroker in the midwestern U.S. calls himself "The Personal CFO for Successful Entrepreneurs."

7. Prepare a Verbal Benefits Statement

Next, you need a *verbal benefits statement* or "elevator speech." In other words, it's what you say to someone when you have only a short time to deliver a compelling message about what you do. A strong verbal benefits statement will generate immediate interest and create a desire to learn more. Just as with your positioning statement, it will also turn off non-qualified prospects.

Let's say you're in an elevator and a man asks, "Hey, I've seen you in the building before. What do you do here?" You tell him, "I'm a financial planner." Typically, he won't know what that means. Or, if you tell him you're an insurance agent, he'll smile politely and get off at the next floor. However, if you say something compelling, you could open his mind rather than closing it.

In a verbal benefits statement—and in positioning in general—what you want to do is link yourself to the payoffs that your clients want most from their money. Here's a universal template for a verbal benefits statement. When people ask you what you do, you say,

> *"I'm kind of like a financial navigator.*
> *I help ———— make smart decisions about their*
> *money so they can ———— ."*

How does this work? Assume you're playing golf with an entrepreneur you haven't met before. He gets around to asking what you do. You simply say,

> *"I'm kind of like a financial navigator. I help successful*
> *business owners make smart choices about their money so*
> *they can spend more time playing golf."*

For most golfers, there are few things they'd rather do than play golf, so this is a strong promise of benefits.

If your verbal benefits statement is on target, a qualified, motivated prospect will ask you for more information. Let's say that, as you're playing golf, the business owner says, "Interesting. How do you do that?"

A typical product pusher would immediately pull out a prospectus and start detailing the wonderful management processes or the incredible tax benefits of his current hot product. Of course this doesn't work. The prospect will run away.

The best response is,

> *"I'd love to tell you, but I don't like mixing business with pleasure, and we're here to have fun today. If you're really interested, give me one of your cards. I'll have my assistant call to set up a meeting. We can't help everyone, but if you come in, I can find out more about your situation and see if we would be able to help you."*

This really hooks interested prospects, because they typically want just enough information to disqualify you. In this process, though, you reverse the selling situation and get them to chase you.

In one fell swoop, you've established the ideal position as the type of financial advisor your golf partner would like to work with. If they're not 100 percent happy with the person they're currently working with, or even if they're slightly *curious*, they'll probably give you a card. This puts you in the driver's seat and allows you to follow up on your own terms. With this tactic, you've just harnessed one of the most powerful marketing emotions: curiosity.

Here's another universal concept you can use:

> *"I help affluent ———— become wealthy ————."*

For instance, say you're attending a dental conference. People ask you what you do. You say,

> *"I help affluent dentists become wealthy dentists."*

Once they understand the distinction, there are few dentists who won't be interested in finding out more about that.

Ask Your Clients for Help

How do you develop these powerful positioning statements? You'll get the majority of the information you need from your research interviews. Ask enough people in a specific niche about their issues and concerns—including asking them for the most compelling thing you could say to make them interested in working with you. Synthesize the responses and write a couple of different positioning statements. Then try them out on your informal board of advisors. Use the ones that evoke the strongest positive emotional response.

Continue to refine your positioning statement so that when you say it to qualified, motivated prospects, they'll leap out of their chairs to find out more about how you achieve those goals for them.

Remember that another purpose of the verbal benefits statement is to turn away unqualified prospects, as one broker did. Because his wife was the editor of a major automotive publication, they attended the Monaco Grand Prix. The broker specialized in restricted stock, so when people asked him what he did, he said,

> *"I help entrepreneurs reposition their assets without incurring fines and hassles from the SEC."*

As you can imagine, most people said, "Boy, that sounds confusing," and they simply wandered off. One individual, however, said, "Oh, you mean like restricted stock?" Bingo. This financial professional had identified a qualified and interested prospect. It turned out he owned a major corporation and had been considering estate planning. He was concerned about his restricted stock issues. They struck up a conversation that eventually led to a major account for the broker.

Maintain a Sense of Humor

One last thought on verbal benefits statements. These are normally delivered in social situations when people ask you what you do. You should say it with a little bit of humor in your voice so the person you're talking with picks up on the fact that you're having fun with it.

Craft Your Elevator Speech

Consider each of the following types of verbal benefits statements as you develop your own.

1. Appeal to people's desire to retire. Since 95 percent of all working people would like to retire, if someone who's employed asks you what you do, you can say,

> *"I help employed people make work optional."*

Another way of saying this is

> *"I help people who are leaving their jobs make smart decisions about their retirement investments."*

2. Associate yourself with your prospects' favorite activities. A stockbroker says to some colleagues at a yacht club,

> *"I'm just trying to help my retired clients make smart choices about their investments so they can spend more time on their yachts."*

3. Associate yourself with your prospects' values. One advisor describes herself by saying:

> *"I'm a financial advisor. I help successful individuals organize their estates so they can leave more to their loved ones."*

4. Tap into your prospects' emotions. A financial planner interviewed a number of business owners. He found they were upset with the state legislature for continually making it harder for business people to prosper. So he developed this verbal benefits statement:

> *"I help successful business owners overcome the financial hurdles created by politicians."*

5. Consider a niche-related position. For advisors who work with medical professionals, here's one that's shorter than the one above, but extremely powerful:

> *"I help medical professionals make smart choices about their money so they can enjoy the financial success they deserve."*

Customize These Segment-Related Verbal Benefits Statements

If you decide to work in a variety of segments you'll need to customize your verbal benefits statement for each segment or niche. Refer to your research interview notes for each market segment as you draft each verbal benefits statement. Watch how people react when you run them by them. Pay attention to body language and voice intonation. See if you get positive responses—or neutral or negative responses.

This section offers some compelling messages for different market niches. Feel free to customize them.

ENTREPRENEURS

As you learned in Step 2, some of the most powerful motivators for business owners are control, independence, and building a successful business. For many business owners, their businesses are their babies and they want them to be successful. What could you say to them, knowing this?

> *"I help successful business owners get control over their personal finances and investments so they can focus their energies on building more profitable businesses."*

SELF-EMPLOYED PROFESSIONALS

These individuals are often very status- and prestige-oriented. It's important to them that other people know they're successful. You could say,

> *"We help professionals make smart choices about their personal finances so they can enjoy the financial success they deserve."*

If you offer asset protection using family limited partnerships, you could say,

> *"We help protect your hard-earned assets from aggressive attorneys."*

SALES AND MARKETING EXECUTIVES

This group primarily wants financial independence and personal freedom. So try this:

"We help our clients make smart choices about their money so they can enjoy financial independence and personal freedom."

RETIREES

Retirees are most concerned about maintaining their financial independence in retirement. You can tell retirees,

"We help retirees make smart choices about their money so they can maintain their retirement lifestyle."

WIDOWS

Typically, one of the most compelling emotional needs for people who have survived the death of a spouse is companionship. So, you could say,

"We help widows simplify their personal finances so they can stop worrying and enjoy more time with their friends and loved ones."

INHERITORS

Inheritors generally feel a strong sense of responsibility to pass along a legacy to the next generation. You could say,

"We help inheritors organize their financial affairs so they can pass on a secure legacy to their children and grandchildren."

DIVORCED WOMEN

People who are divorced often feel overwhelmed by the sudden responsibility of managing their money. Say,

"We help divorced women get control over their personal finances so they can get their lives back on track."

Positioning Evolves as Your Business Evolves

Keep in mind that your positioning tends to evolve as your business evolves. When I first started my company, my positioning statement was "Author, Speaker, Consultant." That described who I was, but there was no promise of benefits.

The second version was "Marketing Tools and Strategies for Financial Professionals." That explained a little about the benefits, but it didn't talk about the payoff.

The third version was "Maximizing Financial Professionals' Productivity and Profits." That started saying more about the payoffs for our clients.

Then we started working more with mutual fund companies. As we developed a clearer sense of our mission and purpose, our tagline took on its current form: "Transforming the Investment Industry." This is a much higher purpose.

Having a strong position is a powerful tool. Not only does it attract qualified, motivated prospects, but it also helps crystallize in your own mind the benefits people receive from working with you.

We all need to start somewhere; don't hesitate to revise your positioning statement as you find a better way to position yourself.

Chapter at a Glance

Positioning is the foundation of all your marketing communication. It's your identity in your own mind and in the minds of your prospects and clients. It's a promise of the benefits your clients will experience from your services.

Your ultimate goal is to become the most desirable financial services provider for your targeted prospects. When you have this position, prospects will be attracted to you because of your expert reputation. Your clients will stay with you because you deliver on your promise.

One of the side effects of successful positioning is what it does for your self-image. When you have a positioning statement, it helps to focus your energies and your thoughts. It can become a self-fulfilling prophecy.

Most people in the industry stand for nothing. There's no edge, clarity, or focus for them. They haven't aligned themselves with the payoffs their clients really want from their money. So their default position is product pusher. Effective positioning can help you differentiate yourself from these generic advisors. Positioning can also

- make you stand out in a crowded marketplace,
- attract ideal new clients,
- increase the perceived value of your products and services,
- maximize your income, and
- help you retain clients.

In the next chapter you'll learn how to package your position to sell it effectively.

Chapter 10 Action Steps

Exercise 1: Think about what you learned in the section "Capitalize on Trends" on pages 197 and 198. In addition to the explosion of wealth and the trend toward fee-based advice, list any other trends you see that might be good to keep in mind as you develop your position. These trends may be national, regional, or local.

Exercise 2: Review "Develop a Unique Selling Proposition" on pages 200 and 201 and focus on your own position. Describe what's different about you and your services in a few paragraphs. Feel free to include specialization, and being the first, biggest, or best. Describe your position using references to the niches you've selected. This is for internal use only.

Exercise 3: How strong is your current position? Answer the questions in "Evaluate Your Current Positioning Statement" on page 205 to evaluate the message you're sending to clients and prospects.

Exercise 4: Develop your new positioning statement. Using your response to the previous exercises in this chapter, come up with a phrase you can include in all of your marketing materials to communicate your position. This should be a shorter version of your unique selling proposition and should invoke a compelling image.

Exercise 5: Craft your verbal benefits statement. This is your elevator speech to open people's minds to the possibility of working with you. You'll use it to answer the question: "What do you do?" in a thought-provoking manner. It should be a few sentences long. Refer to "Craft Your Elevator Speech" on page 209.

Package Yourself
for Success

*After all, you can't expect men
not to judge by appearances.*

—Ellen Glasgow, American novelist and poet

Consider this information from a business card: CAMPBELL & ASSOCIATES. BILL CAMPBELL, PRESIDENT. IN BUSINESS SINCE 1959. Rather uninspiring, isn't it? Bill thought so, too. He was an insurance agent but didn't want to communicate that on his business card because the label was too limiting. He had the right idea, yet he wound up with a card that was not only boring but didn't say anything about what he could do for his clients.

After he conducted some client research interviews, he decided to specialize in estate planning. This allowed him to provide a valuable service to the types of clients he enjoyed working with most. In time, the move would make earning money effort-less for him.

But first he had to reposition his company. He renamed it *Estate Conservation Strategies.* Then he had to get rid of the old, boring card.

A graphic designer put together a simple logo of a moon over a pyramid—a compelling image that conjures up visions of the ancient Egyptian kings and their long-lasting legacies. The new logo and name of his business now spoke to the needs of his clients.

Next, he went to a printer and ordered a presentation folder with his company's name and logo on the front. He also printed newly designed stationery, business cards, and a fact sheet that described his services.

He bundled the materials together and took the package around to all of his existing clients and centers of influence. They discussed the new focus of his business, and he left the packages with them to read and review later.

Shortly thereafter, he called me. Extremely excited, he said, "Steve, I've got some great news to report! I just got a call from a guy who asked me whether I did estate planning. I said, 'Yes, I do.' He said, 'Great. I need to come down and talk to you. My parents are in the import/export business. I'm going into business with them and we need to do some estate planning.'"

A little perplexed at his enthusiasm, I told him that sounded good.

Bill responded, "Steve, you don't understand. I've been in the insurance business for more than thirty years. This is the first time anyone has ever called me out of the blue."

Positioning was the conceptual step. Once he had determined his position, he needed to present it in customized marketing materials so he could begin communicating.

What Is Packaging?

Developing these communication tools is a process known as "packaging." By positioning and packaging yourself effectively, you're more likely to attract people to your services. Previously, Bill had hidden the fact that he did estate planning because he considered himself an insurance agent. But once he was in alignment with the market forces and focused on communicating the benefits for his clients, prospects started calling him.

Packaging is essentially creating communications tools that tell your story. It's the final step in preparing to communicate. Consider it the art of attracting ideal prospects with consistent, user-friendly descriptions of your products, services, company, and yourself. Your objective is to stamp in people's minds the image you want them to have of you. You do this by creating a set of marketing materials that will convey your message in a compelling way.

Packaging includes your marketing literature, brochures, press releases, forms, price lists, presentations, articles, ads, and all correspondence. Each of these marketing tools has a specific use in attracting and landing ideal clients.

By packaging yourself effectively, you can create high visibility, high credibility, and high desirability in the target niches you have selected. Your objective is to use your marketing tools and strategies to get qualified, motivated prospects to meet with you and to feel comfortable sharing their financial information with you. That's a key goal of any financial services marketing campaign.

The image you project also involves subtle things, like your reputation, your business location, your office decor, your ad in the telephone directory, the clothes you wear, the car you drive, and the professionalism of your office staff. All of these coalesce into a single impression—a mental image—of you. They help determine what rung you occupy on the ladder of the mind.

Why You Need to Package Yourself

A word of warning: If you don't have your own marketing literature because you rely on materials from product sponsors, you're communicating that you're a product salesperson. Follow the steps in this chapter to project a more client-centered image.

When you're selling services, you're really selling a relationship. Prospects think to themselves, *Why should I want to have a relationship with you?* In the previous chapters, you worked on some compelling answers to that question. You spent some time thinking about what your company stands for and articulating your position. You came up with a slogan you could tag onto your company name and a statement to use when meeting someone new.

In short, you determined what core benefits you want to communicate to the outside world. That was the hard part. Now it's time to make sure you have a marketing toolkit that will help you reinforce that message on an ongoing basis.

Why is this important? Product sponsors spend large amounts of money on glossy, color brochures, sales presentations, and collateral marketing materials. Their goal is to make their products as desirable as possible, showing consumers the benefits they'll receive.

But you're a client-centered advisor. You're in the financial *services* business, not the financial *products* business. As you make the transition from selling products to selling advice, you and your organization become a larger component of the overall benefits your clients are buying. Marketing materials provided by product sponsors are not enough on their own. You need to promote what your organization does and how you help people.

The challenge is that services are intangible. They can't be seen, touched, smelled, or tasted. This makes it hard for potential new clients to determine the payoffs they'll receive if they decide to work with you— unless you articulate the benefits clearly in your own marketing materials.

Consumers weigh every transaction on a cost/benefit scale. If they know the costs but are fuzzy about the benefits, they won't move forward.

Also, wealthy clients want to work with experts in their areas of need. But they'll know you're an expert only if you tell them. If they don't know about your specialized services, they won't perceive your full value.

Develop Effective
Communication Tools

We're approaching the most important part of the marketing process—*contact*. The goal is to get the right message to the right people at the right time in the most efficient manner possible.

In the seven chapters in Step 5, you'll learn the nuts and bolts of communicating effectively, including the importance of selecting the right channels. But before you can begin to implement your communication strategy, there are several important arrows you need in your quiver.

What kinds of communications tools do you need? To start, you don't need fancy brochures or expensive audio business cards. You just need some simple, clear, benefits-oriented tools. Later, when you pin down your story and your simple tools are working effectively, you can create more expensive pieces. Here are the 12 basic tools every financial services professional needs.

1. Logo and standard ink color, type style, and "look" (design)

2. Letterhead and business cards

3. Customized presentation folder with pockets

4. Corporate overview sheet with purpose statement

5. Brief biography of each key employee in the firm

6. Fact sheet of services, including features and benefits

7. Price list with an explanation of how you charge for services

8. Ideal Prospect Profiles

9. Case studies of people in each niche that illustrate your total solution to their problems

10. Article reprints or copies of articles about the advisor or the firm

11. Speaker's media kit

12. Relationship-building tools

1. Logo

Every big business has its logo. It's a symbol that represents the company and its brand. Do you need a logo? No. But if you have one, it makes you appear more credible and established. It also gives you an opportunity to make a lasting visual impression in the minds of your clients and prospects.

Logos are effective only if they're unique, so don't pick a logo out of your printer's clip art collection. It will make you look cheap. If, in the beginning, you can't afford to have your own logo designed, don't use one at all.

2. Letterhead and Business Cards

If you work in a branch office or have your own established company, you probably already have letterhead and business cards. If you need to design stationery, keep it simple. Professional letterhead is usually printed on high-quality white, cream, or very light gray cotton bond paper. You can select from a number of styles available at any printer.

If you're willing to invest a few hundred dollars in addition to the cost of your printing, you can get a graphic designer to create a personalized stationery design. To create an upscale look, use two colors. They'll make a much stronger impression than one. Have the designer note the colors you select and make sure you have the type styles (fonts) on your computer. That way, you can print your letterhead on plain paper in a pinch.

3. Customized Presentation Folder

Any office supply store has a huge selection of presentation folders. Select a color and style that works with your company colors. Make sure your presentation folder has pockets on the inside front and back covers. You'll use these presentation folders to package additional marketing materials about yourself and your firm. These folders are extremely versatile and never go out of style. They're your all-purpose wrapper for the marketing tools you create to tell your story.

If you're willing to splurge, you can have a printer customize the covers with your logo and company name. Or you can print adhesive labels and stick them on the cover. Look in your telephone directory for printers that specialize in printing short runs of presentation folders. Some printers even do embossing. But don't get too carried away. It's what's inside that counts most.

4. Corporate Overview

A corporate overview is usually one or one-and-a-half pages long. It explains your company's purpose, tells what your company does, and describes the people you can help most. When clients, bankers, centers of influence, or reporters want information about you and your organization, this is a good piece to give them.

The corporate overview is not a glossy marketing brochure, but it could be used to develop a brochure in the future. Corporate overviews are usually printed on company letterhead or simple bond paper. You can use a high-quality color printer to create more impact. I've seen five- to six-page company profiles in this format with color photos to add visual interest.

Write your corporate overview with bullet points to make it easy for readers to scan quickly for the basic story. Focus on your characteristics, benefits, and how you help people.

The beauty of this system is that you can change, upgrade, and improve it instantly. You can also customize it for different audiences. If you add a new service or target a new niche, no problem. The corporate overview can be updated in a minute.

5. Brief Biographies

Your firm is made up of people. Brag about them a little. Use short, four- to eight-paragraph biographies to describe each key employee's strengths and experience. Emphasize past successes that support each person's current role in your organization. A reader should come away with the belief that your people are well qualified for their positions.

Don't use a resume format. That makes it seem like you're looking for jobs. Limit each biography to one page. That's plenty of room to hit the highlights of even your most experienced associates.

Styles for these biographies are changing. Stick to the facts, but make them personal and friendly—not stiff and formal. Clients want to know the real people. They especially want to understand the motivations of their financial advisors. This is a good opportunity to take a stand and state each person's goals. I like to start these biographies with a bold statement about what the person stands for and then prove it with supporting facts.

6. Services Fact Sheet

Include a fact sheet that describes each of the services you offer. It should emphasize the advantages of the services and the types of people

Sample Corporate Overview
Brilliant Investment Advisors

At Brilliant Investment Advisors (BIA), our mission is simple: to provide personalized investment advice that minimizes our clients' financial concerns and maximizes their security.

Jane Advisor, president of BIA, understands that every client has unique needs. Our role is to help you make smart, well-informed decisions about your investments—providing you with greater financial independence, peace of mind, and security.

- Our investment strategies enhance your success by establishing a growing portfolio that optimizes returns and lowers volatility.

- We are affiliated with many of the country's leading investment management firms. They execute the investment strategies dictated by your personal plan. These alliances allow BIA to provide comprehensive quarterly performance reports, detailed tax information, and high levels of advice and service at a reasonable cost.

- Our clients are business owners and professionals, including physicians, dentists, and franchise owners. They are financially successful, experienced, and prudent investors with an average portfolio size of $1 million.

While each of our clients is unique, they all have one thing in common: *They want unbiased investment advice from experienced professionals.* Our clients look to BIA to preserve their capital and provide real growth in their portfolios after taxes and inflation. They have worked hard for their money and look to us to guide them toward financial security in retirement.

Our Approach

When you start working with BIA, we become your "personal chief financial officer," offering the resources to coordinate all of your financial needs. BIA has developed strategic alliances with key professionals who can handle your estate planning, retirement planning, and even your tax planning. We believe that the synergy created by professionals working together makes our team approach more efficient than working with any one of us individually.

Unlike many brokers, we are an independent firm with no proprietary investment products to push. Our approach is different—we are a fee-for-service company.

- We have found that the out-of-date commission system is an obstacle to conscientious advisors because it stresses transactions, which may not always be in your best interest.

- Our fees vary depending on portfolio size, type of assets, management style and, in some cases, performance.

- Because our fees increase only if your portfolio grows, our interests are aligned with yours. We focus on your financial objectives and your future.

Our Investment Process

Before we begin developing your investment strategy, we take a good, hard look at where you are today. We assess your investment goals, available resources, desired rate of return, and risk tolerance. This research allows us to customize a plan to fit your specific needs.

Then we develop a unique Investment Policy Statement—a blueprint that addresses your specific risk versus return concerns. Once that blueprint is in place, we provide personalized investment advice.

Asset allocation is the process of allocating investment funds into different asset classes in a way that enables you to maximize your expected return for a specific level of risk. We have found that it is responsible for more than 90 percent of the variations in portfolio performance—so choosing the right asset allocation for you is our top priority.

But our interest in your success doesn't stop there:

- We carefully monitor its progress, providing you with quarterly reports that summarize your activity and compare it to your goals.

- We make periodic adjustments to rebalance your portfolio, ensuring that our strategies stay on track with your needs.

who can benefit most from them. If you provide both general financial advice and investment advice, divide your fact sheet into two separate sections. You may also include insurance advice if that's one of your areas of expertise.

These services normally involve data gathering and analysis with a specialized software program. Financial advice is usually delivered as a written financial plan, estate plan, retirement capital needs analysis, college funding plan, rollover withdrawals, or tax analysis. Investment advisory services usually involve portfolio risk/return/cost analysis, investment policy statements, and efficient frontier analysis. On your fact sheet, include all of the above that apply. Color charts and graphs will clarify your recommendations.

If you offer additional data analysis services and recommendations, list them. If you have special services for your targeted niches, such as asset protection or business consulting, be sure to include those. For instance, you may want to list retirement feasibility studies for doctors or a business sale analysis for business owners. Clearly state the services available and why or when clients should consider using each service.

Remember that if you list products, your clients are going to associate you with products. List services and you'll establish yourself as a professional advisor.

7. Price List

A price list is one of your most important marketing tools. Once you've packaged your services, you need to determine how much you'll charge for them. Then format this list of prices in the same style as the fact sheet so it's easy for readers to find the cost for each service.

An advisor in Texas told me that after he packaged and priced his financial and investment services, his whole business changed. Before he had developed his price list, his clients would call and ask for specific information. Since he had no idea of what to charge, he often did the work for free. He figured it was good service and would lead to additional paid business, but instead his clients expected more free services. The more free advice he gave, the less money he made.

Sample Biography

Joe Advisor
Joe Advisor Financial Planning
1234 Main Street
Denver, CO 12345

For Joe Advisor, helping people make the most of their financial assets is rewarding work. Joe enjoys guiding his clients as they implement the investment strategies that help them meet their financial and life goals.

As president of Joe Advisor Financial Planning, Joe takes a comprehensive approach to wealth management. He sees his role as helping people make well-informed decisions about their investments and retirement plans—providing them with greater financial independence, peace of mind, and security.

With more than 25 years of experience in the financial services industry, Joe was one of the first financial planners in the Denver area. He was providing financial planning services even before it was widely known as a profession. As a Registered Investment Advisor, he has demonstrated a consistent ability to protect and grow the hard-earned assets of his clients, many of whom have experienced major life changes including retirement, divorce, or the loss of a spouse.

Joe graduated from the University of Colorado with a bachelor's degree in Finance. He holds the Certified Financial Planners designation (CFP), is a member of the Institute for Certified Financial Planners (ICFP), and has been admitted to the Registry of Financial Planning Practitioners.

Joe values education as a way to promote professional excellence. He is an active member of the International Association for Financial Planning and is the past president of the Denver chapter. Joe has also served as a speaker and panelist at various industry programs, including a financial planning program that aired on PBS.

When he's not working, Joe enjoys spending time with his wife Jane and their three beautiful children at their vacation home in Aspen.

Once he developed a fee schedule, he could quote his clients a fee for whatever they wanted done. If they decided it was worth it, he had the money to pay an assistant to do the work. If they decided it was too expensive, he didn't have to waste his time doing the work for nothing. Both his income and his free time increased dramatically.

8. Ideal Prospect Profiles

Ideal Prospect Profiles are one of the most basic marketing tools, but they're often overlooked. You wrote first drafts of these for each of your niches in Chapter 7. Now polish them, if necessary. You should finish with a list of six to ten bulleted items describing those individuals who can benefit most from your services.

The profiles should be printed on your letterhead with the title, "People Who Can Benefit Most From Our Services." Hand these out to clients, centers of influence, and strategic alliance partners. You and your staff should memorize them. This keeps you focused and simplifies the referral process. It also ensures that referrals fit your profile.

Be sure to customize your presentation folder by including the appropriate profile when you meet with prospects. For example, sharing your Ideal Prospect Profile of medical professionals with a prospect who meets this description will demonstrate your commitment to his or her market segment.

9. Case Studies

One key to communicating benefits effectively is to bundle solutions for a group of niche-related problems. This makes it easy for prospects to see the value of working with you. Here's how you do it: Identify problems you can get paid to solve for each of your target segments or niches. Then develop a success story, with examples, that illustrates the common problems faced by those in this group and the services you offer to help solve these problems.

Tell a success story about a client in a specific niche who benefited from your services—making the client the hero of the story. Develop stories like this for each niche, presenting them as one-page case studies. An example would be how estate planning helped keep the farm in the family.

Use these stories to customize your presentation folder for a client in the same niche. These stories will become the foundation for your speeches, the articles you write, and the strategic alliances you create.

To provide a total solution, you should also organize a team of experts to help solve the problems of clients in each of your target niches. Establish strategic alliances with the top experts in your area. Offer referrals to these experts as part of your total solution. Then recap all of these offerings on the back of the case study.

Let's say you target pre-retirees. If you develop a retirement capital needs analysis and an investment policy statement, you can bundle these reports as a "retirement feasibility analysis." Put this in your presentation folder with a cover letter that calls attention to these services, and you've got yourself a bundled financial analysis product.

Intelligent people who are thinking about retiring will usually seek out information to make sure they don't make any mistakes. Let them know you can help them sort out the confusing details. Then present your retirement feasibility analysis in an easy-to-understand format.

10. Article Reprints

No matter what you say about yourself, it's never as powerful as when someone else toots your horn for you. Ideally, your presentation folder will include articles about you and your business. These provide proof that you really are an expert in your field.

Everyone wants to work with a financial advisor who has specialized knowledge. Becoming an expert is the primary way you can create the perception that you're uniquely qualified to add value over and above your competitors. But how do you become an expert? One way is to get your name in print. There are two types of articles that will build your credibility: those written by someone else about you and those actually written by you.

By including article reprints, you can build your credibility with your prospects. Also, the reprints give your prospects the opportunity to learn more about you than they would from your other marketing materials alone. That helps to cement your relationship. You'll learn more about the process of generating articles to reprint in Step 5.

11. Speaker's Media Kit

If you plan to do public speaking, you'll need additional marketing communication tools. At a minimum, you'll need a dynamic brochure that presents you as a credible speaker and a sample tape of one of your presentations. You'll use this to market yourself to meeting planners and other gatekeepers for sponsored seminars.

The most common format is an 8-$\frac{1}{2}$" x 11" double-sided sheet that you can send to meeting planners. It's usually printed in two or three colors. Be sure to have the person designing the brochure make a second version in black and white—and on two pages, rather than front and back—for faxing.

On one side of the sheet should be a picture of you along with a headline that explains who you are:

JOE ADVISOR, FINANCIAL PLANNER

PRESENTS

HOW TO TRANSFER YOUR ESTATE QUICKLY

AND EASILY TO YOUR HEIRS

This side should also include the name of your company, a list of your speaking topics, a list of the benefits your audience will receive, and some testimonials from important people who've heard you speak.

On the back of your speaker's brochure, include outlines or descriptions of several of your most popular presentations. The titles must promise solutions to problems: "Transfer Your Estate Quickly and Easily to Your Heirs" or "The Simple Investment Strategy that Always Works," and so on. Include bullet points that identify what participants will learn.

Make sure your speaker's brochure and your presentations establish your position as an inspiring, humorous, informative, high-quality speaker who uses dynamic visuals and real-life case studies. With all that, who wouldn't want to hear you speak?

After faxing your brochure to a meeting planner, be prepared to follow up by mailing a full speaker's information package in a presentation folder. Include your bio, your speaker's brochure, an audiotape of your speech, a recent black-and-white head shot photo suitable for publication, article reprints, and so on. You should also include a cover letter.

You'll need presentation visuals in PowerPoint, workbooks or handouts, evaluation forms, and a formal step-by-step follow-up system. You'll learn more about these in Step 5.

12. Relationship-Building Tools

Since you're going to be building your business through relationships, you'll need tools that will help you establish them. To generate client referrals, you'll need a referral-generating script, customized pre-approach letters for your hot referrals, and an appointment-setting script. If you're going to work with centers of influence, you'll need a phone script, an interview script, and a thank-you letter.

If you're going to work with strategic alliances, you'll need an appointment-setting script, a confirmation letter, interview questions, a customized liability letter, problem/solution fact sheets, follow-up letters, and additional on-going correspondence. We'll explore these tools when we get to referrals and strategic alliances in later chapters.

Chapter at a Glance

Many advisors find it challenging to bring their company services, products, and position into focus. But those advisors who want to become known as experts must do so. An amateur can sell a mutual fund that has a great track record. But only a professional will have a value-added set of services and compelling messages that offer attractive benefits for targeted prospects.

By packaging yourself for success, you can get the right message to the right people at the right time. Those people who want solutions to the problems you are an expert at solving will seek you out. If your message is compelling and you have presented it convincingly in your marketing materials and communications, then qualified, motivated prospects will contact you. That's about as effort-less as you can get.

By packaging and communicating effectively, you can reverse the selling process. Instead of chasing wealthy prospects, they will chase you!

Chapter 11 Action Steps

Exercise 1: Take stock of your current marketing tools. What's missing? Begin developing the first 11 key materials discussed in this chapter. Be sure each one reinforces your position.

Exercise 2: Have your informal board of advisors review and comment on your materials before they're finalized. And remember: You should update your materials whenever you find a way to improve them.

Step 5

Communicate Your Benefits Effectively

Everyone knows Christopher Columbus discovered North America—whether he realized it at the time or not. But thanks to a clever communication strategy, for many years Europeans believed Amerigo Vespucci was the first explorer to set foot on the continent.

Vespucci claimed to have discovered the mainland of North America before any other explorer. He then traveled widely in Europe lecturing, writing books, and publishing maps of the New World. This aggressive self-promotion eventually led a German cartographer to name the new continent "America" on his maps. In the end, Vespucci retired rich while Columbus, penniless, died in jail.

Vespucci harnessed the power of effective communication.

The moral of the story is this: It's even more important to be an effective communicator than it is to be the first or the best.

In the first 11 chapters, you targeted your niches, conducted your research, crafted your position, and developed the tools you'll need to begin communicating. Much of that work was conceptual and strategic. From here forward, this book will become much more tactically and "how to" oriented. What comes next is what most people think of when they think of marketing.

The seven chapters in Step 5 will give you the nuts and bolts of getting your message out to attract ideal new clients. I call these processes "niche marketing systems."

You'll discover the key channels and tactics for generating qualified, motivated leads and what to do with them once you have them.

Section Preview

- Systemize an effective referral-generating process.

- Leverage public speaking opportunities.

- Implement a powerful public relations campaign.

- Establish profitable strategic alliances.

- Create a systematic process for qualifying leads and setting appointments with referrals from all of the above sources.

Attract Prospects Through Group Presentations

Speech is power:
Speech is to persuade, to convert, to compel.
—Emerson, 19th-century American transcendentalist lecturer
and author, "Self-Reliance"

When driving in San Francisco, I once saw a compelling ad on a bus bench for a hair restoration service. The ad communicated the service's benefits loudly and clearly—and a bit crudely. There was a picture of a balding young man. The ad headline promised, "Grow Hair, Get Babes."

The ad spoke directly to balding young men and promised them something most of them wanted. It solved a problem for them. Any young man who felt romantically challenged and blamed it on his receding hairline would be riveted by the ad. It targeted his emotional pain.

This simple bench ad communicated compelling payoffs to thousands of people each day. Qualified prospects who were interested in these benefits could contact the company for more information via its 800-number.

If you communicate the right message—to the right people, at the right time, through the right channels—qualified and motivated prospects will ask you to help them solve their problems.

Develop Your Marketing Communications Strategy

Once you've packaged and positioned yourself for success, you need to get out there and communicate your benefits to your target prospects as effectively as possible. An effective marketing communication strategy will accomplish these three goals for you.

1. Establish your visibility and credibility.

2. Generate qualified, motivated leads.

3. Systematically screen prospects and set appointments with motivated leads.

Indirect vs. Direct Marketing

As you develop your marketing communication strategy, it's important to keep in mind that some tactics are more likely to lead to immediate results, while others will lay the groundwork for future success.

Indirect marketing establishes your credibility, visibility, and position in the marketplace. Indirect marketing is a soft approach. It often involves offering a value-added message that communicates who you are and what beliefs you have. This type of information is used to educate your prospects to become better consumers of your services.

Here's an example: You write a series of articles for a publication directed to franchise owners about how to do estate planning. These messages create credibility and show readers how you solve problems.

Direct marketing is the better way to immediately generate qualified leads from people who want your help *now*. This type of communication requests a response from the audience. If you call a referral for an appointment, you'll ask for a meeting. If you give a presentation to members of your target niche, you'll give them an evaluation form that invites them to request an appointment. If you write an article, you'll probably offer some free information to people interested in contacting you.

Such tactics as mass mail, cold calls, newspaper ads, public seminars, and TV and radio advertising are *direct, numbers-based communication channels.* Since you aren't interested in attracting the masses, don't use mass media tactics. These tactics may work for selling products to the masses, but they aren't effective for offering services to the elite.

So how do you communicate with ideal prospects if mass mail, cold calls, and newspaper ads don't work? You have two alternatives: credibility-based communication channels and relationship-based communication channels.

Credibility-based channels include speaking engagements, books, magazines, newsletters and the electronic media. Your goal is to appear as a credible source by writing for industry publications and by speaking at targeted niche events. If you're an expert and an advocate for a specific group of people, then editors, producers, and meeting planners will be more likely to perceive you as a valuable resource their audiences would be interested in hearing from.

The second communication pathway is through *relationship-based channels.* Examples include referrals, introductions and endorsements from clients, centers of influence and strategic alliances. These are by far the most effective ways to communicate because you're collecting third-party endorsements. A third-party endorsement is far more powerful than anything you could say about yourself.

5 Ways to Communicate Effectively

To recap, there are two credibility-based communications strategies and three relationship-based strategies that will help you attract motivated, wealthy clients. These lead-generation tactics include

1. speaking in front of target niches (credibility),
2. profiting from the power of the press (credibility),

3. developing a systematic referral generating process (relationship),

4. mixing business with pleasure (relationship), and

5. creating strategic alliances with centers of influence (relationship).

In this chapter and the next one, we'll take a look at credibility-based strategies. This type of marketing paves the way for you and begins relationships with prospects—before they even meet you. It will also inspire the most motivated prospects to contact you. In chapters 14, 15, 16, and 17, we'll explore relationship-based marketing tactics. You'll learn to take relationships to the next level. Finally, in Chapter 18 we'll discuss how to qualify, prioritize, and set appointments with your potential new clients.

Sponsored group presentations, audience-specific media (such as magazines or newsletters), and one-on-one meetings are all effective forms of communicating your benefits to prospects. Each of these works fairly well on its own. But, as you'll see in the next few chapters, each method has its strengths and weaknesses. Your impact will be strongest if you combine a variety of these methods.

To build your credibility and visibility and to generate leads, it's more efficient to communicate to groups rather than to individuals. Speaking to groups in your target niches is a powerful, time-efficient way to communicate your benefits to a large number of prospects at once.

When you finish, people who are interested in your benefits *right now* will invite you to contact them with additional information. One-to-many speaking engagements often generate one-to-one appointments. This chapter will show you how to do this in an effective manner.

Public Seminars Require Enormous Effort

There are two types of group presentations: Those you market to the public and those sponsored by existing organizations or groups. I'm not a fan of public seminars even though I know a lot of "top producers" generate high sales with them. I did public seminars myself in the mid-1980s. But that was then, and this is now. If you like to speak, there are ways to present to qualified audiences with less effort. Here's why I don't recommend publicly advertised seminars any more.

They're Expensive

Financial advisors who use one popular seminar marketing package are reporting costs of over $500 per family unit to fill their seminar seats. Looking at it another way, response rates of one-half to one percent are common. That means up to 99.5 percent of your marketing dollars are wasted.

You may cut the cost to only $300 per family unit with more effective advertising and by feeding your prospects. But that still amounts to some pretty big advertising checks.

These costs are extremely difficult to overcome if you are offering fee-based asset management. Public seminars practically force you to sell high commission, transaction-based products.

Generating leads from public seminars may increase your gross revenue, but your expenses will eat up a substantial portion of your profits. You'll often earn less in net income and work much harder than a smaller producer with a more focused marketing strategy.

There Are No Cumulative Benefits

You can't penetrate rich niches with public seminars. You can't reinforce your message over and over with the same group of people. It's hard to create recurring revenue that builds real value in your business. By going broad and shallow, you don't develop any cumulative benefits over time. If you rely on seminars then stop doing them, your prospect pipeline and your revenue completely dry up.

The Wrong People Show Up

Many of the people who do show up at public seminars are there strictly for information. Some are even your competitors. The vast majority of people who come are Thrill Seekers or Guru Groupies. Most Prudent Investors have such a low interest in financial products that they aren't attracted to financial seminars. Because ideal prospects don't tend to respond, it's difficult to consistently attract and land them with this kind of marketing.

They're Labor-Intensive

Public seminars can be exhausting. Think about all the work that goes into doing one: You need to prepare the direct mail pieces or newspaper ads; you need to develop or customize the presentation and visual aids; you need to present the classes or workshops.

Then there's the follow-up work: calling attendees to set appointments, meeting with interested prospects to answer their questions and qualify them, preparing proposals for qualified prospects. Unless you're a super salesperson, you'll have a fairly low closing ratio because many of the attendees are "just looking."

Overall, the project requires an enormous investment of time, money, and staff. You must factor the cost of your time and your employees' time into the total cost of doing public seminars.

Public seminars worked well when the industry revolved around selling financial products to the masses. If you're lucky, they can still work today. But they're a classic example of massive, random activity to generate one-shot sales. There's a better way to generate leads through group presentations.

Speak at Sponsored Meetings

Many of the advisors I know enjoy speaking. But all of them have come to the same conclusion about public seminars: lots of effort, not enough results. Putting on public seminars turns out to be what my friend John Bowen calls a "real grind."

In the client-centered, fee-based phase of the industry, you need a more sophisticated, lower cost, niche-focused strategy.

Many advisors have used their speaking skills to add value for member of target niches. If you do this right, you'll generate far more profits for the time and money you invest.

Concentrate your presentation marketing efforts on

- trade associations,
- educational institutions,
- professional organizations,
- churches,
- charities,
- outplacement services,
- hospital auxiliaries,
- your alliance partners' clients,
- special interest groups, and
- other targeted communities that have high concentrations of people who fit your Ideal Prospect Profiles. (Chambers of Commerce and other service clubs, with the notable exception of Rotary, are usually too generic and low end.)

I call these targeted presentations "sponsored seminars" or workshops because someone else hosts them. A sponsored presentation is a highly effective channel for generating qualified leads. Here are a couple of key reasons to speak at sponsored group meetings.

You Fill a Need

The meeting planners for organizations have many speaking slots to fill. These groups are meeting already or are looking for to ways to create special events to add value for their members. Many times you can charge a fee and donate it to the group you're speaking for. I've personally been involved in many fund raising events in partnership with associations.

If you position yourself as an expert in your targeted niche(s), program chairs will invite you to speak to their groups. You'll fill a need.

7 Presentation Tips

Deliver your performance with enthusiasm and as much energy as possible. Be sure to keep in mind the following tips.

1. Educate; don't sell. Product pushers will never be invited back or referred. Deliver great information your audience values.

2. Interact with the audience. The more the audience gets involved, the more effective your communication will be. I like to use the word *workshop* instead of *seminar* because it implies interactivity. Develop a dialog with your attendees and have them complete mini-tests and exercises. More involvement equals more leads.

3. Use the case study format. Show your attendees how your story relates to them. This stealth qualifying method helps audience members recognize their need. They'll say, "I want you to do for me what you did for the client in your example."

4. Keep it simple. At one of my workshops, a lady came up to me after I finished and said, "I liked your presentation. But I have one question: What's cash flow?" After that I always used the phrase *checks in your mailbox* instead of *cash flow*. If you want people to follow you, use simple words.

5. Use metaphors and analogies. An advisor in the midwestern U.S. uses farming analogies to illustrate investment concepts. Always explain a new concept by comparing it to something your audience is already familiar with.

6. Show up early. Be sure to show up early on the day you're going to speak. Meet all the key members of the organization before you speak. It's a good idea to greet people as they arrive. Introduce yourself. This helps to break the ice.

7. Use evaluation forms. Make a call for action. Collect the evaluation forms and read them. Refine your presentation based on the feedback. Have your staff set appointments with the qualified prospects.

They'll invite you instead of you having to invite them. That's great marketing!

One advisor stopped conducting public rollover seminars and started conducting in-house workshops for an outplacement service company. His closing ratio went up dramatically, and so did his income. And the company organized the workshops as a value-added service for their clients.

These Presentations
Are High Payoff

There's no cost to you because the organization will promote the event for you. The organization will increase your visibility and credibility at its own expense. All you have to do is show up, deliver an inspiring presentation, and collect evaluation forms from the interested attendees. In addition, the organization will be happy to pick up any of your out-of-pocket expenses.

One of my clients recently spoke for 100 CFOs at an educational workshop sponsored by a Big Six accounting firm. They paid all his expenses, and he got to collect leads from his interested audience members. No matter how much money he spent, he never would have been able to attract such a high-level audience.

You Receive an
Implied Endorsement

You'll wear the halo of an implied endorsement. The simple act of booking you to speak says the organization's leaders believe you to be a trustworthy expert. You gain an aura of credibility, as if the organization had conducted due diligence before selecting you. In a sense, the organization *is* recommending you to its audience. You'll learn how to get these implied endorsements from centers of influence in Chapter 17.

You Make
Multiple Impressions

Market researchers tell us it typically takes seven to 12 impressions to turn a prospect into a client. When you speak or write to the same target audience over a period of time, people start to know who you are and to believe you're an expert in your niche. Multiple impressions establish your position and create trust with your audience.

One advisor works with fire departments in the southwestern U.S. He has been a featured speaker at industry conferences for years. He is now a minor celebrity in his niche. When people need his expertise, they know who to call.

The more your targeted prospects see you, hear you, and hear about you, the more likely they are to come to you when they need help. Your presentation evaluation forms will generate qualified leads every time you talk.

Don is an advisor who had been using mass mail to market public seminars for years. With some coaching, he realized his two nights a week of conducting educational prospecting seminars was way too much effort. Over a four-month period, he converted his "A" clients to fee-based money management. Then he transferred his "D" clients to a younger advisor and helped five of his seven employees find other jobs.

His gross revenue dropped by two-thirds. But his net income remained the same. He says public seminars got him where he is but won't take him to the next level in his business. Now he has created a clearing to identify and attract more "A" clients so he can build a super-profitable business and a wonderful life.

How to Book Sponsored
Speaking Engagements

Go to any hotel on any day or night of the week, and look in the meeting rooms. What do you see? Not surprisingly, you see people meeting. And most of the time someone is in front of the room making a presentation. What's the topic? The speaker is most likely providing information to help audience members achieve their goals or solve their problems.

The speaker could be you. But you need bookings at the right events, where high concentrations of your ideal prospects congregate. You should have identified many of these opportunities during your research interviews.

Speak Wherever You Can At First

The best way to draw attention to yourself is simply to begin speaking. Once you've developed your presentation and created your speaker's brochure, speak anywhere you can at first. As you get better—and become better known—you can become more selective about your venues.

At the end of every talk, ask your audience if anyone knows of another organization that could benefit from your information. Describe your target group. People who liked your talk will invite you to speak to their groups.

You'll usually be asked to contact the educational chairs of the organizations. Ask your advocates if they'll recommend you to their meeting planners. These people are almost always looking for quality speakers who have special information of interest to their audiences. If the groups are in your target segments, follow up and book a speech.

Contact the Right Person

Call the program chairs or meeting planners. Tell them you have a number of clients in their niche. (Your marketing person can do this step.) Briefly explain the problems you specialize in solving. Tell the meeting planners you have put together a presentation that provides the audience with useful information in an entertaining and fast-paced talk. Ask if that would be of interest to their groups.

People who select speakers are wary. Their big fear is booking a speaker who flops—or, worse yet, tries to sell products or services to the audience. If the meeting planners think you're going to push products, they simply won't invite you to speak.

Find Out What They Want

Program chairs are your best source of information to help you design a successful presentation. If you ask, they'll tell you what they want and need. Find out what topics are of interest to the group. Also find out what other successful speakers have done to hold the group's interest.

Program organizers will help you customize a presentation based on your expertise and the needs of their audiences. If you convince them that you're a competent speaker and have valuable information for their audiences, they'll usually find a slot for you.

Send Your Speaker's Kit

The contact people at your targeted organizations will probably ask you to forward some more information about yourself. They'll need this information to sell their committee members on your capabilities.

Fax your speaker's brochure to the contact person. Then mail a full speaker's information package in your presentation folder. Include your brief biography, your speaker's brochure, an audio tape of you presenting a typical seminar, a recent black-and-white photo suitable for publication, any marketing materials from other places you've spoken, and article reprints. You should also include a cover letter. (For help in putting together these materials, see Chapter 11.)

Book the Date

If you position and package yourself as a knowledgeable and entertaining expert, meeting planners will be eager to have you speak to their groups. Before you hang up from your first conversation, schedule a telephone appointment to review your speaker's brochure with the meeting planner. Call at the appointed time. During this conversation, confirm a speaking date, topic, and location. Get all the details and send a confirmation letter.

Don't expect to get paid for presenting at these niche meetings. These meetings are your communication channels. View them as a free opportunity to start a relationship with future clients. It is customary, however, for you to receive reimbursement for your expenses.

Deliver a Compelling Presentation

Speaking before a live group is one of the most persuasive communication mediums available. Every compelling speech has a clear purpose. Usually the purpose is to educate and persuade. Make sure your speech ends with a *call to action*. If you don't want your audience to *do* anything, why speak?

The purpose of your sponsored speeches is to educate the audience to become successful consumers of your services. You need to sensitize them to financial problems that you can get paid to help them solve. Your call to action will usually be to have members of the audience complete an evaluation form and check the box: "Please contact me. I'd like more information about your services."

You can determine how effective you are in communicating with your audience by tracking the percentage of people who invite you to contact them afterward. If they're moved by your presentation—and they're qualified—they'll want to know more.

Create Dynamic Visuals

The state of the art today in presentations is to use Microsoft PowerPoint, or a similar presentation program, and a digital video projector. Slides, overheads, and word processed documents are old technology. They undermine your professionalism. If you're going to speak, you must create dynamic presentations using a laptop computer and a digital projector. If you need help, you can consult one of many graphic design studios that now offer the service of preparing a presentation for digital projection.

Use Case Studies

Case studies create the most powerful marketing stories. Your audience members want to understand what you do and how you can help them. In the service industries, usually the only way to try a service is to buy it. But case studies give potential new clients the sense of having taken a test drive.

The best way for people to understand how they can benefit from your services is for them to hear a story about someone just like them. Tell your audience members a story about how you helped someone in their niche. If they like what you did for the other person, they'll ask you if you can do the same for them. Case studies make it easy for your prospects to decide to do business with you.

Make Your Ideal Prospect the Hero

Make your ideal prospect the hero of your presentation. But customize the details for each audience. If you're speaking to doctors, make your hero a doctor. If you're speaking to widows, your hero should be a widow. Start your talk by describing this individual's situation and personality (demographics and psychographics). People in the audience who fit the profile will immediately recognize themselves and their situations in your story. They'll instantly become attentive.

Clarify and Dramatize the Problem

Explain the problem that you can get paid to solve in detail. The people in your audience who have the same problem will recognize themselves in your story. Focus on a common problem you expect many people in this audience to have. Use a *hook*: Build up the problem and explain in detail why it must be dealt with now.

Use computer projections to visually communicate your key points. Turn your listeners' vague concerns into concrete fears by identifying and quantifying the true cost of their problems. Show them what will happen to them if they don't act now. Involve their senses and emotions as you explain the problem.

Explain the Solution

Once you have their attention, offer a way out. In the final part of the presentation, show your solution to the problem. Generally explain the strategies used to solve the problem. Associate yourself with the payoff of taking action. Never talk about specific products. Keep it simple.

Demonstrate the before and after benefits with your case study. Make the contrasts dramatic and graphic. Use color charts and multimedia elements where you can. Emphasize how happy the clients felt after their decisions.

People in your audience who fit your hero's profile and feel the pressure of the same problem will be riveted by your presentation. They'll be eager to learn how the hero solved the problem. The qualified and motivated people in your audience will then want to know what to do next to solve their own problem.

Call for Action

The final stage is the call to action at the end of your presentation. Since you are a client-centered advisor serving your niche, you'll be very attractive to many people in your audience. Give those who fit the profile, have the problem, and want to solve the problem *now*, an opportunity to identify themselves and request a meeting with you. The best way to systemize this process is to use a standard presentation evaluation form, such as the one on the next page.

Hand out this form as everyone enters the room. Ask them to complete the top part (name and address) while they're waiting for the meeting to begin.

Collect the Evaluations

As you wrap things up, sell your audience members on the benefits of meeting with you. Tell them you're passionate about helping your clients solve these problems. Say you're always trying to improve your presentations, and you'd appreciate their feedback. Ask them to complete the evaluation form so they can help you make future presentations better.

Presentation Evaluation Form

Name _____ Spouse _____

Address _____

City _____ State _____ Zip _____

Day Phone _____ Best Time to Call _____

How did you hear about this workshop? _____

_____

What prompted you to attend this workshop? _____

_____

How valuable was the workshop information?
Poor 1 2 3 4 5 6 7 8 9 10 Excellent

How effective was the presentation of the material?
Poor 1 2 3 4 5 6 7 8 9 10 Excellent

Overall how would you rate this workshop?
Poor 1 2 3 4 5 Excellent

1. YOUR OPINION of today's program? _____

_____

2. What part do you wish we had spent MORE TIME ON? _____

_____

3. What part do you wish we had spent LESS TIME on? _____

_____

4. What was the MOST IMPORTANT IDEA you gained? _____

_____

5. How do you plan to APPLY THIS IDEA? _____

_____

6. How could we IMPROVE this program? _____

_____

May we quote you?   ❑ yes   ❑ no   Initials _____

*Do you have friends or associates who could
benefit from this program?*

_____

Name _____ Organization _____ Phone _____

(continued next page)

> ## The Next Step
>
> *By participating in this workshop, you have earned a one-hour,*
> *complimentary consultation.*
>
> ❑   I want to get started within the next two weeks.
>   Please call me to arrange a consultation as soon as possible.
>
> ❑   QUESTIONS • I'm not sure if I'm interested. I'd like to find
>   out more. Please call me when it's convenient.
>
> ❑   RAIN CHECK • I'd like an appointment in the future.
>   Please call me on _____/_____/_____ .
>
> ❑   NO THANKS • I'm not interested at this time.

I usually say,

> *"Please complete the whole form, including the bottom.*
> *Please check the appropriate box so I'll know how you'd*
> *like to be treated. If you don't mark any boxes, I get*
> *confused."*

They usually laugh, and it seems to improve the response rate.

Your goal is to encourage interested people to identify themselves. These evaluation forms help you refine your presentations to meet the needs and interests of your audience. They also allow you to collect names and telephone numbers of interested people—without irritating the other audience members or the meeting planner. I call this "stealth lead generation."

Chapter at a Glance

Credibility-based communication channels include presenting targeted group educational workshops and writing articles for targeted publications that serve your segments, subsegments, and niches.

Relationship-based channels include generating referrals and introductions from clients, centers of influence, and strategic alliance partners. All of these methods of lead generation are effective. But combining them will give you the greatest marketing impact.

Speaking at public seminars is a high-cost, high-effort method of generating leads. You can improve your results dramatically if you speak specifically to members of your target niches at sponsored meetings.

Speaking for groups is a powerful way to communicate your benefits to a large number of prospects at once. An evaluation form is your tool for efficiently generating feedback and identifying qualified motivated leads.

Turn to Chapter 13 to learn about another powerful credibility-based approach: implementing a public relations campaign.

Chapter 12 Action Steps

Exercise 1: Make a list of the local associations that serve your target niche(s). Contact these groups to book speaking engagements.

Exercise 2: Customize your presentation materials for speeches to each target niche. Be sure to include colorful visual aides to hold your audiences' attention.

Exercise 3: Deliver your first speech to a sponsored forum. Review your evaluation forms and modify your presentation based on the feedback you receive. Have your staff contact any leads, qualify them, and schedule appointments.

Profit From
Public Relations

*A man's success in business today
turns upon his power of getting people
to believe he has something
that they want.*

—Gerald Stanley Lee, author, *Crowds*

couple of financial advisors wrote an article about estate planning for shopping center owners. The article ran in a glossy publication called *California Center*—a magazine for mall owners in California.

Then these advisors used a combination of marketing techniques, including direct mail targeted to the list of *California Center* subscribers. When a shopping center owner responded to one of their direct mail letters about estate planning, they scheduled an appointment for an initial interview. The two financial professionals went out to talk with the prospect, but they found he was resistant and cold. He participated in the meeting with his arms crossed in a way that communicated, "Go ahead. Try to sell me."

About halfway through the interview, one of the advisors said, "Did you happen to see our article in *California Center?*" The prospect went to a shelf and pulled out the magazine. He said, "Oh, this is you guys, isn't it? You wrote this article?" They nodded in agreement.

From then on, his attitude improved. As soon as he realized they had written an article that was impressive to him, his behavior changed completely. He opened up and told them the details of his situation. Ultimately, he became a great client.

You can see from this story the awesome power of public relations to influence perceptions. It's a very important positioning tool.

The Benefits of Public Relations

Public relations is defined as an organized set of activities designed to communicate your position, promote your business, and make sure that your targeted prospects know who you are. There are two goals of your PR activities. One is to get articles published with your name as the author; the other is to be interviewed by the media. Basically, you want to generate articles *by* you and articles *about* you.

When you want to communicate your benefits to thousands of people at once, nothing works like a public relations campaign. The media can give you broad exposure in your targeted segments. Public relations is an excellent vehicle for establishing credibility and visibility. It locks your name and your position in the minds of your prospects.

Let's say you're a millionaire looking for someone to help you with your personal finances. Wouldn't you feel more comfortable with a highly visible expert than with someone unknown to you? Financial advisors who are interviewed on radio and TV or who appear in magazines and newspapers are perceived as knowledgeable, competent experts. People assume the media would never run an interview with an incompetent amateur.

With PR you can create and nurture your desired image. Public relations has five great benefits for you.

1. It can establish you as a trustworthy expert.

2. It can bolster your visibility in your target markets.

3. It can generate leads—both directly and indirectly.

4. It can shorten the sales process.

5. It's free or low-cost.

Public relations can literally make or break your career.

Getting published creates more credibility and status than buying ad space. When one of my articles is published, I often get speaking engagements, consulting projects, and telephone orders for cassette tape programs. All this is possible for little effort and no cost.

What Editors and Producers Don't Want

You can achieve your goals if you help the members of the media achieve *their* goals. Let's start with what the editors and producers don't want.

After reading one of my articles about PR, a financial advisor submitted some articles for publication to a couple of local magazines. He was rejected outright by some editors, and others offered to publish his articles as *advertorials* or *special reports* (paid editorial) if he purchased the ad space. He was frustrated with his lack of results, so he called me for advice.

I asked him to tell me about the articles. He said, "My firm has already written a number of articles for its reps. All I have to do is put my name on them." I asked him what the articles were about. He responded that one was called, "How to Get Higher Income From Your CD Money." Another one was, "Annuities for Tax Deferred Growth."

So I asked him, "How do those articles address the problems or meet the needs of the magazines' readers?" He said he wasn't sure they did.

Next, I asked him, "Who are the readers of the magazines?" Again, he didn't know.

Then I told him why he was being rejected by the editors: "Your topics are all product-oriented. The editors probably think you're trying to use their magazines to sell products to their readers."

"Well, yes, that's exactly what I'd like to do," was his response.

I said, "If your primary goal is to use their magazines as advertising vehicles, isn't it reasonable that they charge you for that privilege?"

People who want to use magazines or other media for their own commercial purposes constantly bombard editors and producers. If you try this approach, you'll almost always be rejected or charged the going rate for ad space. And, incidentally, you won't get much response from this kind of blatant product pushing.

What People in the Media Do Want

Many people believe you need a PhD to be considered an expert. The truth is that an expert is someone who understands public relations and gives good interviews. Most advisors assume that the TV shows that just interviewed their competitors conducted massive searches to find the most competent experts in the field. They don't realize that a large percentage of everything they see or read in the media is the result of public relations activities.

Members of the media simply don't have the resources to do extensive research and background checking for every article. They often count on freelance journalists and PR specialists to contact them with compelling story ideas. Then they select the topics that will help them sell their magazines (or TV programs or radio shows) to their respective audiences.

Keep in mind there are tremendous opportunities for getting published today. There are now more than 17,000 magazines in the United States alone. This includes the magazines and newsletters published by more than 22,000 trade associations for their members (not all trade associations publish formal newsletters).

If you assume that 17,000 publications need just two major articles each month, that's 34,000 articles each month or 408,000 articles each year. That's a heck of a lot of articles! And that doesn't even include the

A Positive Twist on
Radio Broadcasts

A growing area of PR is to produce your own audiocassettes instead of writing an article or getting interviewed. Audiocassettes don't create quite as much credibility as a major media story, but they can be easy and inexpensive to produce.

One advisor went to a small local radio station and asked if he could do a series of shows on financial planning. The radio station agreed to sell him six half-hours of air time for $25 each. To keep things simple, he interviewed a different financial service professional for each show.

He kept the topics generic but addressed subjects he knew would make him sound knowledgeable. He recorded each show and made copies for $2 each. This included a quality label with the name of his show, the topic, and his 800-number.

These tapes of his live radio show were given to prospective clients before they came in for an initial interview. They helped to establish his credibility and to build a good case for the particular service or product he wanted them to know more about. The advisor told me that those $2 tapes generated many hundreds of thousands of dollars in new accounts.

thousands of newsletters that serve niches—or the ever-expanding realm of electronic publishing on the Web.

Then what do editors want? Fortunately, the editors of many of these publications have a common problem you can help them solve: They have little or no budget for articles. They need free articles that address the needs of their unique audiences. By solving editors' problems, you can achieve your goals of increased visibility and credibility.

How to Get Published

You don't want your articles to appear in just any publication. You want to be published in magazines and newsletters that have a large number of your ideal prospects as readers. A good way to find out what magazines your prospects read is simply to ask your favorite clients what magazines *they* read. Pay particular attention to trade or professional magazines. General circulation consumer magazines and newspapers are harder to get into, and they reach a much more diffused audience.

Select Your Target Publications

Go to the library, and use the current *Encyclopedia of Associations* published by Gale Research to look up specific trade associations. Then contact the trade associations, and ask for a new member kit. It will tell you all about the association and will usually include a current issue of the association's publication.

Also, consider buying the current edition of *Writer's Market* (Writer's Digest Books). This book and the CD-ROM that comes with it are published annually and list roughly 2,000 magazines and offer tips directly from the editors about the types of article ideas you should try to pitch.

If you're targeting industry or consumer magazines, you can find a more comprehensive listing in another annual publication called *SRDS* (Standard Rate and Data Service, published by Cahners) at any good library. Cahners also maintains a Website that provides access to a list of online media kits as well as Websites for business publications and consumer magazines. Go to *SDRS Media Kit Link*™ (www.srds.com/cgi-bin/srds/mediakitlink/mediakitlink.cgi) to check it out.

Once you have uncovered the name of a magazine you want to learn more about, contact the advertising sales department of the magazine and ask for a *media kit*. The kit will tell you how many subscribers the magazine has and provide you with a detailed breakdown of reader demographics. Often a recent copy of the publication is included.

Then ask the sales department to transfer you to the editorial assistant. Request a copy of the publication's *writer's guidelines*. This is a document that magazines have on file to share with prospective writers that offers specific guidelines to be followed, as well as tips for submission.

Study the magazines and their reader demographics to determine which ones you want to approach. Concentrate on those magazines with wealthy audiences whose readers are likely to have problems you can solve.

Your best bet is to begin by writing for small local publications before you contact the big guns. Smaller publications are more likely to run a positive "puff" piece about you and your services. My first articles were published in the newsletters for local IAFP chapters. The editors couldn't be very particular about their writers because they were desperate for material. I used those first couple of published articles to establish myself as a credible writer.

After you have a few articles under your belt, work your way into more prestigious publications. Many people try to get into *Forbes* or *Money Magazine*. The reality is you may never get there.

No matter what publication your article is printed in, the reprints will be far more powerful than a brochure. They'll help you establish your credentials for more influential publications and the electronic media.

Contact the Editor

Decide what topics or article ideas you want to suggest to the editor. Your best bet is to use the exact same topics as you use in speeches. You already know the subjects, have detailed outlines in PowerPoint (discussed in the previous chapter), and know the audience is interested. You'll simply have to tweak the information and shorten it to fit into the space available.

I usually call the editor directly. His or her name appears on the masthead of the magazine in the first couple of pages. But keep in mind that some editors accept article ideas only in writing. Refer to the writer's guidelines to determine if this is the case. If so—and you ignore this request—you'll seriously diminish your chances of success.

Simply tell the editor,

> *"I'm a financial advisor. Many of my clients read and enjoy your excellent magazine. The reason I'm calling is that many of my clients are concerned about* [mention a specific problem you want to solve]. *I specialize in helping people solve that problem. I'm wondering if your readers would be interested in an article on the subject?"*

If you're on target, the editor will say, "Well, yes, I think they would be interested. Have you ever written articles on the subject before?" This is a buying signal. The editor is trying to determine whether you're a reasonably competent writer.

Once you've passed the writer's competency test (or the editor's desperation test), the editor will discuss the topic with you in more detail. At this point, the editor will probably suggest a *slant* or *angle* that will best suit the readers' interests.

The editor will often ask you to submit an outline. You can turn your PowerPoint presentations into outlines for each article. Include copies of any other articles you have written (known as "clips") to help establish your credibility.

Also include a cover letter stating that you'd prefer to submit the article on a "first rights" basis. This reserves the copyright for you so that you can publish the article later in another publication. However, some publications will buy articles only on an "all rights" basis.

The editor will then return your outline to you with comments, changes, and an assignment letter for your signature. The letter serves as a contract and will state the terms of your agreement to write the article—including the pay rate, copyright agreement, whether or not you're entitled to free reprints, and the submission deadline. Now you officially have an assignment.

Write the Article

This is where I lose many financial advisors. Most of us are much better talkers than writers. Plus the thought of spending all that time at a computer instead of with clients seems expensive. Don't worry. There are two painless ways to write your article.

You can try dictating it into a tape recorder and then having it transcribed. Prepare for your dictation by filling in the details in the outline you submitted. Also gather any reference materials you might need. If you have given the presentation a few times, dictating will be a snap. After it's transcribed, make your final edits. This method will cut your writing time down to one-third the time it would take you to type your article. And that assumes you're a decent typist.

If you don't want to dictate and transcribe, here's another option: Pay a freelance writer to interview you and turn your knowledge into an article. This is called ghostwriting and is very popular with busy professionals. You don't really think Lee Iacocca wrote his own autobiography, do you?

Have your ghostwriter or transcriber give you a double-spaced hard copy of the article and an electronic copy on disk so you can edit and restructure if necessary. Print out the final copy with your name on it, and send it along with the disk to the magazine's editor.

Be sure to respect the deadline, or you won't be asked to write for that publication again.

If you want to maintain good relationships with your editors, don't offer the same article to another publication in the same industry. If you submit the article to another, non-competing publication, customize it for the audience of the next publication. Subsequent publications should be on a "one-time rights" basis only. This means the article was published before and may be published again.

As far as your writing style goes, don't worry if it isn't perfect. Editors will correct grammar and punctuation mistakes and will polish your copy to make you sound brilliant. That's what editors do; however, do your best. Most editors are not fond of rewriting an entire article and would hesitate to work with an author who consistently provided poor copy.

Your ultimate goal should be to become a regular columnist for your targeted magazines. This will give you constant exposure to your ideal prospects.

How to Get Interviewed

Once you've had a couple of articles published, you're ready to be interviewed by the media. You can use the following techniques for print, radio, or TV.

First, you must develop a media or press kit. This is an information package that describes your credentials and communicates your message. A press kit normally includes at least the following five items:

1. a biography listing your accomplishments and credentials,

2. a publicity photo that makes you look like a successful business executive,

3. any relevant articles you have written,

4. information about your company, its products, and its services, and

5. a press release announcing a new development in your business or some other newsworthy event or information.

You already should have developed most of this material and a presentation folder in Chapter 11.

The press release can be your "hook" that interests the media in you. Remember to make yourself the star. You want to be perceived as an expert problem solver—not a product pusher.

Contact the Producer or Editor

Once you have prepared your press kit, target the members of the media you feel will be most interested in your story. Base your selection on research. Don't waste time contacting media sources if you don't know what audience they target. In most metropolitan areas, you'll be able to buy a book of local media sources, usually compiled by local PR firms. Use it as a master list.

There are two approaches you can use for getting interviewed. One is to present yourself as a credible source who members of the media can

5 Tips for Successful PR

Public relations, when handled well, is a powerful tool for gaining visibility and credibility. You can use it to get media stories about you and by you in targeted niche publications. Here are five tips.

1. Tell success stories. When you speak, tell success stories. When you're interviewed for the media, tell success stories. When you write articles and columns, tell success stories. Talk about people who solved problems. Don't talk about products. When you tell a success story, people can see themselves benefiting from your services.

2. Focus on multiple impressions in niches. Use PR to establish your expertise and to maintain a high profile in your niche(s). Focus on communicating with your targeted prospects—not the mass market. You'll need seven to 12 impressions to turn a typical prospect into a client. With PR, you can maintain a constant presence in your markets.

3. Include a call to action. As you paint the picture of your hero in a case study, readers recognize themselves. As you describe the problem, they feel the pain because they also have the problem. When you explain how you solved the problem, they'll be excited. Be sure to include your contact information, or at least the name of your business and the city and state where it's located so readers can find you. You can also offer a free gift or information to generate interest.

4. Use reprints. The best thing about magazine articles is the reprints. After you generate some articles written about you and by you, you'll want to buy reprints from the publishers. Add the reprints to your presentation folder to enhance your credibility. When you have a number of reprints, choose the best ones for each situation.

5. Work with an expert. The subject of PR is so broad it needs its own book. Consider hooking up with a true PR professional, and harness the tremendous power of PR to help you build your credibility and visibility in your targeted niches.

interview when they need a local slant on a specific topic. The other approach is to present yourself as someone they should interview right now because you have timely information of topical interest to their audiences.

Most markets have radio programs that focus on financial topics. It's a good idea to start with one of these shows. Unlike magazines, some radio stations have programs on which you can pay to be interviewed. This practice is much more accepted in radio and TV than in magazines or newspapers, so don't ask a print editor if you can pay to be interviewed.

Prepare for your interview by bringing a list of questions the host can ask you. Practice delivering short answers to the questions. Use each opportunity to show that you're a trustworthy, knowledgeable expert who cares about clients.

It's usually an imposition for the studio to record your interview. Make arrangements with a friend to tape the interview when it airs.

Every time you're published or interviewed, you can add the tape or article reprints to your media kit. You can work your way up from small, local media to more prestigious national media. Eventually you'll become established as an expert in the segments you want to serve.

Generating Qualified Leads

One of the complaints I hear is that PR takes too long to generate business. This can be true. As mentioned on the previous page, market researchers have determined it usually takes seven to 12 impressions—or prospect contacts—to make a sale. One of the benefits of PR is that you can make an impression on many people at one time, and you can reinforce your image over time with additional articles or interviews. Eventually these multiple impressions result in indirect sales leads.

But most of my clients want to generate sales *now*. Here are some proven ways to turn your PR activities into immediate income.

When writing articles, use the case study format just as you would with a PowerPoint presentation. Make your ideal client the hero, and focus on problems that you can get paid to solve. Write these case studies as if they actually happened to one of your clients.

Be sure to end the article with a short biography that includes your purpose statement, the name of your company, and the city in which your business is located. Include your telephone number and e-mail address if the editor will let you.

When this article is published, it will be read by several thousand or even tens of thousands of your ideal prospects. If your readers fit the profile of your hero, have the same problem as your hero, and want to solve it, they'll call or e-mail you. This is what I call "direct response PR."

You can also generate qualified leads from radio and TV interviews by offering free information. Tell the audience you have reprints available of an article you just wrote. Or offer a free special report, a checklist, or a cassette tape. Ask audience members to call your office and leave their names and addresses. Then send them information packets with return reply cards offering respondents a free one-hour consultation.

Putting It All Together

One of my first consulting projects was for an attorney who specialized in asset protection. His primary business was creating family limited partnerships and offshore trusts for wealthy professionals and business owners. Because the field was new at the time, there wasn't much competition. That made work, if you could get it, very profitable. My job was to help him get more work.

The first thing we did was reposition his services from "Comprehensive Estate Planning" to "Asset Protection Planning." Our basic promise of benefits was to "protect your hard-earned assets from aggressive attorneys." We targeted doctors who had malpractice insurance cost problems, business owners, key executives, manufacturers, and board members of smaller corporations.

We conducted a few public seminars to see what would happen. Because the topic was new at the time, we had a good turnout: 50 or 60 attendees total. At one seminar, three different couples owned mobile home parks.

It turned out that an aggressive law firm in San Diego was systematically organizing class-action lawsuits against mobile home park owners throughout southern California. The most popular cause for action was failing to maintain their parks at a high enough standard. In many cases, rent control prohibited the owners from raising rents. This meant the owners didn't have the money to renovate or upgrade older parks.

It sounds like these mobile home park owners had some serious problems, doesn't it? We had identified a perfect niche for this attorney's specialized service. After he did asset protection planning for a couple of these park owners, I conducted research interviews with them.

I discovered the lawsuits had every mobile home park owner in California scared to death. And my client had the cure. By making it difficult for attorneys to collect settlements, asset protection planning discouraged them from filing suit in the first place. Our mobile home park owners were so well protected that attorneys realized it wasn't worth their time to sue them.

I contacted the editor of the biggest trade magazine in the mobile home park industry and offered to write an article explaining how to solve this huge problem. He was eager to publish this valuable information for his 3,500 readers. We didn't get paid, but we did get to put the attorney's name and telephone number at the end of the article.

We paid a college English professor $1,000 to interview the attorney and ghostwrite the 2,000-word article. When the article was published, the attorney's telephone started ringing. He received more than 40 calls from interested prospects. When the smoke cleared, he had picked up three wealthy new clients worth over $122,000 in legal fees.

That article became the foundation for his media kit, PowerPoint presentations, and presentation folder. Soon he was speaking for mobile home park associations all across America. The last time I saw him he was on his way to conduct a workshop on an Alaskan cruise for a national mobile home park owners association. He had found his rich niche.

Chapter at a Glance

Public relations is one of the very best ways to market financial services. It builds credibility and visibility with your targeted prospects. You can become very popular with editors and producers if you help make their magazines, newsletters, and radio and TV programs attractive to their audiences.

The members of the media have an insatiable need for knowledgeable experts who have useful information for their readers and viewers. So position yourself as an expert problem solver.

Your goal is to get published in targeted magazines and interviewed by credible media sources. Doing this can bring you tens of thousands of dollars of free publicity. Follow the direct response techniques suggested in this chapter to maximize your immediate payoff.

Chapter 13 Action Steps

Exercise 1: Make a list of the local associations and publications that serve your targeted niche(s). Charge your person responsible for PR with getting you exposure with these groups.

Exercise 2: Use information from your research interviews to develop a "story" or "hook" that will interest your target market. Work with your PR or marketing person to develop this idea into a query for a magazine article. Send the query to several magazines read by your target niche. Be sure you contact the magazine editors to introduce yourself and offer yourself as a source for upcoming articles.

Exercise 3: Land a writing assignment, write the article, and get it published. Get reprints and add them to your marketing package, speaker's kit, and media kit. Send reprints to your key clients, prospects, and centers of influence.

Bury Yourself
in Referrals

In this world, we must help each other.

—Jean de La Fontaine, 17th-century French poet

M any years ago, a good friend of mine and I were giving presentations to a group of insurance agents. Bill did a great job, and people loved him. On a one-to-ten scale, he would have scored a 9.5. I didn't do too badly myself. I probably would have scored an 8.5. Most of the other speakers weren't as polished or experienced as we were.

Afterward, we had lunch with one of the other speakers who had given a solid 7.0 presentation. As we discussed the day's events, she mentioned that she had received five referrals from the person who'd hired us. Surprised, Bill and I looked at each other and asked, "How did you do that? How did you get the referrals?"

She replied, "I asked for them." Bill and I were dumbfounded. Each of us thought to ourselves, *I can do that.* Right then Bill and I both vowed to create a *systematic* process for generating qualified referrals.

I've since learned that financial advisors who consistently get great referrals have a systematic, almost automatic process for generating them.

How Ideal Clients Want to Meet You

Russ Prince, a well-known market researcher, recently conducted a survey of 879 individuals with more than $1 million invested with money managers. He published the results in his excellent book *Cultivating the Affluent* (Institutional Investor, 1995).

Prince and his associate Karen Maru File surveyed these wealthy investors to determine how they preferred to meet their advisors. The top six answers indicated one form or another of referrals. Yet, when he later asked financial advisors what type of marketing help they wanted, the highest vote was given to direct mail. Direct mail seems easy, but it's expensive, it takes a lot of time, and it requires much more effort than getting your clients to market for you.

Tiburon Strategic Advisors conducted a similar survey. See the results in "Why Referrals Are Crucial to Your Business Success" on the next page.

Being referred or introduced to a qualified prospect is a direct form of marketing. The goal is to add so much value for clients and centers of influence that they feel eager to encourage their friends and associates to use your services. You'll learn more about adding value and making your clients ecstatic in upcoming chapters.

There is nothing you can say that's as compelling as a happy client recommending you to his or her close friends. This is practically essential for attracting huge accounts.

At the higher end of the food chain, almost all business takes place through referrals and introductions. Through a solid endorsement, the trust your client has in you is transferred to his or her friends. You earn the friends' business by proving your trustworthiness and value to your client. In short, you become more referable the more client-centered you are.

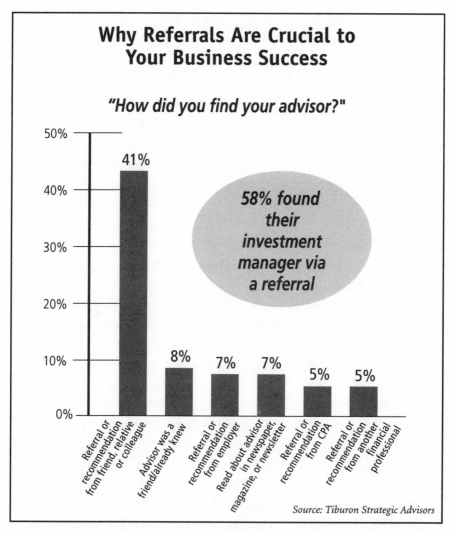

Why Referrals Are Crucial to Your Business Success

"How did you find your advisor?"

58% found their investment manager via a referral

- 41% — Referral or recommendation from friend, relative or colleague
- 8% — Advisor was a friend/already knew
- 7% — Referral or recommendation from employer
- 7% — Read about advisor in newspaper, magazine, or newsletter
- 5% — Referral or recommendation from CPA
- 5% — Referral or recommendation from another financial professional

Source: Tiburon Strategic Advisors

If you rated some common marketing communication channels for effectiveness, the results would look something like this (on a scale of one to 1,000):

Communication Channel	Marketing Effectiveness Score
1. Letter	1
2. Phone call	10
3. Face-to-face meeting	100
4. Introduction from an enthusiastic third party	1,000

Clearly, the last approach is one you need to master.

Harness Human Nature

Survey after survey indicates that referrals are the best way to build a super-profitable financial services business. That's how almost all wealthy prospects want to meet you. Look at your current client base. I'll bet most of your wealthiest, smartest, and most appreciative clients came to you through referrals. It's human nature.

Think about this: What if you weren't in the financial services industry, and you received a $2 million inheritance. Let's say you wanted to find someone to manage your money, but you didn't know anyone personally. Would you respond to an ad in the paper? Would you look in the yellow pages? Would you wait for someone to call you to offer a hot investment product? Probably not. These are the things an uninformed, unconnected, naive person would do.

If you're like most intelligent, well-educated, reasonably sophisticated people, you would ask your friends, business associates, and professional advisors something like this: "Do you know a competent, trustworthy financial advisor who can help me make the right decisions with my money?"

You would do this recognizing there could be substantial undesirable outcomes if you made bad financial decisions on your own. And you'd know there's always risk working with someone new. You would appreciate it if someone you trusted could recommend a financial advisor. It would solve a big problem for you.

When it comes to their money, Prudent Investors know they can't afford to make mistakes. And the reason advisor referrals work so well is that they overcome the natural fear of making such an important decision.

If you apply your Ideal Prospect Profile and the research and positioning strategies you learned in earlier chapters, you'll be a client-centered advisor. All you need is a systematic process for generating qualified referrals from influential clients and centers of influence.

You may never need to spend any more money or effort on marketing. Your enthusiastic clients, strategic alliances and centers of influence will become your marketing apostles.

Why Doesn't Everyone Market Through Referrals?

If referrals are so powerful, why don't all financial advisors build their businesses around them? There are three reasons.

First, most advisors aren't very referable. They aren't client-centered advisors with specialized knowledge and services for targeted niches.

Second, most advisors don't have a clear idea of how they add value or even who could benefit most from their services. If you don't know why people should refer you to their friends, don't be too surprised if your clients and professional colleagues don't know either!

Third, most advisors don't have an effective referral *process*. They just wing it. They say something inane, such as, "Who do you know who needs a financial advisor?" After the tenth client says, "Gee, I can't think of anyone," the advisor stops asking.

An advisor who attended one of my workshops explained her referral process to me. She told me that when she met with her clients, she "beat them up" until they gave her referrals. When I heard that, the first thing that went through my mind was, "Boy, I bet they really look forward to those quarterly meetings. They probably bring you the names of their newspaper carriers just to get you off their backs."

The goal is not to "beat up" your clients until they throw you a couple of names. The idea is to educate them about what you're looking for and to enlist them in the process of helping themselves by introducing you to their friends.

Many advisors do get some new clients using the "autopilot" referral method. In other words, if a client mentions the advisor to a friend and the friend is highly motivated and calls the advisor, then the advisor gets a new client. It's effortless. But many of these referred prospects become "C" or even "D" clients.

Most advisors accept the new high-maintenance, low-payoff clients because they don't have any better way to get new clients. They also accept these low payoff clients to keep from offending the referral source. As we discussed in Step 2, this can reduce your hourly income and your quality of life.

This bleak scenario won't happen to you because you've followed the strategies in the previous chapters. You're now client-centered and, therefore, highly referable. Your clients and centers of influence will be eager not only to refer but to actually introduce their friends and associates to you. But how and when do you generate referrals?

The 4 Best Times To Ask for Referrals

Once you decide you're going to generate referrals on purpose, you need to establish "trigger" times for which you'll have trained yourself to go into a referral generating mode. The process should become automatic and almost subconscious. It should be just a natural part of your normal client interactions. There are four great times for you to generate referrals:

1. during research interviews,
2. when you initially meet potential new clients,
3. when you start the business relationship (by opening the account or selling the policy), and
4. when you meet to review your client's financial situation and goals.

During Research Interviews

As you learned in Step 4, when interviewing clients or centers of influence, you should always show them a profile of the type of person who can benefit the most from your services. Make sure the person depicted in the profile is in the same niche as the person you're interviewing.

Several of the questions you ask during the interview will help you gather referrals. You'll ask such questions as, "What do you think of the profile?" Learn what improvements you should make. Should you make it more specific? Should you make it less specific? Should you target certain niches, communities, neighborhoods, or organizations? Ask the people you interview to focus on specific people they know who fit your Ideal Prospect Profile.

Tell them you're constantly looking for new ways to improve your business:

> *"I want to learn how I can add the greatest value for my*
> *ideal clients. I'd like to interview some of your colleagues*
> *who fit my profile to get their perceptions. Who do you*
> *know who could give me useful insights?"*

Tell them you're looking for people who are helpful, open-minded, friendly, and curious—people who are willing to talk and express their views. When they give you the names of people who fit your profile, explain that you won't try to sell anything. Make sure they understand that your agenda is strictly research-oriented.

In research interviews, you're often referred to people who fit your profile and need your help right now. I'll explain how to identify these prospects and what to do with them in Chapter 18.

When You Initially Meet Potential New Clients

Minnesota Fats was one of the world's greatest billiards players. He explained his success by saying that with every shot, he set himself up for the next shot. You should use this strategy to develop an effective referral process.

When you first meet a potential ideal client, explain how you help people. One of the best ways to do this is to show your Ideal Prospect Profile and say,

> *"I can't help everyone, but you are exactly the kind of*
> *person who can benefit most from my services."*

Your potential new clients will be excited when they realize that you offer specialized knowledge and services for people just like them:

> *"I don't think of the people I do business with as clients*
> *but rather as partners. We work together to help each*
> *other achieve our goals. If we decide to work together I'll*

make a commitment to you to use all my knowledge and resources to help you achieve your financial and personal goals. But I'd expect the same level of commitment from you. If I help you, would you be willing to help me achieve my personal and financial goals?"

Explain to new clients that you primarily build your business through referrals:

"The more successful my business is, the more resources I have to help my clients. Over the years, I've found there's nothing I can do to build my business that is nearly as powerful as an introduction from a happy client."

Ask,

"If I do an exceptional job of meeting and exceeding your expectations, would you have any reason not to introduce me to your friends and business associates who can also benefit from my services?"

This is sometimes called the "deal before the deal." It lets your prospects know the terms of how you'll work together. It also demonstrates that your interests and theirs are in sync. Once you have a commitment, you have set yourself up to receive excellent referrals and introductions later. When you first agree to work with new clients, make sure you set the expectation that you'll help each other in long-term, mutually beneficial relationships.

When You Start the Business Relationship

Bill Bachrach, the top sales trainer in our industry and the friend I mentioned at the beginning of this chapter, has developed an incredibly powerful and simple technique for getting new and existing clients to refer people to you. Here's my version of his powerful process.

After you have completed the delivery of a valuable service for your new client, start with the four most powerful words in the English language:

> *"I need your help. There are two primary ways I can spend my time. One is marketing and the other is working with my clients. I believe the best use of my time is helping my clients make wise decisions that will help them achieve their goals. But, like any businessperson, I must also market my business to keep it healthy and growing.*
>
> *"Ideally, I'd like to spend all my time helping my clients. How would you prefer I spend my time?"*

Of course, most of your clients will say they want you to spend your time helping your clients. Let them know you agree:

> *"If you can help me build my business, I can focus more of my time on serving you. I'll constantly be on the lookout to find better ways to help you achieve your goals. But I need you to constantly be on the lookout to help me identify people who could benefit from my services. Does that sound fair?"*

All reasonable people will think this is a fair arrangement. Remind them of "the deal before the deal" that they agreed to honor. Tell them you've found that the best way to find any professional service provider is through referrals. Explain that introductions are even better. Take out a written profile of your ideal prospect and tell them,

> *"This is a profile of the type of person who I have found can benefit the most from my services."*

Allow the new client to review the profile. Ask for feedback. Then tell the client what you want him or her to do:

> *"Your part of our partnership is to constantly be on the lookout for people like this. Who do you know who fits this profile?"*

If you're talking with a retired person, for example, be sure you show him or her a profile of a retired person, widow, or someone else he or she is likely to know. It won't do much good to show a retired engineer a profile of a doctor.

> *"When you run across people who fit this profile, I'd like you to introduce them to me, or give me their names so I can introduce myself to them. Is that all right with you?*
>
> *"I won't try to sell them anything. But I will contact them to see if there is any way I can help them."*

Notice that at this point you haven't asked for referrals. You have asked for introductions and the names of people who fit your profile. If they give you some names, great. If not, don't worry. This is just the beginning. You'll learn more advanced techniques for generating referrals later in this chapter.

Let your clients keep the written profile. Tell them you're always looking for ideas and strategies that will help them meet their goals. Reinforce your hope that they'll always be on the lookout for people like them who could benefit from your services.

Don't pressure your clients and make them feel uncomfortable. Simply remind them that it's beneficial to them, to you, and to their friends if they introduce you to other people who fit your profile.

Your ultimate goal is to *train* your clients to always be alert for ideal prospects they can introduce to you. This education process takes time. But it does work. Remember, people learn through repetition. If you repeat this process every time you meet, clients will begin to bring you names when they come in to see you.

Soon you'll have an army of happy clients trying to help you, so you can focus more of your time on helping them. By focusing most of your attention on meeting your existing clients' needs rather than chasing reluctant prospects, you create stronger relationships and much happier clients.

When Reviewing Your Clients' Financial Results

One of the great things about the fee-based asset management business is that it gives you the opportunity to meet personally with your clients a few times a year. Most clients think this is so you can service their accounts and review their investment performance. But another great reason is to ask for referrals. (Even if you aren't offering fee-based services, you should meet with your "A" and "B" clients at least once a year.)

Mike, an advisor who gathers over $1 million in new managed accounts per month, is a former pilot. Every time he meets with a client, he uses a checklist. He learned to do this when he was flying. As he addresses each item he checks it off the list. The last item on his checklist is to ask for referrals. He uses the "How would you prefer I spend my time?" dialog explained above.

Mike's clients soon learn he's going to ask for their help each time they meet. They expect him to say,

"Who do you know who fits this profile? Would you be willing to introduce me to them over lunch if I treat?"

After a few meetings, they come prepared with names and are eager to share them with Mike. That simple referral technique consistently generates leads that turn into over $12 million a year in new investment assets.

Some advisors think their clients won't want to refer them because they fear the quality of service may go down. That's true if they're the only person providing the service. But if they have a well-organized business that can absorb the growth, this won't be a problem.

If you sense this type of reluctance among your clients, you need to make sure your business model is client-centered. Then point out that the time you'll save in marketing will be more than enough to absorb some new accounts. The ultimate result will be a healthier business that can support more and better services—a win for both new and existing clients.

Be patient with this process. Remember, people learn through repetition. Don't expect them to remember who can benefit the most from your services the first time. But after three or four times they'll get the hang of it, and they'll feel excited about introducing you to their friends who can also benefit from your expert services.

Maximize Your Quantity and Quality

The most productive referral strategy is to generate as many quality leads as possible. Then get your referral source to personally introduce you to the high-potential prospects. Start by encouraging your referral sources to identify as many people as possible, as long as they reasonably fit your profile.

Ask for referrals at every opportunity, and you probably won't have much trouble getting them. You may not end up with 50 or 100 referrals every time you ask, but you should average at least five to ten reasonably qualified leads.

Help Your Source Focus

Sometimes your clients and research subjects want to help you, but they just can't think of anyone. In that case, you'll have to help them focus on people who fit your profile. Here's how to maximize the quantity and quality of your referrals.

When people start giving you names, write them down on a note pad. Say things like, "Who else?" "Go on," "Great!" and "Any more?" Don't try to qualify the referrals at this point. That comes later. When your clients run out of names or have difficulty coming up with names, focus them on specific communities of people.

Ask clients, "Do you belong to a church?" Then say, "Who do you know at church who comes closest to this profile?" Usually you'll get a couple of names. Then say, "What about your neighbors? Do any of your neighbors match this profile?"

Ask clients about their family members, co-workers, business contacts, hobbies, or sports activities. If they golf, ask about some of the people at the golf club or some of their golf partners. What you're doing is identifying specific groups of people your clients know. By narrowing their mental focus to small groups, they can more easily pick out specific people in those groups.

Take the stand that your referral sources are doing their friends a favor by introducing them to you. Remember, if you're truly a client-centered advisor, their friends will thank them for introducing you. It's a classic case of win-win-win.

Generate a Long List of Names

If your sources have trouble thinking of referrals, say, "A great way to jog your memory is to go through your address book." If they're happy with your services, they should be delighted to do that for you.

Once your referral source has given you all of the names he or she can think of, you'll probably have a positive problem. A number of the advisors I work with have been literally overwhelmed with qualified leads. One got 66 leads. Another got 88 leads. The highest number I've heard of is 300. Don't worry. You'll learn how to prioritize your referrals in Chapter 18.

Advanced Referral-Generating Techniques

When people know you have specialized knowledge and services, they're usually eager to refer others to you. This is especially true if you have clients who are friendly, open minded, and helpful. But occasionally you'll have a "hard case." The following story illustrates how you can use advanced referral techniques to generate referrals even from reluctant clients.

An advisor I know works with many Japanese Americans, although he isn't Japanese himself. When he conducted his initial research interviews, he saw proof of something he had known all along. Japanese Americans are reluctant to refer people. It's a cultural issue relating to privacy.

We brainstormed about how to get referrals from one of his best clients, a Japanese electronics executive. We decided the best approach was to take a list of names of other local electronics executives. We thought this client would probably know some of the people on the list. The advisor's goal was to gather background information, industry insights, and names of good people to interview or work with.

To learn more about referral reluctance we added an additional question to the research interview: "Can you tell me why Japanese Americans are so reluctant to give referrals, and what I can do about it?" Often when you ask someone to explain an objection, people talk themselves out of it. But in this case the executive told Carl it was a cultural thing, and he couldn't change it.

Carl said he understood and showed the executive his profile of the person who could benefit most from his services. They discussed the profile, and Carl produced the list of executives he had compiled earlier. Carl said, "I know you aren't comfortable referring me, but would you be willing to go over the list and give me your insights about people you know? I'm trying to prioritize them as 'A,' 'B,' or 'C' potential new users of my services."

The executive reviewed the list and identified "A," "B," and "C" prospects. He also gave Carl background information about the different individuals and their companies.

Then Carl said, "I know you aren't comfortable with me using your name, but normally if I was referred to someone, I would send them a copy of a letter like this. If they were interested in meeting, I would set up an appointment. If they didn't want to meet with me, I wouldn't bother them again."

He produced a copy of a referral letter customized for the electronics industry. The client read the letter, looked at the list, and looked back at the letter and said, "You can use my name on a letter like this."

Carl was surprised at first. He recovered quickly and went back to his list. He had his client help him customize letters to the "A" prospects. Almost magically this reluctant referrer became a great referrer. That day Carl learned how to harness human nature to master the referral process.

Later, Carl said he believed the executive changed his position because he felt comfortable Carl was going to try to help his associates—not harass them. His vague fear disappeared once Carl explained his follow-up process. The client began to see more benefits and fewer risks. When your clients understand your agenda, goals, and commitment to helping people, their reluctance disappears. They start actively looking for ways to help you achieve your business goals.

Chapter at a Glance

If you use these techniques effectively, within a year you should be able to identify ten key centers of influence and clients who could each refer one ideal client per quarter (four per year). That would be 40 new clients per year. If each new client had an average account size of $500,000 (or equivalent insurance sale), that would be $20 million per year from this very simple marketing tactic: referrals.

Consistently generating qualified, motivated, and wealthy clients is a key goal if you want your marketing to be truly effort-less. By mastering the art of referrals, you'll end up with a positive problem: You'll be buried in qualified leads. If you truly partner with your clients and help them achieve their goals, they'll reciprocate and help you achieve your goals.

You'll generate more high-quality referrals than you can possibly handle.

And this is just one source of qualified, motivated leads. Turn to the next chapter to learn about other ways to generate qualified leads effort-lessly.

Chapter 14 Action Steps

Exercise 1: Develop a script for asking for referrals in your own words. Take what you found in this chapter and adapt it so it will sound natural coming from you. You may want to make a few different versions—with minor adjustments—depending on the type of person you're addressing, such as new prospects, new clients, existing clients, and research subjects.

Exercise 2: Now try it! Ask the next person you meet with for referrals. After your discussion, evaluate how successful you were and how well the process worked. Make modifications to your script based on your experience.

Mix Business With Pleasure for Fun and Profit

To affect the quality of the day;
that is the art of life.

—Thoreau, 19th-century American advocate of
individual rights and author, *Walden* and "Civil Disobedience"

Imagine having so many well-connected clients in your target niches that when a big change is about to occur, you're one of the first to hear about it. My friend, Hal, enjoys this privilege because he's invested the time to understand his niches' issues and to get to know the key centers of influence on a personal level.

He is a master at working the grapevine and piecing together information. When a retirement wave is about to hit, someone always lets him know. He instantly taps into his intelligence network, calling influential individuals to find out the terms and likely prospects for each wave of downsizing. Because he's done such a good job for his clients, they're happy to give Hal information and to recommend that their friends work with him.

Other advisors are banging on the doors trying to get into this niche, the lucrative oil industry, but Hal is firmly entrenched. He dominates his niche because of his specialized knowledge and strong relationships. He's planted deep roots in fertile soil. Now he's cultivating his garden and effort-lessly enjoying an abundant harvest.

Adopt Rich Niches With People You Like

You've already done the legwork to make sure that the niches you target will be those you enjoy. This implies that you'll like the people in these niches—either you have common interests or you feel connected with them for some other reason—so that you'll naturally have a good time with them and they'll naturally have a good time with you.

Of course, people have a tendency to like people who are similar to them. Shared interests often build solid foundations for new friendships. I have seen advisors build great businesses on their interests and passions: golf, boating, wine appreciation, gardening, sports, hot cars, and horses.

When I first heard about Dick, he had broken into one of the richest niches in America: a high-end country club in Palm Springs, California— the city with more millionaires per capita than any other in North America.

Dick was a stockbroker who had just moved to the area. He decided he needed to meet wealthy people if he wanted to build a profitable investment business. So he joined one of the finest golf clubs in town and he befriended the starters, buying them simple gifts at Christmas and tipping them well during the year. He told them: "Don't start me with the good golfers, start me with the *wealthy* golfers."

Every day at 1 P.M., he'd leave work to play golf. Each day, Dick spent four to five hours with three new people, the vast majority of whom were multimillionaires. Most of them were retired business owners who had cashed out. They all had investment portfolios.

When his golfing partners asked him what he did, Dick told them he was a stockbroker. He said he used a hedge strategy that reduced risk in the market. He admitted that the strategy didn't beat the market. But he said that wasn't his goal. Dick told them, "Most of my clients already have a lot of money. They just don't want to lose any."

He went on to say, "My clients would much rather focus on improving their golf games than worry about their investment portfolios. I help them simplify their investment decisions so they can spend more time playing golf."

As I explained earlier, this line captivates any serious golfer. Dick found the ones with plenty of time and money sat up and paid attention. They'd usually ask him for more information.

He'd use the "curiosity hook" to gauge their interest: "I don't like to talk about work while I'm playing golf. But, if you're interested in finding out how I might be able to help you, give me your card. I'll have my assistant contact you to set up a convenient time for us to meet."

This simple niche-adoption and lead-generation strategy helped Dick generate over $500,000 in commissions in his first year in Palm Springs. By the end of his fourth year in business, Dick was generating close to $4 million in annual gross dealer concessions. He became the firm's fastest rising star by playing golf every day.

The funniest part of this story is that the other advisors in his office wished they could play golf as much as Dick did, but they said they were too busy trying to build their businesses.

Dick found the perfect way to combine his personal interest with his business interest. He was able to adopt and penetrate a rich niche and become very successful in the process. He had fun and made good money with very little effort. The other advisors had the wrong strategy. And working extremely hard following the wrong strategy is never going to be as effective as having the right strategy and cruising along effort-lessly.

Build "Share of Mind" in Your Target Niches

Each of these success stories of advisors who have adopted a rich niche is about creating what marketers call "share of mind." As compared to a share of market, you capture a share of each person's awareness in a particular segment or niche. This means that you have penetrated your target niche so thoroughly that your name and reputation has left an indelible impression on a great number of people. As a result, whenever there's a need in the niche, you are the first one to be called.

You can deliberately create share of mind by increasing your presence and popularity in a niche. You can go to the places your ideal clients frequent (such as the golf course); you can host parties they are likely to attend (you'll read more about this in the pages to come); you can even start a business just like theirs.

The advisor you read about in Chapter 5, a Texan who took my enthusiasm for the franchise niche to heart, eventually bought two specialty auto repair franchises. When he goes to the company conventions, he's the only financial advisor in a sea of successful franchise owners.

To purchase one of these franchises you must have at least $750,000 in net worth and prove that you have the skills to run a business. This means that everyone in this niche is pre-qualified by the parent company. That's just the minimum net worth. At the conventions, there are two groups: younger owners who are focused on growing their business and older, wealthier owners who are thinking about cashing out.

Because he is a franchise owner himself, he has a lot in common with the other owners. This advisor owns this niche. He is now conducting research interviews and building strategic alliances with some of the most influential owners and corporate executives.

His goal is to systematically help the wealthy, older franchise owners transition out of the business. He'll help them reduce taxes on the sale, set up an estate plan, and manage their portfolios for the rest of their lives and for the next generation.

Oh, there's one last thing. He's found the franchise business to be very profitable. He's earning over $100,000 net income from his new stores. And since he hired professional managers, it takes almost none of his time. That's pretty effort-less.

Throw Parties for Clients and Their Friends

To thoroughly adopt and penetrate a market niche, you need to stay on the minds of your top 20 to 100 clients and centers of influence. And you need to come up with a system for consistently getting introduced to their friends and associates. You can use phone calls and letters to stay in touch, but you also should host events that don't incorporate any financial information at all.

Remember that Prudent Investors don't have a very strong interest in financial products. That's why they have you. They'll be more likely to show up and bring a friend to a social event than an educational one. So associate yourself with the payoffs that your clients want—not the products.

A proven technique for increasing your share of mind, having clients associate you with benefits instead of products, and creating and opportunity to meet more people in your target niche is to host a party. In honoring clients and encouraging them to bring their friends to an enjoyable social gathering, you're not asking your clients to provide you with a list of referrals. Instead, you're generously including their friends in whatever celebration or event you're planning. Again, what you're doing is adopting a niche, just as Hal did with the oil industry or the Texas advisor did with franchise owners—you're just doing it with a little champagne and caviar.

Since birds of a feather flock together, many of your clients' friends will be at the same economic level as your clients. They'll have money to invest, too. You're building relationships and adding value with people in a rich niche before you ever discuss business with them. And you're able to do this because you and the prospects have a common friend—your client.

What will make your clients want to invite their friends to your events? There's the obvious benefit of getting to enjoy an activity with people they care about. Go out of your way to exceed your clients' expectations and focus on creating emotional payoffs and good feelings. If you help your clients achieve their goals, they'll want to reciprocate by helping you achieve yours.

When they ask how they can help you, tell them,

"Constantly be on the lookout for people just like you who could benefit from my services. Just introduce me to these people when you run across them. And be sure to bring them along with you to next month's fourth-of-July picnic."

Use the referral processes described in Chapter 14 to educate your clients about the benefits of introducing you to their friends and associates. Then invite your clients to bring friends to any and all of your special events. If they frequently bring new people to your functions and are always looking for people who can benefit from your services, they will build your business for you.

Help Retirees Celebrate Their Achievements

Companies with attractive retirement plans and a solid base of long-time employees over 55 years old comprise a lucrative niche for investment advisors. This is rollover heaven. But most companies today won't let advisors present workshops or prospect actively on their premises. How do you penetrate lucrative rollover niches when the front door is closed? You invite qualified people to participate in one of your fun events!

When people retire from a company they have worked at for many years, often they're depressed. They're leaving behind their income, their identity, and many close friends. They may be feeling a sense of grief because of these losses. You can put a happy spin on the retirement situation by turning it into a time of celebration. Offer to host a retirement party for your recently retired ideal clients and the people close to them.

Throw a Small Retirement Party

Let's say your client, Bob, is retiring from a long career in the aerospace industry. Invite the retiree and ten to 20 of his best friends to an intimate gathering to celebrate 25 years at XYZ Company. Most of the retiree's friends will have large rollovers, too.

Have your client help you plan a fun party to celebrate his newfound freedom. Consider hosting the party close to work on a Friday afternoon. Make it easy for Bob's friends to attend.

Send out invitations on your letterhead to a short mailing list supplied by your client. Have your assistant or marketing person confirm attendance with phone calls. Make sure everyone knows you're sponsoring the event and that you'll be the master of ceremonies.

Try to make it exciting and memorable. Have your assistant or marketing person help you decorate the room. Work with your client to come up with a theme to add meaning and substance.

At the party serve wine, beer, and non-alcoholic drinks. Avoid hard liquor. Work within a reasonable budget of no more than $50 per person.

Just make sure your guests really enjoy themselves. When people are laughing and having fun, they naturally like the person who's making it all possible—you. You'll become the captain of your own rich niche!

Schmooze the Guests

Be a good host, honor your client, and get to know your guests. Provide name tags for everyone to help facilitate conversation. Make sure you mingle. Create a reason to speak, at least briefly, with every guest. Work on building rapport and having fun. Don't talk about financial services at all.

If people ask you what you do, tell them,

> *"I make sure people like Bob don't have to worry about their financial security when they retire."*

See how they respond. Then turn the conversation around to them. Get them talking about themselves, their work, and their plans for retirement. Ask them, "When do you plan to retire?" Then ask, "What are your plans for the future?" Get them talking about their retirement plans.

If they are curious about your services, say to them,

"I'd love to show you what I do, but right now is not the best time." Ask them, "Are you really interested in how I help people make smart choices about their money so they can maintain their retirement lifestyle?"

If they say, "Yes," then say,

"If you give me your phone number, I'll have my assistant call you to set up a convenient time for us to get together."

Then get their numbers so your marketing person can follow up to qualify and meet with them.

Generate Qualified Leads

At the end of the party, thank everyone for coming and have everyone toast the guest of honor. Then announce that the party is coming to a close and say, "Before you go, I need your help." Hand out retirement party evaluation forms. Use the same form as you created in Chapter 12, changing the headline to read, "Bob Smith's Retirement Party." Customize the form to gather information on the location, time, entertainment, etc. Use this information to make your parties better in the future.

Ask everyone to complete one. Include at least one important question on the evaluation form: "Would you like to meet with [*your name*] to plan your retirement and your retirement party?"

Any of your guests who are thinking about retiring will want to talk with you. Those who already have financial advisors will be impressed with you and your party. If they like you, they may want you to provide them with a second opinion"on their investment or financial strategies.

Usually, your guests of honor will look for ways to encourage their friends to get to know you better. They may suggest that their friends take you for a "test drive," or free initial interview. Be open to giving second opinions and offering "get acquainted" services to make it easy to start relationships with these people.

Build value-added relationships in your niches and people will look for ways to do business with you. It works the same way with other niches as it does with retirees. You can always ask individuals you'd like to get to know better if you can do a research interview with them.

Widows Just Want to Have Fun

Many advisors enjoy working with wealthy widows although it's a difficult niche to penetrate because it's usually hidden and fragmented. As people age, they tend to go out less and less often. As they get older and their hearing and eyesight decline, widows and widowers often become isolated and lonely.

But as my mom, a 76-year-old widow says, "Girls just want to have fun!" More than anything else, isolated widows long for companionship. If you help fill that emotional void, you can add huge value for this group, while dramatically increasing your share of mind. A great way to meet wealthy widows' need for companionship is to throw birthday parties or other special events for them and, of course, their friends.

Find out what would make a fun outing for your widowed clients. Have them invite up to seven of their close friends (who are also likely to be wealthy widows). Keep the number small so you can get to know everyone. You'll probably need to arrange transportation for this group.

An advisor I know recently took a widow and five of her friends to a birthday lunch. He loves to work with widows, and he hit it off with them right from the start. He now has five of the six wealthy widows as new clients. And they're planning more events as you read this.

More Ideas for Fun Events

A financial professional in the midwestern U.S. decided to stop mass marketing for new clients and instead focus his marketing budget on his existing clients. He decided his clients could be his secret marketing weapon if he treated them right and enlisted them in the process of helping him.

The result: He has become one of the most successful financial professionals in America. He interviewed his best clients and found out they liked dancing, gardening, cruising, and golf. Follow his lead and host events such as the following five:

1. Valentine's Day dance: Host a Saint Valentine's Day dance for your clients, prospects, and their friends. Hire a live band to play their favorite music. Decorate the room with flowers and nostalgic items to celebrate a simpler time. Associate yourself with love, romance, and the good old days.

2. Gardening clinics: Host a spring gardening clinic right after tax season. Find someone like a county extension officer from the local university to make a presentation for a small fee. Invite your clients, prospects, and centers of influence.

3. Golf clinics: Host an annual golf clinic and tournament. Sponsor a fairly well known—but not too expensive—golf pro to provide instructions the day before the tournament. Set up a hospitality tent. Play the role of master of ceremonies. Be sure to meet everyone.

4. Open houses: Host an open house during the holiday season. Offer hot spiced cider and holiday treats. Block out the whole day for the event and encourage attendees to spend it catching up with old friends and meeting new ones. Treat your clients like extended family members.

5. Cruise ships: Try an annual cruise. Sponsor the cruise and market it, but have your clients pay their own way. There are plenty of opportunities on a week-long cruise to bond with many new people. This is *effort-less*, client-centered marketing at its best.

Your goal in creating fun things to do with clients is to meet as many people as possible who have a high probability of needing your financial advice—now or in the not too distant future. Then look for ways to build relationships, rapport, and trust before the subject of business comes up. Ideally, they'll let you know they're interested. You won't have to chase them.

When you set up social events celebrating one or more of your clients, they will become your marketing apostles and your most effective salespeople. They will do a more effective job than you can.

Bottom Line: Get Out of the Office and Have Some Fun

When I was a wholesaler, I became good friends with Don, one of my top producers. We did seminars together, and we went on many joint sales calls to see clients and prospects. At one point, I realized he wasn't all that organized or even particularly persuasive. Even so, he was one of the top producers in his firm nationwide. I asked him, "Don, to what do you attribute your success as a financial advisor?"

I was intrigued by his answer. Don said, "Steve, the main reason I'm such a big producer is I'm *out of the office a lot.*" He continued, "In fact, the second biggest producer is out of the office more than anyone except me." Don knew his competitor would actually do more business if he'd simply get out of his office even more.

Don believed the secret to success was to spend as much time as possible out among prospects. And he knew there weren't any prospects in his office.

He worked a bit with individual investors, but his primary niche was much more profitable. Don decided many years ago to target small cities in Arizona. He knew that even a small city usually had a substantial treasury and had a definite need for professional investment advice.

He developed a list of all the small cities in his state. He found out when their city council meetings were held. Then he drove all over the state attending these meetings. Within a year he was friends with many of the key centers of influence in each community. They were the people running the cities and their treasuries.

Eventually, Don had a large percentage of his state's small cities as clients. Each city typically had multiple investment entities. So each one was extremely lucrative for Don.

He told me other brokers made cold calls to the city treasurers from the big cities. "But," he said, "they'll never do business with these cold callers. We've been friends for years. I take them to lunch. We talk on the phone. Our wives and kids are friends. I even know the names of their dogs. There's just no way anyone can compete against the trust and relationships I have built with these people."

Chapter at a Glance

You want to create a fun business and achieve the highest payoff for your effort. Earlier you selected two to three target niches you felt passionate about serving. Now it's time to adopt and start serving those niches.

You learned in the previous three chapters about several strategies for generating leads. This chapter offered a fourth strategy: combining your own interests with those of your prospects. This synergy helps you to market naturally and to have fun building your business.

Service the people in the niche even before they become clients. Start the relationship with some common interest or activity. They'll think of you when they need you.

To heighten your profile and presence (share of mind) in your target niche, show up where your best clients hang out or congregate. Or create your own events and attract people to them. Develop a reputation of what you stand for and like to do. Associate yourself with the payoffs your ideal clients want from their money. Play golf and plan parties to celebrate meaningful events in your client's lives.

All of these activities will lead you to your clients' friends and other new prospects. You'll become a valuable resource for them and, ultimately, they'll become your ideal new clients. You'll attract a community of people with common personalities, wants, needs, concerns and desired payoffs. You'll have created your own rich niche.

Chapter 15 Action Steps

Exercise 1: Identify one social activity that would be appropriate for you to plan for each of your target niches.

Exercise 2: Give it a try! Planning the first event of its kind will take a little longer than subsequent events. Put together a budget and outline the details. Then work with your assistant or marketing coordinator to pull it all together.

Identify Potential Strategic Alliances

Men can do jointly what they cannot do singly;
and the union of minds and hands,
the concentration of their power,
becomes almost omnipotent.

—Daniel Webster, 19th-Century American orator and political leader

You "met" Dan, an advisor with $100 million under management, in Chapter 3. You may remember that he provides fee-based asset management through a third-party money manager. He gathers the assets and handles the client relationships. The investment management company handles the money.

Dan gathered his tidy pool of assets in only five years. He works out of an executive suite, so he has no employees. During those five years he also started a family and earned his master's degree from a major university. How did he do it?

More than half of his $100 million under management came from a strategic alliance with a high-level estate planning insurance professional. This and other strategic alliances provide him a high quality of life by giving him the free time to do other things. Is he just "lucky" to know the "right" people? He may be fortunate, but he's also smart. And he's not alone.

A financial planner in central California landed a $4 million account after her first meeting with a new strategic alliance partner. It was the biggest account she had ever opened.

An investment advisor in the northeastern U.S. developed a strategic alliance with a local accounting firm. Over six years, he captured $175 million in managed accounts. The first $100 million came from the accounting firm's clients, and $75 million came from referrals to their friends and associates.

An estate-planning professional in Georgia established strategic alliances with two local accounting firms. He's now conducting estate-planning workshops for the accountants' wealthiest clients.

Bring All of Your New Skills Into Play

I've witnessed many effort-less success stories unfold when financial advisors established mutually beneficial relationships with other organizations and professionals. But building a profitable alliance requires careful planning and advanced marketing skills. You'll need to bring everything you have learned up to this point into play. By reading through the material and completing the exercises in the previous chapters, you've positioned yourself as a client-centered advisor. You've earned the right to take your business to this higher level.

This book is focused on the ultimate objective of making you extremely attractive to key centers of influence and their wealthiest clients. You can't *sell* these sophisticated professionals on working with you. You have to be the kind of advisor they want to work with. Once you've developed an inspiring vision of success, targeted profitable niches, researched to understand your prospects and to identify specific opportunities, and positioned yourself as a trustworthy problem solver, you'll be attractive to accountants and other centers of influence.

While you should continue developing leads from other sources—such as speaking, PR campaigns, and referrals—the best use of your marketing time is developing strategic alliances. Alliances are a terrific way to tap into rich niches of successful business owners, key executives, professionals, retirees, divorcees, and widows. When you create strategic alliances with centers of influence, their client bases become your rich niches.

Use My 4-Step Process

Over the past six years, I have developed an extremely effective process for developing mutually beneficial relationships with accountants, attorneys, investment bankers, and other centers of influence. Advisors who master this niche-marketing tactic often report the first new clients they get from alliances are the wealthiest clients they have ever had.

My approach involves four key meetings between you and your prospective strategic alliance partner. We'll cover the first two meetings in this chapter as we focus on finding opportunities. Chapter 16 will walk you through the next two meetings. It'll explain how to win over an alliance partner and how to work together not only to solve clients' problems, but your partner's problems, as well.

The strategy is much like the financial planning process. First, you gather soft and hard data so you can analyze it and make some decisions. Then you clarify potential partners' goals, obstacles, and concerns. And finally, when you know exactly what they want to accomplish and what they're willing to do, you make specific recommendations that will help them achieve their goals. If

Create a Profitable Strategic Alliance in 4 Meetings

1. Identify qualified potential partners.

2. Identify specific opportunities.

3. Prioritize your partner's interests.

4. Present your recommendations.

you've listened carefully and your recommendations make sense to them, they will be eager to work with you.

Using this process, advisors throughout North America and Australia are creating strategic alliances with accountants, association executives, attorneys, consultants, casualty agents, life insurance specialists, investment bankers, and money managers. My technique works *everywhere* because it identifies and harnesses hidden demand for your services. It's a systematic process for identifying how you can add the most value for your partners, their clients, and yourself.

It also works because it's based on the marketing concept of identifying the right people to work with. You shouldn't spend any time trying to sell to people who won't recognize or benefit from the value of your services. Your goal is to identify potential partners and attract them. You shouldn't be chasing them.

Don't Take the Shortcut

Many financial advisors want to get to the sale as quickly as possible. That attitude may prevent you from ever developing a mutually beneficial strategic alliance. If you use the process described here, you'll have the highest probability of creating profitable long-term relationships Business will come effort-lessly—once a trusting relationship is firmly established.

Don't try to shorten this four-meeting process by having fewer interactions. Over time I've purposely added steps to create more opportunities for building relationships through understanding, trust, and rapport. As you've learned in this book, the shortest road to phenomenal results is not usually a one-step tactic.

I will illustrate the process using accountants as our example, because they're the gatekeepers of society's wealth. Once you understand the process, you can apply it to any other center of influence you want to work with.

What's in It for Them?

Many accountants are obtaining licenses to sell securities and offer financial advice. But because they generally have a high need for certainty, most accountants will never want to personally offer investment or insurance products. Instead, many will create strategic alliances or joint ventures with client-centered financial advisors—like you.

Several investment and insurance companies are now offering fee-splitting arrangements with accounting firms. But ethical accountants won't recommend you to clients, no matter how much they profit, unless they trust you. That's why this process is based on trust and relationship-building conversations, not product-selling or revenue-sharing conversations. Those can come later.

Furthermore, a strategic alliance partnership isn't simply about exchanging people's names. Sharing referrals isn't an effective system because participants keep score. In other words, if you give your partners more referrals than they give you, you'll be upset with them. And vice versa.

The question to ask is not, "Are we even?" but, "Am I achieving more of my goals by working with this person than I could without the alliance?" Think of it this way: Strategic alliances are about creating a bigger pie. They aren't about how many slices each person gets. Both parties work together for mutual benefit. And, ultimately, the biggest beneficiaries are the clients. That's what makes this process powerful.

If you use the tactics outlined here and in Chapter 17, you may never have to split fees and commissions or share revenue. You'll discover new and unusual ways to add value for your partners instead. Ultimately, if you do decide to share revenue, you'll be able to dictate the terms and work only with the most ideal partners.

Position Yourself as an Expert

It's critical to build a solid position and expertise in your chosen niches before you approach accountants. It's common for them to receive five to ten phone calls every day from other financial professionals looking for referrals. But accountants see a tremendous amount of risk in giving generic product pushers access to their client bases. What if the product pushers turned out to be incompetent, unethical, or just too aggressive? They see their role as protecting their clients from salespeople.

Well-connected professionals, particularly accountants and attorneys, don't want to work with generic financial advisors. But if you've established yourself as an expert in your niche—with specialized knowledge, services, and alliances that can help a specific group of wealthy clients solve their problems—potential strategic alliance partners will be enthusiastic about working with you.

Your expertise reduces their risk and significantly increases the benefits they can offer their clients. They'll be eager to work with you to provide their clients with total solutions to their financial problems.

Greg, a financial planner I know, created a strategic alliance with my banker. He did a financial plan for her, and then she introduced him to her top clients. She had an investment broker in her bank lobby, so I asked her why she was working with Greg instead of referring clients to her bank's broker. She replied, "Oh, he's a product pusher. But Greg's a top-notch financial advisor." Greg was positioned as a client-centered expert. And because of that, he secured their partnership.

The Difference Between an Alliance and a Joint Venture

Scott, an advisor in southern California, created a strategic alliance that has evolved into a joint venture. The key change is that he and his partners set up a new company and will share the profits. The investment banking firm specializes in helping owners of pharmacies, funeral homes, home medical care companies, and convalescent homes sell their businesses. Together, Scott and the investment banking firm are developing a new company to provide money management services to the investment banker's clients after they sell their businesses.

The alliance partners already have $10 million of their clients' sales proceeds earmarked for money management to start the new business.

And they typically sell $3 or $4 million worth of business every month. So there's a huge flow of money in motion that will soon find it's way into the new company.

It's important you understand the difference between these two business models. In a classic *strategic alliance*, no money changes hands. Instead, both parties benefit in other ways. A *joint venture*, however, involves the two parties setting up a shared company and splitting the revenue.

A Word About Revenue Sharing in Joint Ventures

If your relationship progresses and the accountant eventually asks you about revenue sharing, be open to the possibility. But make sure any agreement fairly compensates each party based on effort and expertise.

A good idea is to set up a separate business. Share the net income after paying all expenses and a reasonable salary to anyone who works in the business. A 50/50 profit split is a reasonable place to start negotiations. Don't give away a huge part of your gross commissions and fees just because the accountant has the clients. Remember, you have the expertise that makes this strategic alliance possible.

Meeting 1: Identify Qualified Potential Partners

I have found it typically takes up to a year to develop a highly profitable relationship with strategic alliance partners, so start by being very selective as you choose your partners. You want to be sure you're investing your time with the right people.

As you assess potential partners, keep in mind the distinction between *centers of influence* and *strategic alliance partners.* Centers of influence have influence over ideal prospects. Strategic alliance partners are centers of influence who have many of your ideal prospects as their clients. So as you begin to search for alliance partners, start by considering centers of influence in your niche.

Focus on Partners
Who Add Value

There are many different strategic alliance partners you can work with, but accountants often turn out to control the most profitable prospects. Each accountant typically has 100 to 200 clients. And their clients are in rich niches: They're business owners, key corporate executives, professionals, wealthy retirees, widows, and divorced women. And remember, when you establish a strategic alliance, your partner's client base becomes one of your rich niches.

The good news is that there are more than 400,000 accountants in the United States today. But most of them won't make good partners. You're looking for *exceptional* accountants. I define these as entrepreneurial, market driven, client-centered, value-adding accountants. You want partners who are open-minded and fun to work with.

There are three different levels of accounting services: 1) bookkeeping (sometimes called "compilation"), 2) auditing and tax or regulatory compliance, and 3) at the top end, consulting services. You want to avoid the bookkeepers. Also avoid the people doing auditing and compliance. They're providing traditional accounting services and aren't really adding value above the core product.

But those who do consulting—business development consulting, computer consulting, fee-based estate and financial planning, and consulting in other areas—are adding value. These accountants are actively looking for better ways to help their clients achieve their goals. They tend to be more open to strategic alliances.

Typically you'll find ideal accounting firms have three to ten professionals and one to three support people for each professional. Local firms are usually easier to approach and develop relationships with than large regional or national firms.

Target the Rainmakers

Often the firm's partners have assigned one individual to be in charge of business development. Many times it's one of the younger, most entrepreneurial associates. These people are often called the "rainmakers" in their organizations. They're receptive to new ideas—both by virtue of their personalities and because their partners expect them to generate new clients. These are the individuals you want to identify and build relationships with.

Your ideal accountant prospects will be the chief rainmakers in their firms. They're roughly 40 years old and work with highly successful clients. Accountants who offer consulting services—even financial planning or estate planning—are ideal candidates for strategic alliances.

You can identify these accountants through your clients, by reading local business publications, and through referrals from attorneys, bankers and other accountants. Start by identifying any accountants you know. They may not be top priority candidates. That's fine; it's a good idea to practice this tactic on low-risk prospects. Then you can work your way up to your ultimate targets: the best and the brightest in the marketplace.

Pre-Screen the Candidates

Once you've identified a likely prospect or firm, call the office. Ask the receptionist who's responsible for business development. Say the following:

> *"I'm trying to identify a high quality accounting firm that I can develop a strategic alliance with. Would you please send me a company information package?"*

You can have your marketing person gather this initial information. When you've received materials from ten to 15 accounting firms, review it all. Look for signs indicating which firms are marketing-oriented and entrepreneurial. Try to identify five companies that communicate an intent to add value beyond traditional accounting services.

When I asked one compliance-oriented accountant about his ideal client, he put his thumb and forefinger about one inch apart and said, "a tax return this thick." That was not the answer I was looking for, so I said, "Thanks, but no thanks." That's the best thing to do with a tax preparer, or an auditor, for that matter. They usually don't have a high caliber client base and aren't open to new ways to add value.

Use your meetings with potential partners to screen out the firms that aren't appropriate. The interview questions provided in this chapter will help you find accountants you'd enjoy working with and who have the types of clients who match your Ideal Client Profile. They should be open to working with other financial professionals. You should feel comfortable referring your best clients to them because you may need to do this in the future.

Call to Set Up the First Meeting

Referrals are always the best way to meet any professional, so try to get a strong introduction to the accountant. Once you've identified a couple of qualified candidates, it's time to set up the first meeting.

When you call, say the following:

> *"Joe Smith referred me. I'm doing some research to identify one or two accounting firms I can create strategic alliances with. My goal is to develop additional business for both our firms. I don't know if it makes sense to develop a strategic alliance with you or not, but since I've heard such good things about your firm, I'm willing to invest some time to explore the possible benefits— if you are."*

If you're talking to the right person, he or she will be interested because the entire accounting industry currently has a strong need to develop additional revenue sources. Bright accountants are looking at strategic alliances as one of the primary ways they can grow. If an accountant isn't interested in meeting you, obviously you called the wrong person. Simply go to the next one on your list.

If anyone seems interested yet resistant, find out what the concerns are. Address them. For example, you can say,

"I'm not talking about referrals because, frankly, they don't work that well. What I am talking about is working together to better help our clients achieve their goals and also to develop additional business for both of our firms."

If someone asks about sharing in your commissions or fees, say you're open to that possibility, but you would want to know more about the accountant and the firm before you would seriously consider such an arrangement.

When you find accountants who are interested, schedule meetings and ask them to bring information about themselves and their businesses so you can determine how you might be able to work together. It's likely you already have this information from your screening process, but requesting it sets the tone of the first meeting. It puts your prospective partners in the position of trying to sell you on why you should work with them, rather than the other way around. If you do it correctly, you've reversed the selling process.

Send a letter confirming the time and place of each meeting. Recap the key points in the scripts above.

Because of the tremendous explosion of tax preparation and accounting software, entrepreneurial accountants worth their salt are always looking for new ways to expand their businesses. By discussing a strategic alliance instead of referrals, you're positioning yourself as someone they should be interested in working with. The right accountant will be eagerly awaiting your first meeting.

Meet to Determine Compatibility

Normally, financial professionals take accountants to nice restaurants for lunch and tell them how smart, honest, trustworthy, and technically competent they are. Then they give them three business cards and say, "If you know of anybody who needs financial advice, please have them call me." Then the accountant usually goes back to the office and drops the cards in the round file—along with all the other cards from smart, honest, and technically competent financial professionals.

You want to reverse the process so you're in charge.

To prepare for your first meeting, create a series of questions that will help you get a better understanding of the accountant's company and the types of clients he or she serves. Print out two sets of these questions on your letterhead under the title "Business Profile." Refer to the questions in "Business Profile Questions to Determine Compatibility" on the next page for examples.

When you meet, say,

> *"The purpose of this first meeting is to get to know each other and to learn more about each other's firms. We should be able to discover together if it makes sense to consider developing a strategic alliance. My goal is to enable both our firms to more effectively achieve their goals."*

During your interview, use the business profile questions to guide your conversation. Give one copy to the accountant. He or she will be impressed that you're so prepared. Use the questions just as you would in a research interview. Here are some tips to make these information gathering meetings as productive as possible.

- Learn as much as you can about the accountant's firm and his or her key issues and perceptions.

- Listen specifically for indications of rich niches, money in motion, and pools of capital.

- Use the questions only as a guide. Remember, your goal isn't just to get through these questions, but to use them to identify opportunities and build relationships.

- Take notes on a legal pad, then asterisk those points you'd like to explore in more detail.

- Once the accountant has run out of steam on a specific question, ask additional questions to probe more deeply.

Business Profile Questions to Determine Compatibility

As you sit down for your first meeting with a potential strategic alliance partner, your goal is to gauge compatibility. Here are some business profile questions to get you started. Bring your list to the meeting on letterhead.

1. "Tell me about your business."
2. "How many professionals do you have in your firm?"
3. "How many support people do you have?"
4. "What types of niches or services are your specialty?"
5. "Approximately how many of each type of client do you have?"
6. "Describe a typical client in each niche."
7. "How would you describe your ideal client?"
8. "How many ideal clients do you have in each niche?"
9. "How do you define your role for your clients?"
10. "What goals do you have for the future of your business? Where do you see your business going in the next couple of years?"
11. "What experience have you had working with other financial professionals?"
12. "What are your thoughts about offering financial planning, investments, money management, or estate planning services to your clients?"
13. "What are some of the biggest challenges you face in your practice today? What challenges do you see in the future?"
14. "Tell me about your biggest marketing successes."
15. "What's important about success to you?"
16. "Why should a potential client do business with you instead of any other accounting firm? In other words, what makes you different from and better than other accounting firms?"
17. "If we were able to generate additional business for both of our firms, would you be able to handle the additional workload?"

Normally, this initial interview process takes about 90 minutes. I suggest you conduct it in the accountant's office. It'll give you a chance to check out the environment and get a feel for his or her business personality.

If the accountant asks you about your business, respond briefly and stay focused on the accountant. Give him or her your marketing package that you developed in Chapter 11. Your goal at this point is to listen to qualify your potential partner and determine compatibility, not to sell yourself. Let the other person do 80 to 90 percent of the talking.

Make a Decision

When you have completed the interview, you must make some decisions. Do you like this person? Does the accountant have the kinds of clients who can benefit from your services? Could the accountant add value for your current client base? Would the accountant make a good business partner? Is he or she open to creating a strategic alliance?

If not, thank him or her for the meeting. Remember, you're in charge, not the accountant. Say the following:

"I don't see any way I can add much value to you or your clients at this time. It doesn't seem like a good match. Let's leave the door open for future opportunities, but for now I want to try to find a more natural fit."

But if you are satisfied that the person has passed your initial screen, check to see if it's mutual:

"Based on what I've heard so far I think we could work together. What do you think?"

During this first meeting, you're looking for the accountant to give you positive feedback as a sign of interest in a strategic alliance with you. A financial professional in Texas was somewhat surprised to hear an accountant say: "You know Jim, we've got most of the pieces in place. But you just might be the missing link in our entire organization." In other words, the firm was already looking for someone like Jim. Nothing could be so effort-less as satisfying an existing demand for your products and services.

If your potential partner expresses interest in you, too, offer to meet again, this time in your office. That way the accountant can meet your staff and see your environment. I'm assuming you're proud of your office, and it will make a good first impression. Tell the accountant the next step is for him or her to learn more about you and to identify specific areas you may be able to help each other with. Schedule a time to meet in a week or ten days. Don't come across as too eager.

Meeting 2: Identify Specific Opportunities

To prepare for the second meeting, print the points listed in "Accounting Industry Issues" on the next page on two pieces of your letterhead—one for you and one for the accountant.

When the accountant arrives, show him or her around your office and introduce your associates. Then sit down to discuss the five key industry issues. Say something like the following:

> *"Our marketing consultant has identified five key issues that the accounting industry is facing today. My goal is to find out more about the issues and opportunities your firm is facing so I can determine how I may be able to add the most value for you and your firm.*
>
> *"I've found that, for a strategic alliance to benefit my partners, I need to eliminate or reduce some of the key obstacles that are keeping them from achieving their goals."*

Give the accountant one of your prepared outlines of key industry issues and ask for his or her thoughts, feelings, and experiences with each issue. Use these questions as a starting point for a meaningful discussion. Listen to what the accountant says and how he or she says it. Watch body language. Probe for perceptions. Find out his or her greatest fears and concerns.

Accounting Industry Issues

Dozens of top financial advisors and half a dozen accountants helped me create this strategic alliance process. By interviewing them, I was able to identify some of the key issues or concerns facing the accounting industry. Your goal is to help your partners solve or at least minimize three to five of these issues.

1. Liability

2. Client retention

3. Revenue generation

4. Business development

5. Competitors offering a total solution to solve their clients' financial concerns and problems (financial products and services)

Try to understand what the accountant sees as the biggest problems now and in the future. Look for opportunities in the problems.

The ability to quickly and professionally get to the key points is a core competency of effort-less marketing. It's the key skill that separates you from all the product pushers in this industry. It's important to note that many advisors are reluctant to ask such detailed, personal questions in the second meeting. But you wouldn't be having this meeting if you hadn't established rapport and trust during the first meeting.

Not only does getting to the point help to differentiate you from product pushers, but it also allows you to start adding value immediately. In one of the meetings I conducted, I was going over these industry issues with an accountant. In the middle of my questions he turned to me and said, "Steve, these are exactly the types of questions I should be discussing with my partners."

That's a strong position: I'd just met this gentleman (an advisor had set up this meeting after pre-qualifying the accountant), yet we were talking about extremely important and sensitive business issues. He was dying to talk to someone about them, but he hadn't even broached these subjects with his partners.

Remember, accountants are looking for advice, direction and solutions to these and other problems. Until now they haven't had anyone to talk with. You just may be the person they have been looking for.

When you get to the last item on your list, ask the accountant this question:

"What are some of the key financial concerns your clients have that are outside the scope of your practice?"

This is where you discover hidden opportunities in the accountant's existing client base.

It's common at this point for accountants to say many of their clients need estate planning, or they have a number of doctor clients who are thinking about retirement and need retirement planning. Or perhaps they have a few widows who have inherited a number of brokerage accounts and real estate, and they want to consolidate and simplify the management of their assets. Bingo! Goldmine! Opportunity!

Try not to show your excitement if the accountant answers this way. You should expect it. The right accountants have many clients who need the services of a competent, client-centered financial professional. That's why he or she is talking with you.

Remember, when clients have financial problems or concerns, they'll usually ask their accountants for help first. So, accountants are really the lightning rods to the major financial issues and concerns that wealthy individuals have. And many of the problems that financial success creates can't be solved by accountants alone. They require a team approach to provide the total solution.

Make special notes of the specific opportunities, issues, or concerns you can get paid to solve. Explore the ones that interest you most. But don't recommend any solutions at this meeting. That comes later. If the accountant can't think of any problems his or her clients have, then it's time to ask specific questions. Your goal is to get the accountant thinking about individual clients for whom your expertise could add value.

If you go through a series of questions to identify specific opportunities, and the accountant can't think of any clients who have those concerns, then move on to the next accountant. This one has a client

Clients Seek Help from Accountants First

One of the key questions a business owner will ask an accountant is how to keep a family business in the family. This is obviously an opportunity for estate planners. Some other common concerns clients raise include the following.

- What to do with excess profits
- How to invest the proceeds from the sale of a business or other assets
- How to manage their company retirement plans prudently
- How to minimize the administrative hassles in a pension plan
- How to simplify the management of large investment portfolios
- What to do about excessive activity in investment accounts (churning)
- How to find an advisor who's more sensitive to their needs
- How to reduce taxes when they sell their businesses
- How to reduce volatility or risk in their portfolios

base with low net worths, doesn't listen to his or her clients, or isn't telling you the truth. In any case, cut your losses and move on.

In this second meeting you have three messages to deliver and think about: 1) You have a professional office and staff, 2) you understand your potential partners' problems, and 3) the most important message—there are ways they and their clients can benefit greatly from your services.

You can communicate all three of these messages with a research interview. It's a learned skill: The more you do it the better you'll get. The better you understand accountants and their clients, the easier it will be to uncover hidden opportunities that you and the accountants can work on together.

Once you've completed your second data gathering interview, if appropriate, thank the accountant for his or her time and set up a third meeting a week to ten days later to discuss your thoughts about how you might work together. Arrange to meet in the accountant's office.

Explain you'll think about everything you've discussed and run it by your associates. When you meet again, you'll bring some specific ideas to the table.

Chapter at a Glance

After you've interviewed four or five potential partners, you should start to see some patterns. You've asked the exact same questions and probably received completely different answers. Some of the accountants will be focused on compilation, tax, and audit services. These accountants aren't looking for ways to add value for their clients, so they aren't good prospects. At the other extreme are the unusual accountants who help their clients build their businesses and solve the problems their wealth has created.

The most important part of this strategic alliance process is identifying the right people to work with. Don't try to turn a turkey into an eagle. Invest your time in finding and building relationships with the eagles. They already have a need and a desire to work with someone like you. They have the best clients and are the most fun to work with.

In the next chapter you'll learn how to develop mutually beneficial relationships with the qualified, motivated potential partners you've identified.

Chapter 16 Action Steps

Exercise 1: Identify between ten and 15 accounting firms in your community that qualify as potential strategic alliance partners. Ask your best clients who they use and get referrals from other professionals you respect. If you need more prospects, try looking in business journals and other publications. Finding them there would indicate the companies are marketing- and growth-oriented. Call them and request company literature.

Exercise 2: Call to schedule your first meetings with five accountants. These will be your practice interviews, so don't worry if they're not your ideal partners. Create a list of interview questions that will help you scope out the accountants' businesses. Refer to "Business Profile Questions to Determine Compatibility" on page 311 for examples.

Exercise 3: Meeting 1—Conduct your first meetings in the accountants' offices. Record notes about important discoveries. Did you hear about money in motion, pools of capital, or other opportunities? Your objective: To identify potential strategic alliance partners and to screen out incompatible individuals.

Exercise 4: Prepare for the second meeting by printing out the list of top concerns of accountants. Refer to "Accounting Industry Issues" on page 314 for a template.

Exercise 5: Meeting 2—Conduct your second meetings in your office. Your objective: To position yourself as a knowledgeable, client-centered advisor with a professional staff and office. And, more important, to start the accountant thinking about specific clients who could use your help.

Create Profitable
Strategic Alliances

*In the middle of a difficulty
lies opportunity.*

—Einstein, German physicist and
developer of the Theories of Relativity

O ne year after their first meeting, the rainmaker in an accounting firm called Greg, an advisor who had initiated a relationship with him. The accountant told him the partners had made a decision to have Greg manage the company's pension plan. He also said, "We've just purchased a pension administration firm with more than two hundred accounts totaling over two hundred million dollars. We'd like you to help our new clients manage their money prudently."

You don't need many strategic alliances like this to build a super-profitable business. But it often takes patience. Greg had all but given up on this accounting firm when his contact called him with the good news. The key is to identify early on which centers of influence you're going to invest time cultivating. You learned to do that in the last chapter.

In this chapter you'll learn the second phase of the most powerful marketing tactic of all: Generating pre-qualified, pre-sold wealthy clients through strategic alliances. By applying the interview techniques you learned in the previous chapter, you should now know three to five accountants who would make strong strategic alliance partners. To establish a business relationship, you'll have to reduce their perceived risk and increase their perceived benefits. Here's how.

Think Win-Win-Win

In this next phase, you'll work with potential partners to create a winning structure for your relationships. The first thing you must do is review the goals you identified in the first two meetings. Next you need to determine how you can create win-win-win partnerships. You also must know what obstacles might stand in the way.

Many times your potential partners' goals aren't solely based on money. As you probably learned in your first few meetings, quality of life and developing efficient business models are also big concerns for many professionals. You'll find each potential ally has a unique bundle of wants and needs, based on his or her situation and perceptions. The more effectively you can position your alliances to provide the payoffs your partners want, the better they will work. If you add enough value, you may never need to share your revenue.

The plan is to develop a formal working relationship that creates synergy. By working together as a team, you create a bigger economic pie for everyone to share. The clients win big, the alliance partners meet their goals, and, of course, you'll be paid well. No one will begrudge your compensation if you've added value.

Prepare a Brainstorming Form

Take out your notes from your meetings and put on your thinking cap. You're going to plan a brainstorming session. It'll help you determine your potential new business allies' hot buttons and where to start the relationships. If you're fuzzy on some points, don't worry. The objective is to use this form at the next meeting to clarify their perceptions, goals, and motivations.

You'll need to create a brainstorming form for each prospective partner. This marketing document is a simple outline with three sections. The first section is a list of goals. The second section lists the issues, concerns, and challenges (obstacles to success). The last section lists areas of potential opportunity to work together—where you can add the most value.

This document should not describe specifically how you'll work together. If you make a premature recommendation that isn't attractive, you run the risk of losing credibility and momentum. You may never get a second chance to recover. This document is designed to help you discover what your potential partner is ready, willing, and able to do to get started.

Prepare for a Brainstorming Session

At the top of a sheet of your letterhead, write "Strategic Alliance Brainstorming Session—[*Your Company Name and Potential Partner's Company Name*]."

Based on your interview notes and insights, prioritize three to seven points under each of these three headings.

1. List your potential partners' goals.
2. List issues, concerns and challenges.
3. List opportunities to help your potential partners and their clients achieve their goals and solve their problems.

Goals

In this section, list the key goals you gleaned during your interviews. List any specific goals mentioned. Prioritize the goals as well as you can.

Also include common goals you can assume, such as

- working fewer hours,
- charging on a value billing basis to increase hourly revenue,
- developing bundled services that a staff person can handle,
- attracting more appreciative clients, and
- providing value-added services to improve client retention.

You can add value by mentioning goals any good businessperson should have. You're expanding the horizon of what might be possible in a partnership with you. Customize this for each individual.

Key Issues

In this section, list any key obstacles or concerns that came up during your meetings. For instance, you'd note if an accountant is thinking of selling his or her company or moving offices, if one of the partners is retiring, if many of the clients are retired or widowed, if the partnership is breaking up, if the firm is having trouble getting good employees, and so on.

Don't expand on this list with your own ideas. Stick to the specific issues confronting each person or company. These issues are often about resources or vague fears. They're points you should be aware of, but they aren't really goals.

For example, one estate planning attorney's partner was a good technician but horrible with clients. These types of issues are critical to understand, but they're not your job to fix. Focus on the most pressing concerns the accountant mentioned both for themselves and their clients.

Strategic Alliance Opportunities

Financial problems for potential partners and their clients can be big opportunities for you. Once you discover specific areas of "pain" or unmet needs, you should determine how motivated they are to solve them.

These strategic-alliance opportunities usually fall into three categories:

1. helping the person with estate planning or investment management services (usually a retirement plan),

2. solving problems for clients that are outside the scope of the person's or firm's expertise (such as consolidating a widow's scattered investments into one comprehensive portfolio), and

3. developing the business (such as generating revenue and attracting new ideal clients).

Focus on solving problems for existing clients. Attracting new clients is a future possibility, if you work well together and run out of existing clients to help. But if a partner doesn't have clients who could benefit from your services right now, he or she isn't right for you. Invest your energies finding the right relationships.

The goal is to identify existing problems you can get paid to solve—problems you believe a partner will be motivated to act on. The two most common problems I've found are estate planning and investment management. (This applies to both accountants and their clients.)

Once you've completed this exercise and have the issues on paper, you need to find out if you and the other person are thinking along the same lines. It's time to share your thoughts and determine the best place to start.

Meeting 3: Prioritize Interests

Hold this meeting at the potential partners' offices. This is where they are most comfortable. You can tell a lot about the level of interest by the way you're introduced and by who else has been asked to attend the meeting.

Your goal for this meeting is to conceptually agree on the specific areas in which the two of you could create synergy by working together.

Share the brainstorming form. Go over each section and each point. Ask for feedback. Watch body language, and listen to tones of voice. Ask for help in prioritizing the items. The basic dialog goes like this:

"We've identified a couple opportunities for working together; however, I need to clarify the areas where I can add the most value."

Hold a discussion about the different opportunities to add value and to provide a total solution for some of his or her clients. By involving your strategic alliance partner, you jointly design the ideal business relationship—for both of you.

A Typical Brainstorm Discussion

As an example, I'll use an accountant in southern California who specializes in estate planning for wealthy business owners and their widows. This accountant fit our criteria and was an outgoing, entrepreneurial professional. He was not licensed to sell securities and insurance. He wanted to identify other financial professionals to help him provide a total solution for his clients.

In previous meetings, he had said many of his clients were wealthy widows whose husbands had left them with some stock and three or four pieces of real estate. Many of them needed help simplifying and consolidating their investment assets.

During this brainstorming session I suggested one strategic alliance possibility was to develop an estate consolidation feasibility analysis for wealthy widows. He expressed enthusiasm, so I said, "I'm not sure how it would work, but we might be able to gather information and analyze it in a systematic process."

I suggested that his assistant could analyze the data and create reports on a value-billing basis. Then the accountant's firm could do the analysis and estate planning, and the financial advisor could design a prudent investment plan and provide any necessary insurance. This way we were creating new business for the accountant and the advisor from the accountant's existing client base.

The accountant lit up when we started talking about the potential tax issues and planning strategies. We focused on using charitable remainder trusts to reduce capital gains taxes when clients consolidated real estate and brokerage accounts into fee-based, managed accounts.

Identify Specific Areas of Interest

Float "trial balloons" to see which areas your potential strategic alliance partners are most interested in. Then solicit their ideas, concerns and thoughts about business opportunities. Remember, you're not trying to sell them anything. You're trying to determine what they're most interested in "buying."

Be sure to include personal financial services, if appropriate. Once you have identified and explored the key possibilities, ask the accountant to prioritize them for you.

Sometimes you can't identify any mutual areas of interest. Or someone seems to be interested but has a lot of excuses. In these cases, you've run into a dead end. To find out for sure, say the following:

"I've run all my options past you and haven't been able to identify any opportunities to add much value. I'm kind of out of ideas. What are your thoughts on how we might be able to work together?"

If your potential partner can't think of anything either, you should cut your losses and move on to another center of influence. No sense beating a dead horse. You're looking for people who have a clearly defined need for your services and clients who want your help right now. Say that you'd like to keep the lines of communication open, but you don't see any way to move forward right now.

If you have found some way you're sure you can help the person and his or her clients, proceed to the next step.

Develop a Presentation to Explain Benefits

Once you're clear on the areas of opportunity both of you would like to pursue, you must prepare a few more marketing tools. You need a liability letter and one or more financial strategy fact sheets. You'll use these to explain the benefits of your plan to the accountant.

Prepare a Liability Letter

Liability is one of the unspoken concerns that most professionals and particularly accountants have. They're not just worried about being sued. A more subtle risk is losing clients' trust after referring them to incompetent or unprofessional advisors.

Customize the letter shown in "Sample Liability Letter" on the next page and print it on your letterhead. You'll use this to reduce their concerns about you hurting their relationships with their best clients.

Prepare One or More
Financial Strategy Fact Sheets

To prepare the fact sheets for presenting your financial strategies to potential partners, focus on the most pressing problems they indicated key clients want to solve. You'll create a separate fact sheet for each problem, which you can print on your letterhead.

Title the document with a succinct headline that promises to solve the problem. (See the example on page 328.) Create headings for three sections in each fact sheet:

1. The Problem,
2. The Solution, and
3. People Who Can Benefit Most.

Under each heading, list three to five points to define the key concepts. They should be concise; one page is plenty.

Create a customized version of a Financial Strategy Fact Sheet for each opportunity the accountant expressed interest in. I've given you an investment example ("Simplify a Large Investment Portfolio") and an estate planning example ("How to Keep the Family Business in the Family") on pages 328 and 329. If you find other opportunities, follow the format to develop your own fact sheets.

The headline is your promise of benefits. Write it just like the headline of an ad. It expresses the essence of your value-added services. Once you get a strong headline, the rest of the fact sheet should be easy. Just keep it short. It's a discussion document, not a complete plan.

Sample Liability Letter

[Printed on Letterhead]

Client Name
The Valuable Business
123 Millionaire Way
Fat City, CA 90000

Dear [*Name*],

The enclosed Investment Policy Statement is presented for your review and implementation. The recommendations are based on the objectives and risk tolerance you established at our previous meetings. I am confident that this plan will give you the highest probability of achieving your investment goals.

Please understand that I take full responsibility for these recommendations and the implementation of this plan. Your accountant, Terry Numbers, has not endorsed the specific investments in this plan nor performed any research on the specific investment managers included in this plan. Of course, I have conducted the due diligence necessary to confidently make the enclosed recommendations.

I strongly encourage you to discuss the tax consequences of this plan with Terry to ensure it will meet your tax objectives.

I look forward to implementing this plan with you.

Sincerely,

Dale Brilliant, CFP, RIA, ChFC

Sample Financial Strategy Fact Sheet
Simplify a Large Investment Portfolio

THE PROBLEM

Individuals managing large investment portfolios face the following.

- Financial insecurity caused by feeling out of control of investment processes and results
- Information overload caused by the volume and complexity of statements
- Limited time, expertise, or interest to spend on personal finances
- No formal financial or investment plan

THE SOLUTION

Work with a Registered Investment Advisor to develop and implement a personalized investment management plan.

1. Define clients' risk tolerances and objectives.
2. Design and implement investment strategies.
   - Tailor an investment strategy and asset allocation mix to meet client's investment objectives.
   - Diversify investment portfolios to minimize risk and volatility.
3. Monitor performance and maintain asset allocation.
   - Compare performance relative to the clients' goals.
   - Re-balance portfolios to maintain proper diversification.
4. Provide value-added services.
   - Produce quarterly reports detailing transactions, income, and realized profits and losses.
   - A personal advisor will answer questions and recommend options.

PEOPLE WHO CAN BENEFIT MOST

Serious investors (not savers) will benefit most if they

- would like to feel in control of investment direction, minimize transaction costs, and avoid expensive mistakes;
- want to simplify, streamline, and systemize the investment management process; and
- have over $250,000 in cash and/or securities.

Sample Financial Strategy Fact Sheet

How to Keep the Family Business in the Family

THE PROBLEM

An owner of a successful family business wants his children to continue operating the business when he retires. However, the following costs
may force liquidation of the business when he and his wife pass away.

- Federal estate taxes
- Probate fees
- Administrative fees
- Outstanding business loans

THE SOLUTION

Work with a competent professional to design and implement plans.

1. An estate plan that minimizes death taxes and expenses by
   using the following.
   - Wills
   - Living trusts
   - Life insurance trusts
   - Buy-sell agreements

2. Design and implement a business plan that provides liquidity to
   - pay off business debt,
   - replace management talent,
   - supply operating capital, and
   - fund buy-sell agreement.

PEOPLE WHO CAN BENEFIT MOST

Children who are active in the management of a capital-intensive,
family business *or* owners of a capital-intensive, family business if they

- have a net worth of more than $1.6 million,
- are 50 to 70 years old,
- have/are children actively involved in management, and
- have a business more than 15 years old.

Under "The Problem," list the specific problems identified for you in the last meetings.

Under "The Solution," offer a strategic process rather than a product solution. For instance, "work with a Registered Investment Advisor to develop and implement a personalized investment plan," not "invest in a managed account." Briefly explain the process you would use.

Under the third section, "People Who Can Benefit Most," summarize the Ideal Client Profile that you developed in Step 2. Use net worth and income figures to qualify potential candidates for your services.

Meeting 4: Present Your Recommendations

Now that you have a total solution to problems you know people want to solve, you're ready to see how motivated they are to get started. It's usually best to conduct this fourth meeting in your office where you're in control.

Introduce the liability letter first. Produce a copy and say,

> *"Before I explain how we might be able to work together, I need to discuss one very important point: liability. As I'm sure you're aware, we live in a litigious society. So whenever we work together to help a mutual client, I will always provide you and the client with a letter like this.*
>
> *"This will clarify for our clients where your areas of liability and responsibility are and where my areas of liability and responsibility are."*

Let the person read the letter, and ask for feedback. Some people will be very interested in the letter and give you ideas about refining it. Others will tell you they aren't worried about liability. But all of them will be impressed that you're thinking about their needs. Once you have addressed the liability issue it's time to present your ideas for working together.

I'll use the example of an accountant who has a lot of widows who want to consolidate their late husbands' scattered investments into simplified portfolios.

Give the accountant a copy of the appropriate financial strategy fact sheet and introduce this document:

"You mentioned that many of your clients are widows with large investment portfolios, and many of them would like to consolidate and simplify their late husbands' scattered investments. That's great because that's one of the areas I specialize in. In fact, I put together this fact sheet to explain the strategies I use."

This is where the strategic alliance really starts to take shape. You'll show the accountant how you can solve or minimize many of his or her key concerns. By the time you're finished the accountant should see that by working together you'll provide a total solution for clients. Discuss each of the three areas on the fact sheet: problems, solutions, and people who can benefit most.

Problems

Remember you're discussing problems the accountant told you many clients have. These aren't vague generalities. Specific individuals probably recently asked the accountant for help in these areas.

Say something like this:

"I've found that if we don't solve problems for our clients, they might go to other professionals to solve those problems. And when that occurs, we risk losing our best clients. By working together in a strategic alliance, we can deliver more comprehensive solutions for our clients. That creates a stronger bond and a greater chance of keeping them for life."

Discuss this concept with them. Once they understand how you can help them fend off the competition and increase client retention, move on to the next section.

Solutions

When you discuss the solutions, say something like this:

"In a strategic alliance, it's critical that all parties benefit. Ultimately, the biggest payoff goes to the clients. But we also need to make sure that it's profitable for you and for me."

Let's continue to assume you're discussing widows who want to consolidate their scattered assets. You can tell the accountant that when you sell real estate and liquidate brokerage accounts, obviously there will be tax considerations. Explain that you like to be as tax efficient as possible. Ask about his or her interest in preparing a tax plan to minimize the taxes.

Tell your potential partner that either you can gather the data, crunch the numbers, and provide them for review, or he or she can do the tabulation. Ask the accountant how he or she would like to work together. Normally the response will be, "Why don't you do the work, and I'll just review it?"

Another possibility is to determine if you can gather the data and have an assistant at the accounting firm do the work on a value-billing basis. That means the accountant can bill by the project rather than by the hour. This is typically more profitable for accountants and is more desirable business for them. Help your partner discover an easy new revenue source that someone else on his or her team can support. You're introducing the accountant to a way to generate additional revenue—with very little effort.

When you talk about a problem, typically the accountants visualize specific clients who have mentioned that problem recently. But when you talk about the solution and you explain how they're going to generate revenue, they often think of additional clients who could also benefit but have not yet asked for help.

Your objective is always to think about how partners can benefit without creating too much work or giving them money out of your pocket. Once they understand the revenue-generating opportunities, move on to the next step.

People Who Can Benefit Most

The goal in this step is to identify specific people who would be good candidates for the solutions you have presented. By now you have addressed four of the five key industry issues. You have showed how, by working together, you can: 1) reduce liability, 2) help retain his or her best clients, 3) generate additional revenue from existing clients, and 4) solve client problems that are outside the scope of the accountant's business.

Now you're going to help with one of the most important issues: developing additional ideal clients for your partner's firm. At the end of the meeting, ask this:

> *"How many clients do you have who may be interested in taking a look at a solution to this problem?"*

Since this is one of the key issues he or she has mentioned earlier, you know there should be clients who want and need your help right now. Be ready for four or five clients who need your help right now. Say,

> *"Let's invite them to an informal meeting here in your office to explain how we can help them. But to make this profitable for you, I suggest we invite them to bring a friend who wants to solve the same problem. That way we can generate additional clients for both of our firms."*

This process will show how you can create a more compelling package of benefits to attract new clients by working together. That's called synergy. It's what strategic alliances are all about. You've just become your partner's unofficial business development officer.

Offer a "Test Drive"

Many times people will seem eager to get the benefits but will hesitate to commit to introducing you to their clients. If you run into this situation, don't worry. It's normal. Remember, they wouldn't be doing their jobs if they didn't show some skepticism.

The way to overcome this skepticism and finally win the person's trust is to take him or her for a test drive of your services. Simply say,

> *"I couldn't help noticing your hesitation. It's difficult to determine how we might work together with clients. To get to know each other better, why don't you take our services for a test drive."*

Offer to prepare an Investment Policy Statement, financial plan, estate plan, retirement plan, or whatever is appropriate for the individual's personal situation. Explain the value (from your price list), but offer to do it for free in the interest of developing the strategic alliance.

One advisor was trying to develop a strategic alliance with a firm with five accountants. They had more than $3 million in their own retirement plan. He found out it was invested in multiple bank CDs and the rest was loaned to clients. He offered to develop an Investment Policy Statement for the firm. When they read the IPS, they gave this advisor $300,000 to invest. As the CDs matured and the loans came due, more money was on the way.

Whenever possible, try to turn your strategic alliance partners into your clients. It's a powerful position for you if the accountant says, "There are a lot of competent financial advisors here in Wealthville, but I work with [*your name*] as my personal financial advisor."

If you have completed the exercises in this book, you'll have a systematic, value-added, client-centered process. Your potential partners will be impressed with your processes and professionalism. Once they know you better and understand more clearly how you help people, they should be eager to introduce you to their most motivated clients.

Work Together to Solve the Clients' Problems

You're almost home now. If you've gotten this far, you're working with some great partners. There were many points along this road at which they could have disqualified themselves. But they passed the test. They trust you, understand how you add value, and want to work with you. They have many clients who need your help, and they're ready to introduce you to some of their most motivated clients.

You still have one major hurdle to jump before you can start working with all these wealthy clients. Here's how to set up face-to-face client meetings so you and your new ally can work together to help your mutual clients.

Invite Clients to an Informal Briefing

Help your new partner go through his or her client base and identify those individuals who are most motivated to solve the problems you discovered in the second meeting. Invite the clients to an informal meeting at your partner's office. The best way to do this is to have your marketing person take care of it for you. If you delegate this to your new partner, it may never happen. Many people have severe "call reluctance" and zero marketing skills.

Tell the your partners,

> *"One of the benefits of working in a strategic alliance is each party has different core competencies. My team is good at marketing. So just give us the information on the clients you want to invite, and we'll prepare the invitations and have you approve them. Then we'll mail them, and I'll have my marketing person call to confirm attendance. This is easy for us."*

Make sure they know they will be in control of the process but won't have do any of the marketing. Point out that these clients have already expressed interest in the subject and should be thrilled to hear a solution.

Invite Your Partners' Clients to Attend a Meeting

In creating an invitation or letter, follow these guidelines.

1. Use the headline from the financial strategy fact sheet.

2. Keep it to one page.

3. Be sure to tell clients to bring friends who are also interested.

4. Get your strategic alliance partners' approval and put it on their letterhead with their signature.

5. Invite five times the number of people you want to show up— 25 to 50 is a good range for the invitations.

6. Send the letter out two weeks before the meeting.

7. Have your marketing person follow up by phone. He or she should ask the non-attendees if they would like to meet at another time or if they would be interested in the future.

8. Be sure your marketing person calls the participants the day before to remind them about the meeting.

Meet With Clients

Meet in your partner's office or conference room, and be sure he or she is present. It helps to build trust if your alliance partner is there to introduce you and answer questions.

Five to ten people is the perfect group size. Focus on quality, not quantity. With a smaller group, it's easier to build rapport and start relationships. During a one-hour meeting (don't exceed the time people have agreed to give you!), take the following steps.

1. Introduction: Have your partner introduce you and explain why he or she wanted the people attending to meet you.

2. Discussion: Use a financial strategy fact sheet to review the promises of benefits, the problems, the solutions and the people who can benefit most. Use it as a discussion document to get the conversation rolling.

3. Illustration: Use case studies to explain how you have helped other people. Your goal is not to sell them on the details but to get them interested in the solution and to feel good about you. Charm them with your empathy and caring; don't sell them on your technical skills.

4. Call to action: At the end, ask who would like to learn more about how you can help them with this or any other investment or financial matter. Take the names of interested people. Have your marketing person set up individual initial data gathering interviews with hot prospects.

Implement Solutions to the Clients' Problems

Work closely with your partner to implement solutions to the clients' problems. Make sure he or she is involved in the process, but maintain control over the client relationships, and generate as much revenue for the accounting firm as possible. Keep the conversation focused on making a bigger pie for everyone. Be sure to send out the liability letter to both your partner and the clients.

Once you've satisfied one or two clients, ask them to send your partner a note thanking him or her for introducing you to them. This will reinforce your relationship and prove to your new strategic partner that you are adding value for clients.

One word of warning. Never ask your partners to endorse your recommendations in front of clients. That's why you're there: to take the liability. If they wanted to endorse insurance or investment products, they would probably be selling them without you. Your partners want to work with you so they can stay objective.

Build the Long-Term Relationship

You've started the relationship. Now you must cultivate it. Add value by providing tax information and easy-to-read statements, simplifying your partners' lives as much as possible. Continue to keep the communication channels open and explore other opportunities where you might be able to develop additional business for everyone.

Help your partners position to attract ideal new clients. And, if appropriate, involve other centers of influence in your alliances. Once you've started a great partnership, you can become your partner's informal business development officer. It will strengthen the relationships and your own business.

Chapter at a Glance

By creating a team of professionals that offers a "total solution" to their clients' problems, you can generate additional revenue for alliance partners, keep their clients happy, attract more clients just like their ideal clients, and make yourself a ton of money. You'll also out-position any existing or future competitors.

But you can do this only if your partners trust you. If they don't, they won't share their best clients with you because their risk is just too high. So don't start with a "bribe" (offering to split revenues). Determine how to build trust and add the most value. Then, if you ultimately develop a formal joint venture, you can work out a fee-sharing agreement. At this point, you'll be in a position of strong bargaining power.

This process works well because it allows you to zero in like a laser on the key problems in your partners' client bases. By positioning yourself as a problem solver and reducing stress for your partners and their clients, you establish yourself as a trustworthy resource.

Of course, not every candidate will respond well to this process. Many will frustrate you because they need your help but are unmotivated or fearful. But all you need is two or three key strategic alliance partners who allow you to help them solve problems for their clients. Your business will take off like a rocket.

By identifying the pent-up demand for your services and bundling solutions to meet that demand, you can establish powerful strategic alliances. You can use this exact same process with attorneys, investment bankers, association executives, consultants and any other center of influence who has clients just like your ideal clients.

This process will often take a year to bear significant fruit. It's common to pick up some business early on, but the biggest payoffs will come as you develop trust and rapport with the alliance partner, and he or she starts sending you bigger clients.

Everything you have learned in this book is designed to help you penetrate the highest strata of wealth in our society. You'll meet ideal clients through people they already trust. That trust will be transferred to you. If you follow the strategies in this chapter and the previous one you'll earn the right to create alliances with your community's most influential people.

It will transform your business in a fundamental way. The average net worth of your clients will go through the roof, and every new client will be pre-qualified, pre-sold, and happy to pay for your advice.

That's the way it works for client-centered financial advisors. The market forces drive their businesses to phenomenal, effort-less success.

Chapter 17 Action Steps

Exercise 1: Draft your Brainstorming Form. Refer to "Prepare for a Brainstorming Session" on page 321 for guidelines.

Exercise 2: Meeting 3—Meet to prioritize the accountant's interests. You should leave this meeting having agreed on some specific solutions you could work together on.

Exercise 3: Write your Liability Letter and develop or customize one or more financial strategy fact sheets. Refer to "Sample Liability Letter" on page 327, "Simplify a Large Investment Portfolio" on page 328, and "Keep the Family Business in the Family" on page 329 for guidelines.

Exercise 4: Meeting 4—Present your recommendations for working together. Your objective of this discussion is to come away with the partner's agreement to introduce you to their key clients. Try to leave the meeting with a list of 25 to 50 clients you can invite.

Exercise 5: Following the guidelines in "Invite Your Partners' Clients to Attend a Meeting," invite the clients to the orientation meeting. Hold the meeting and gauge client interest in one-on-one follow-up discussions.

Exercise 6: Solve problems for your partner and his or her clients. Build the relationship by continually looking for ways to add value.

Qualify and Meet With Ideal Prospects

Whenever you see a successful business, someone once made a courageous decision.

—Peter Drucker, American management consultant, professor, and author, *Management: Tasks, Responsibilities, Practices*

n the previous six chapters, you learned how to bury yourself in excellent leads. That's what I call a positive problem. Leads are good. But you must be able to turn ideal leads into ideal clients. Otherwise, all of your marketing efforts will be wasted.

Qualifying leads and setting appointments should be a systematic process in your organization. Each team member will play an important role. The process must be smooth and efficient to minimize effort and maximize profits.

Make lead generation and the marketing activities associated with it a game. See how creatively you can use all the strategies discussed in the previous chapters—speaking, PR, referrals, events, strategic alliances—to generate the number of leads you need to achieve your goals.

Move to Round 2 in the Selection Process

Once you have generated leads, you must qualify and prioritize them. Since you have a finite amount of time, you must meet with only the most motivated and qualified prospects. You have an Ideal Prospect Profile describing the people who can benefit most from your services. You know who they are demographically and psychographically. Identifying prospects who fit your Ideal Prospect Profile was the first round in your selection process.

But how do you know if the ideal prospects you've identified are receptive to starting a relationship with you right now? You need to look for clues about transitional events happening in their lives. You also need to determine if they meet your minimum financial requirements, will be fun to work with, and are willing to pay for your services.

Remember the classification system of "A," "B," "C," and "D" clients. Keep in mind that you're looking for the *Prudent Investors,* specifically. Focus on the "A" and "B-plus" prospects only—the eager and the motivated Prudent Investors. Qualifying and following up with the best prospects is the second round in your selection process.

Use a 12-Point Qualifier Form

In addition to your Ideal Prospect Profile and your more detailed Acceptable Prospect Profile you can use "12-Point Prospect Qualifier" on page 343. It's a questionnaire that will help you determine how qualified and motivated your individual prospects are.

You can use it with referred prospects and prospects who call your office. If you generate leads from presentations and public relations, you can use the form on the phone or when you first meet with new prospects. Rate them on a 12-point system. The higher the score, the more likely a prospect is to become an ideal client.

Assume all of the leads rate zero until you discover otherwise. Prospects in the nine and above range are essentially "pre-sold." They're so hot to buy that all you have to do is take the order. If you identify prospects in the six and under range, you'll have to work harder to move them through the decision-making process.

Complete a 12-Point Prospect Qualifier for every lead that your organization contacts. Use your database to record the scores. Track the number of monthly leads you're generating and the total average points from all prospects. This will give you data to track your lead-generating performance trends from month to month.

Refine your Ideal Prospect Profiles and your referral conversations until you're consistently getting introduced to motivated prospects scoring nine and higher. Determine whether you're generating enough leads to meet your sales goals. Turn up the heat on the lead generation activities if you need more. Your goals should determine your activity level.

Remember that being very selective about who you take on as clients is an extremely important part of this business. You can't be all things to all people. You have a clear idea of

---

12-Point Prospect Qualifier

Put a check next to the true statements.

Prospect's Name : _____

Date: _____

In addition to meeting the Ideal Prospect Profile, this prospect:

- ❑ Meets my minimum financial requirements
- ❑ Is in one of my target niches
- ❑ Was referred to me by a happy client or center of influence
- ❑ Is highly motivated to solve a specific financial problem
- ❑ Knows I'm an expert in his or her area of need
- ❑ Is ready to take action soon
- ❑ Has realistic expectations
- ❑ Likes and trusts me
- ❑ Is honest with me
- ❑ Is easy to work with
- ❑ Lives or works close to my office
- ❑ Is influential with many wealthy friends, clients or associates in my target niches

___ TOTAL YES ANSWERS

1–3 = Poor (D) 4–6 = Marginal (C)
7–9 = OK (B) 10–12 = Ideal (A)

Comments:

_____

_____

_____

the types of clients you can make the most money from and have the most fun with. They'll also be able to benefit most from your services.

You can get some of this information from your referral sources. Then you'll have to actually talk to the prospects to answer the remaining questions.

Call-ins and workshop attendees who asked for appointments will already be eager to meet with you. You or someone on your staff must prescreen them to maximize the use of your time. It's a good idea to prepare a simple qualifying script for the person who sets appointments for you. Make sure this person refers "C" and "D" clients to another advisor who will take care of them.

Get Help Prioritizing Referrals

It's one thing prescreening people who contact you or ask you for an appointment. But what about your referred prospects? You can't follow up with all of them. How do you decide which ones to contact? Simple. When Alan, an advisor in Toronto, got 66 names of high-tech entrepreneurs, he asked the referral source for more information. When you run into this situation with referrals, say,

> *"I have time to contact only a few of these people. Which ones do you think could benefit most from my services? Why?"*

You can also ask,

> *"Are any of these people going through any major financial transitions?"*

Mention retirement, death of a spouse, and sale of a major asset. Let your referral sources think through the names as long as they want.

Alan identified five "A" prospects and discussed them with his client in detail. When Alan asked about transitional events, his client perked up right away. He remembered that one of the business owners had just asked him for advice. "He sold his business and has over $6 million he needs to invest right now." I call that a hot lead.

Money in motion has to go somewhere. It might as well be to you. If the prospect sold a business or received a rollover, ask how much money was involved. If the source doesn't know, ask him or her to estimate.

At this point, you've identified and discussed all the ideal hot prospects. Now you need to dig deeper into the remaining prospects. You want to identify any potential new clients or, if you aren't buried in qualified leads yet, you may want to identify people who would be receptive to participating in market research interviews.

Focus on the next best set of prospects. These are your "A-minus" and "B-plus" candidates. Tell your referral source:

> *"There are three distinct groups that interest me.*
> *Number one: People who need my help right now, who*
> *we've already identified. Number two: Experts who could*
> *help me understand the market and identify hidden*
> *opportunities. Number three: People who fit my profile*
> *and can give me useful insights and suggestions for better*
> *ways to serve their niche. Would you help me determine*
> *who belongs in each category?"*

Then ask,

> *"Would you tell me a little about each of these remaining*
> *people so I can prioritize them?"*

Help your referral sources identify the best people for you to meet. Tell your referral sources about your minimum account sizes. Use your 12-Point Prospect Qualifier form. Get as much information as possible about each person's situation and motivations. Focus on finding pools of capital and money in motion.

Ask for Introductions to Ideal Prospects

Referrals are a good step toward starting new relationships with ideal clients. But they are only the first step. *Introductions* are a much more powerful way to start relationships than just calling or writing to referred prospects.

Recognize that an introduction requires a higher level of commitment from referral sources. And it takes them more time. If you've truly impressed your clients and centers of influence, and they know you're committed to helping people like them, they'll be happy to help you by *introducing* you to all of their closest friends and associates.

Once you've received referrals, explain to your referral sources that, if they're willing to introduce you to their friends, it'll create a stronger foundation for a long-term relationship between you and your new prospective client. Tell them,

> *"If you really think these people could benefit from my services, I'd like your help making sure they perceive me as a trustworthy, client-centered expert instead of a typical product pusher. I've found that a personal intro- duction is the best way to start almost any relationship. Wouldn't you agree?*
>
> *"Would you be willing to introduce me to your friends and key associates who could benefit most from my services?"*

You may want to remind them of their original agreement to be constantly on the lookout for new clients for your firm. Also, remind them that if they help you market, you can spend more of your time constantly looking for better ways to help them achieve their goals. Share your business goals, and enroll them in helping you achieve them.

Meet Face to Face

Meeting socially is an especially powerful way to start lifelong relationships. It's normal for people to introduce their friends this way. If you're working with clients you truly like, they'll like you and want to share you with their friends.

Suggest that you, your client, and his or her friends get together for lunch or a drink after work. You can take them out to dinner, host a small dinner party at your home, or have one catered at your client's home. Or find a common interest or activity. If you golf, play tennis, or sail, these are great ways to meet. Keep it social instead of business-oriented. You want to start the relationship as a trusted friend, not as just another financial professional.

When you meet, try to discover what each prospect is interested in. But avoid any heavy financial or investment discussions. Focus on building the relationships and determine if you would enjoy having them as clients. If you discover you can help them, let them know it. See how they respond to your verbal benefits statement. It should prompt them to ask for more information. Give them just enough to create more curiosity:

"I'd love to tell you more about what I do and to explore how we might be able to work together. But now is not the best time. If you're really interested, why don't you give me your phone number, and I'll have my secretary set up a time for us to talk?"

Get their cards or numbers and permission to have someone from your office contact them. Later, have your marketing coordinator call to pre-screen and set up initial prospect meetings in your office.

If they don't ask you more about your business, you can always ask them if you can conduct research interviews to learn more about their niche or their situation. After your initial meetings you can ask your clients for feedback. Have them describe what they think the next step should be. They'll typically be glad to play the role of matchmaker.

Meet Over The Phone

Use telephone conference calls for introductions if distance or time make it difficult to meet face to face. I often use this technique for introducing two of my friends who I think would benefit from getting to know each other. I schedule the call and then call my two friends or business associates at the appropriate time.

I get the ball rolling by explaining the reason I'm introducing them, and then I hand the ball over to the appropriate party. If needed, I guide the conversation to help them discover specific opportunities or areas of mutual interest. Then I let them decide how they want to proceed. This is the role your clients would play.

It just takes a little commitment to your success and a small amount of time. If your clients are impressed with you and your services, you'll be surprised how eager many of your clients will be to help you.

What to Do If Your Client Won't Make an Introduction

Sometimes clients won't take the time or make the commitment to introduce you to referred prospects. If an introduction is not forthcoming, ask your sources for their permission to contact the qualified referrals:

"Would you recommend that I contact them?"

If they think it's a good idea, ask,

"May I use your name?"

Then ask for help customizing your referral letters for each prospect you want to contact. (See the Referral Follow-Up Letter on pages 350–351.) Sending out referral letters and then phoning prospects is your second choice option. It's a far less powerful form of meeting prospects. Always try for an introduction first.

Send Customized
Introductory Letters

Let's review. You've gathered a long list of referred prospects. You've screened out any "C"s and "D"s. You've identified the hot prospects and arranged to be introduced to as many as possible.

Ideally you'll have plenty of clients to talk with, but if you haven't received enough introductions to ideal new prospects, you'll want to go to Plan B: Customize and mail out letters of introduction to high potential prospects. Remember, do this only if you haven't received enough introductions. Introductions will lead to stronger relationships and quicker results.

Gather Details to Help You Customize Your Letter

If it looks like a letter is your best option, be sure to get your client's help in customizing it for your referrals. Pull out a sample referral letter and ask your referral sources for help:

> *"Would you give me your insights on this letter?*
> *How would you respond if you received a letter like this?*
> *How could I improve it? If you were me, how would you*
> *customize this letter to connect with people? What should*
> *I say that would interest them in talking with me?"*

Explain how you'll follow up with a phone call after the letter is received. Say, "If they're interested in my services, we'll get together for a meeting. If they aren't interested, I won't bother them again."

In the process of customizing the letter, learn key information about the referred individuals. Try to identify their current situations in life, their hot buttons, and their concerns. Dig for any background information that can give you insights into each individual's motivations and qualifications. Use the 12-Point Qualifier to determine their levels of motivation and how well they "fit." Take detailed notes to use when you're customizing the referral follow-up letters.

Send a Referral Follow-up Letter

Use a tape recorder to dictate a customized letter for each prospect you want to meet. Review your notes, and hit the hot buttons for that individual. Stay as close to the standard format as possible to streamline your process. (See "Sample Referral Follow-up Letter" below.)

Have your marketing coordinator type these letters for you. Proof the letters, and sign final copies in blue ink. Be sure the envelope says "Personal and Confidential."

Sample Referral Follow-Up Letter

Mr. John Doe
20 Toronto Lane
Toronto, CANADA M4T 3B3

Dear John:

Rich Smith asked me to contact you, and I promised him I would. I'm a friend of Rich's, and for the past three years, I've also been his financial advisor.

Rich said you own a very successful high-tech company. He also said you're thinking of selling your business, and he thought you might benefit from my expertise. Rich wanted you to know about some of the integrated tax, estate, and investment planning strategies we've used to help him.

Like you and Rich, I'm also a business owner. For the past 15 years I've specialized in helping successful entrepreneurs plan and achieve their financial goals. I provide comprehensive investment and financial advice to help my clients address the following issues.

- Minimizing taxes on the sale of clients' businesses and on their investment portfolios

---

- Clarifying their personal financial goals and developing and implementing customized strategies to achieve them

- Developing a business succession plan that frees them of their businesses and frees up their capital so they can have more fun

- Eliminating worries and ensuring that taxes, costs, and delays are minimized when their estates are transferred to their heirs

Top Notch Investment Counsel applies institutional investment management strategies to individual portfolios. For each of our clients we develop a customized, written Investment Policy Statement. This allows our clients to control the overall investment process while leaving the day-to-day management to our team of professionals.

Rich wasn't sure if you'd be interested in talking with me, but he thought you'd be the best person to make that decision. I'll call you on Tuesday morning to see if it would be mutually beneficial for us to meet. I look forward to speaking with you.

Yours truly,

Alan R. Advisor, CFP
SJA/mlc

P.S. If you would like to talk with me but won't be available on Tuesday morning, please call me, or my assistant, Susan, on our direct line at 000-000-0000 to arrange a convenient time to talk.

Train Your Clients to Endorse Your Services

Let your clients know that the people who receive your letters are likely to call them once they read them:

"Would it be OK if they called you to ask about me?"

Make sure you know what your clients will say:

"If they asked, what would you probably tell your friends about me?"

Listen closely to the answer. Draw out a thorough response. Your clients will articulate the benefits they've experienced personally from their relationship with you. This question will force them to verbalize their subconscious thoughts about you. It'll probably strengthen their conviction about the value of your services.

Train your clients and centers of influence to be effective introducers, referrers, and spokespersons for your firm. They should vouch for your character, trustworthiness, expertise and service. When their associates ask about you, your clients should be your marketing apostles and sell your services for you.

Think about this process from the prospects' point of view. They get letters saying their friends asked you to contact them. If they're interested in the benefits mentioned in the letters, most people would call the referral sources to find out what they have to say about you. Then your referral sources will clearly communicate enthusiasm for your services and personally recommend or even endorse you.

Once the prospects contact the referral sources, you're in. Remember, an endorsement is 1,000 times more persuasive than a letter alone.

Call to Qualify the Prospects

When your letters are mailed, your assistant or marketing coordinator should schedule follow-up calls and note them in your calendar. Have this person remind you to make the calls exactly when you said you would. If you're unavailable at an appointed time, have your marketing coordinator make the call.

Give prospects ample time to receive the letters and to call the referral sources to check your references. These first conversations will set the stage for solid, long-term business relationships.

When you first contact a prospect, mention your referral source by name in the first sentence. Your prospect needs an anchor to connect you with. Ask if the letter has arrived and whether they've had a chance to read it yet:

> *"Hi, this is Alan Advisor. Rich Smith asked me to contact you, and I promised him that I would. Did you receive the letter I sent you last week? Did you have a chance to read it? Rich thought it might be mutually beneficial for us to meet. What do you think?"*

When prospects are agreeable, pre-qualify them (see below) and then schedule an appointment.

Answer Any Objections

This is a true story about contacting prospects and answering objections. When Alan called to set an appointment, at first the prospect refused to meet. He had received the letter, but he hadn't spoken with the referral source.

The prospect had a natural reluctance to meet with someone he didn't know. But Alan knew what this prospect's key concerns were. So he said, "Rich told me you're concerned about reducing taxes on your investments."

John responded, "That's true."

Alan continued, "He said you're also interested in getting control over your investments and setting up your estate."

John replied, "Maybe we should talk. What did you say your name is again?"

Because he knew how to direct the conversation, Alan was able to overcome the prospect's natural reluctance to discuss his situation with someone he didn't know. Use the information your referral source gives you to focus prospects on problems they want to solve.

If you determine a prospect isn't at all interested in your services, it's usually helpful to know why. Say, "You obviously have a reason for not wanting to meet. Would you mind telling me what it is?" This will usually smoke out hidden objections. At least you'll understand more clearly why the prospect has made this decision.

Ask for the Appointment

If the prospect would like to meet, finish prequalifying him or her:

"As you might imagine, I can't help everyone. The people who can benefit most from my services usually have ———————— in investable assets. [Or refer to total estate value. Use the appropriate qualifications for your business.] How well does that describe you?"

If the prospect meets your minimum, say,

"Great. If we were to meet, what would you want me to help you with?"

Discuss his or her needs and your services. Use your 12-Point Prospect Qualifier form, if appropriate. Ask more about the prospect's situation, goals, and obstacles.

If the prospect meets your minimum requirements and it seems like a good personality match, set a time to meet in your office. If he or she doesn't meet your minimum requirements and doesn't seem like he or she would be an acceptable client, refer him or her to another financial advisor who you trust:

"Because of my minimum fee structure, it wouldn't be cost-effective for us to work together. So, if you'd like, I'll refer you to a competent advisor who is a better fit for your situation."

Tell Them What to Bring to the First Meeting

Make sure your prospects are ready to do business when they come in. You're supposed to simplify and streamline their personal finances. During your phone call, tell them,

"To make our first meeting as productive as possible, you'll need to bring a few items with you. Please bring — ———, ———, *and* ———. [List things such as tax returns, information about trusts, bank statements, brokerage statements.]

"You're welcome to leave this information in your car until we both feel comfortable about working together. That way, if we decide to move forward, you'll have what we'll need. We won't waste a minute of your time."

This will help prospects to be mentally prepared to do business with you. These aren't social meetings. Truly motivated prospects will want to share their situations with a client-centered financial professional.

Send a Confirmation Letter

Once you set an appointment, have your marketing coordinator send a confirmation letter. Include a map to your office and an information package about you and your firm. Also have him or her call the day before to confirm the appointment. These additional impressions will create positive reinforcement that your organization is professional, follows up, and has good systems and procedures in place.

Meet to Start a Business Relationship

This book is about becoming a client-centered marketer so you can create more and better selling situations. To properly cover the subject of sales would take a second book. I just want to point out two key things about the selling process that I've learned over the years. In the client-centered phase of the industry, your focus should be on starting relationships, not making transactions.

Advise, Don't sell

The best sales tactic is *not to sell*. Instead, advise your wealthy prospects. Take the pressure off. Calm them. Assure them that you can simplify and organize their financial affairs. Be a client-centered problem solver. And keep the conversation focused on the payoffs they want from their money and your services.

The more they feel you're pressuring them to make decisions, the more prospects will resist. Use subtle reverse psychology. Suggest that you may not be able to meet all their expectations. Get them to tell you what it would take to earn and keep their business. Ask them what they would want you to help them with if you did work together. Mention that your services aren't cheap. Ask them if they have considered solving their problems on their own.

Then offer to help them get what they want. The wealthier clients know that investing and risk management are not exact sciences. They want straightforward information, great service, and expert advice to help them take control of their personal financial affairs.

Develop a Systemized Sales Track

There are many good books about sales. I highly recommend Nick Murray's book: *The Excellent Investment Advisor* (The Nick Murray Company, Inc., 1996), and Bill Bachrach's book: *Values Based Selling* (Aim High Publishing, 1996). Both are written for financial professionals. You should use these books to develop your own customized sales track.

Having an organized sales process is an essential element in your overall effort-less marketing strategy. If you follow the strategies in this book, you'll be so attractive to your ideal prospects that you probably won't have to "sell" them in the traditional meaning of the word.

The New Client Information Form

Let's look at the sales communication tools you'll need for one-on-one meetings. The first tool is a New Client Information form. You'll use it to quickly qualify new prospects and to determine how you can help them. Use this form whenever you meet with a prospect in person.

You or your marketing coordinator should have qualified prospects before you agreed to schedule any time with them. Then this form will help you to quickly gather the financial and personal information needed to have a meaningful conversation to explore how you could add the most value for each prospect.

Refer to "New Client Information" on pages 358 and 359 as you develop your form. Make it useful to your business model and your target markets.

If you have each new prospect complete this form before you meet, it will cut the time you spend collecting hard data in half. Have your receptionist ask new prospects to complete the form when they come into your waiting room: "to allow your advisor to add as much value as possible in the time allotted." This form can cut a two-hour initial interview down to one hour. It covers all of the most important financial information and each prospect's goals and concerns.

Since you'll have most of the hard information, you can concentrate your discovery process on the softer but more powerful human motivations. You can spend your valuable time getting to understand your prospect's values, goals, priorities, dreams for the future, and concerns. It allows you to concentrate on building trust and rapport instead of gathering data. Creating a shared vision of an inspiring future for your clients is a great way to create a strong bond between you.

Create a New Client
Introduction Presentation

Another important marketing tool you'll need is a graphic presentation that explains what you do and how you help your clients. This can usually be a hard copy of your PowerPoint presentation that you use for speaking engagements (described in Step 4). It should tell your story and explain how you help people. If you use your corporate overview for the first few slides and then show case studies of how you help people, it will quickly illustrate your benefits to new prospects.

Print it on a high-quality color printer on good paper and put it in a classy binder. Normally, you'll use this powerful communications tool at your first or second meeting with new prospects. Use charts and graphs to illustrate key benefits and to build credibility and desire for your payoffs. Include examples of statements and "deliverables" of reporting services that you offer. You'll usually show these at your second, or "account opening" meeting.

Keep your presentation materials generic. Use them to sell your prospects on engaging you for some sort of professional analysis or plan. That's the first step to starting a lifelong, mutually beneficial partnership.

New Client Information

Name   Spouse   Date

Address   City   ZIP

Phone/day   evening

Workshop(s) attended

To make our first meeting as productive as possible, please answer the following questions to the best of your knowledge.

1. How did you hear about our firm?

   Radio   Letter   Article   Newspaper   Friend

   Workshop   Professional Referral

2. Please indicate your age group. ____ 18–30   ____ 31–45
   ____ 46–60   ____ 61–75   ____ 76+

3. Which of the following do you have?

   Life Insurance   Living Trust   Long-Term Care Insurance

   Health Ins.   Disability Ins.   Medicare Supplement   Will

   Mutual Funds   Stocks   Bonds   Managed Accounts

4. Who do you currently get financial advice from?

   _____

5. What is the purpose of today's visit?

   _____

---

6. What is your primary financial goal or concern? _____

_____

7. If you were able to accomplish #6 above, what would it mean to you personally? _____

_____

8. Below are listed some of the benefits of our professional services. Please check the benefits you feel would be the most helpful to you in achieving your objectives.

   A __ Establish a savings plan to accumulate wealth

   B __ Plan for my children's education

   C __ Professional help in selecting investments

   D __ Plan for my financial security in retirement

   E __ Professional management of my investment portfolio

   F __ Reduce my insurance cost and analyze my insurance needs

   G __ Reduce my taxes and increase my income on highly appreciated assets

   H __ Prepare my tax return

   I __ Reduce my taxes

   J __ Prepare my estate plan

9. Which three of the above are most important to you at this time? *(List in order of importance.)* 1. _____ 2. _____ 3. _____

10. Which investments do you feel most comfortable with? _____

_____

11. Which investments do you feel least comfortable with? _____

_____

12. What is your current combined gross annual income?

   Under $50,000 $50,000–$100,000 $100,000–$250,000

   $250,000+

13. What is your combined investment net worth, excluding car, home and furnishings?

   Under $100,000 $100,000–$250,000 $250,000–$1,000,000

   $1,000,000–$3,000,000 $3,000,000+

Chapter at a Glance

Generating qualified leads is the critical function of your marketing activities. But even more important is a systematic process to follow up, contact, qualify, prioritize, and meet with every high-quality prospect possible. And you need a systematic prospect conversion (sales) process. This is the critical link between marketing and generating revenue.

Follow up with only the most qualified and motivated prospects. Make it a goal to have too many ideal prospects. Raise your standards and make sure prospects pass your qualifications before you invest your time with them.

Ultimately, you can create a systematic machine that consistently produces a predictable flow of ideal new prospects. Systematically converting your ideal prospects into great clients is a core competency of every effort-less marketer.

If you build your business around fee-based products and services each year you'll generate more and more recurring revenue from repeat customers. You'll start building predictable, growing revenue. Then you can be even more selective about who you decide to take on as clients.

Chapter 18 Action Steps

Exercise 1: Meet with your staff to create a systematic process for following up with referrals. Define specifically who will be responsible for each step.

Exercise 2: Carefully prepare and refine a script for appointment setting.

Exercise 3: Write a sample referral letter for your company. You'll use this to show your clients when you're asking for referrals. Be prepared to adapt it for specific prospects based on feedback from your clients.

Exercise 4 Have your assistant create prospect qualifier and new client information forms using the ones in this chapter for guidance.

Exercise 5: Test your new system on your next referral. Continue to evaluate and refine your processes.

Transform Your Business and Your Life

n the classic film *My Fair Lady*, a Cockney street urchin becomes the belle of the ball. Professor Henry Higgins vows, "I'll make a duchess of this draggletailed guttersnipe. We'll start today!" With Higgins' help, Eliza Doolittle transforms herself from a starving beggar into a desirable, aristocratic woman.

Higgins was successful because he knew exactly how to make Eliza attractive to London's high society. His in-depth knowledge of the people enabled him to package and position her perfectly for this elite niche.

The preceding chapters gave you processes and tools you need to transform yourself and your business to match perfectly the wants and needs of wealthy people in your target segments and niches. You'll play both Henry Higgins and Eliza Doolittle as you develop in-depth people knowledge and transform your business to provide exactly what your ideal clients want and will pay for.

Exceed your clients' and your own expectations.

This final section of *Effort-less Marketing* will guide you beyond marketing. You'll learn how to make your clients ecstatic by providing exceptional client service. I'll give you a glimpse of my vision of the future. My goal in these last two chapters is to inspire you to imagine and create a super-profitable business and a wonderful life for yourself and, ultimately, a better world for everyone.

Section Preview

- Keep your best clients for life (or longer).

- Add value through emotional payoffs instead of products.

- Put more meaning, purpose, and joy into your work.

- Help create a win-win-win world.

Make Your Clients Ecstatic

Do what you do so well that your customers come back and bring their friends.

—Walt Disney, American filmmaker and amusement park founder, Disneyland and Walt Disney World

One autumn, a small group of the world's top marketing executives met at an elite conference in a chateau near the French Riviera. David Ogilvy, the famed advertising man, was the star attraction at this exclusive event. He had promised to unveil a guaranteed technique for increasing the effectiveness of any marketing campaign.

The crowd hushed as Ogilvy ascended the stairs to the stage. He had traveled far across the Atlantic to share his brilliant strategies to this expectant group of creative directors and copy writers. The world's most brilliant marketers leaned forward to hear the wisdom from Ogilvy's lips.

He said, "In all my years as an advertising man, I've learned there's one strategy that's guaranteed to improve dramatically any marketing campaign." He paused and then revealed the secret: "The guaranteed way to make any marketing campaign more effective is simply to *create a better product*."

Ogilvy told the group that he'd never found a marketing strategy that could consistently overcome the handicap of an inferior product or service. Marketing a poor product is a big waste of money. Product returns eat up all the profits. Potential customers quickly learn to avoid the product in the future. And they warn their friends.

The Most Powerful Marketing Strategy

Your superior set of products, services, and delivery methods is your competitive advantage. It's one of the fundamental benefits that makes your firm stand out in a crowded marketplace. It's the core reason clients want to work with you.

A small amount of focused marketing of a high quality, highly desirable product or service will generate growing sales. Your happy new clients will come back for more and bring their friends. The more marketing resonance you create, the less time and effort you'll have to spend on marketing. Your clients and services will speak for you. Word-of-mouth buzz is extremely powerful.

In other words, developing a superior "total solution" is an essential component of a super-profitable financial services business. It makes you universally attractive to your targeted clients. It makes all of your marketing activities more profitable and effort-less. Show the ideal prospects your perfect solution, and they'll become clients for life.

I wrote this book to help you transform your current business into a client-centered business that offers a better "product" to your ideal clients. This isn't about offering a better insurance policy or investment vehicle— but a better *you*. You need to learn to provide better service and a higher level of thinking than you have in the past.

Keep Your Clients for Life

Management consultant Peter Drucker said, "The purpose of a business is to make and keep a customer." Drucker understands the lifetime value of a customer. But in a sales-centered financial services business, the goal is to make the sale. In fact, the average client stays with a transaction-oriented stockbroker for only two-and-one-half years.

In the old days, you got paid for completing a *transaction for the manufacturer*. But when you're offering a fee-based service, you're really providing a service-based *relationship for the client*. You work for the client, and your work is never done. Your client-centered business focuses on processes, not business events. To offer this new, higher level of service, you must transform your organizational structure to provide more customer service support.

Your goal is to make and keep your ideal clients happy for life—or even for multiple generations. By providing ongoing service, your team can generate recurring revenue. This growing recurring revenue will be the financial foundation for your super-profitable business.

By helping your investment clients with their estate planning needs, you can manage their assets for more than one generation. Every family will eventually have to deal with business or estate succession. You're the logical person to manage the assets and the transfer of title to the heirs. Make it your goal to serve three generations of investors from the same family.

Add a Concierge to Your Team

Since we're in the client-centered phase of the industry life cycle, products are commodities. Your organization needs to add more value through personalized services. But you need to focus *your time* on building and managing the business.

To leverage your time and transform your service, you'll eventually need to hire a phenomenal customer service person. (As your recurring revenue grows from fees, some of your revenue can pay for this new employee.)

I see this new employee as a CFP who doesn't like to sell, but who loves to provide great advice and follow-up. This person is highly organized and easily brings order to your clients' chaotic financial affairs. Such a person could start to conduct periodic meetings with your "C" clients while you spend most of your time with your "A" and "B" clients.

The ideal person should have great technical and administrative skills and be a concierge at heart. The job should consist of constantly thinking of ways to delight your best clients. This person should get a lot of psychic income from solving problems and providing great customer service. I like to call this person the "director of warm fuzzies."

This is a critical element of effort-less marketing—making sure your existing clients are totally satisfied with your services and are happy to pay for them. You want clients who will stick with you. Happy, long-term clients who you can partner with are your biggest marketing assets.

"Nichemanship" Streamlines Customer Service

You're probably wondering how it would be possible to deliver such a high level of service to all of your clients on an ongoing basis. Your customer service person will do most of the work. And you don't have to offer exceptional service to all of your clients.

You need to offer this concierge level of service only to your best clients. If they're all in one or two niches, providing great service and meeting their special needs should be easy. Narrowing your acceptable client profile is the only way you can provide exceptional service.

You need to develop a system that incorporates common products and services to avoid having to resort to mass customization, which is far too time consuming. To make your clients ecstatic, you must be able to systemize your administrative work and customer service. That means your clients must all share a similar mix of products, services, problems, and concerns.

Compete on "Total Experience," Not Products

You don't have to provide superior investment returns or the cheapest insurance costs to keep your clients happy. That's good news since you can't control free markets. But you do have control over the service and the experience your clients have with your firm. Focus your attention on adding value in those areas where you have some control.

The critical points of contact between your organization and your clients should result in a stronger relationship—just as car repairs created a stronger relationship between Saturn owners and the Saturn company. And like Saturn's, your service must be fast, friendly, accurate, and professional.

By providing exceptional service that satisfies the financial and emotional needs of your clients, you'll forge a strong bond between your clients and your company—no matter what happens in the markets.

To provide value beyond your core products, you have to involve both the logical left brain and the emotional right brain. You must provide both financial high-tech and personal high-touch. Prudent Investors value a structured and disciplined investment management process. It makes them feel everything is under control.

Focus on the Emotional Payoffs

How can you consistently go beyond your core products to make your clients feel good every time they have contact with you or someone from your office? How do you identify and cater to the deep psychic needs that all human beings have? What emotional payoffs do wealthy clients want, and how can you align yourself with these powerful payoffs?

You must hire the right team and set up efficient administrative systems that deliver outstanding service to your clients. This is a core competency. But beyond great service, you must offer more personalized services.

Money and financial instruments have no intrinsic value. They're only a means to an end. You need to begin to associate yourself and your organization with the emotional payoffs that make your clients feel wonderful. Take a clue from Mercedes Benz. They say they don't sell transportation. They sell status. Don't sell financial products. Sell control, security, peace of mind, and respect. If you do, your clients will never leave you.

Obviously, different clients have different motivators. But there are five payoffs that almost everyone wants:

1. to simplify and consolidate their financial affairs,

2. to feel in control of their financial affairs,

3. to feel secure,

4. to feel important (loved, wanted, respected, and valued), and

5. to have fun.

If your clients associate you with these five benefits, they will be ecstatic with your relationship. Create a project team of staff members to dream up new and better ways to make your clients feel both important and secure.

As financial products and services become commodities, you must constantly strive to add value as your clients define it. Involve them in co-creating the services you offer them. Continually ask your clients what great performance means to them. Then organize your business to give it to them—effort-lessly.

Associate Yourself with Your Ideal Clients' Favorite Things

To cement the bond, associate yourself with things, ideals, or activities your ideal clients value most. Let's say you like to play golf. Work to attract many other avid golfers as your clients. Purposely associate yourself with great golf experiences. Sponsor annual trips for your clients and their friends to exotic golf resorts. Host a couple of golf clinics for your clients and their friends. Watch golf videos together. Start a golf appreciation club. Become your clients' golf cheerleader.

In addition to the tangible financial benefits you'll receive, you'll associate yourself with the things in life that are most important to your clients. Since your prospects really want these payoffs from their money, your total package of financial services is extremely attractive to them. It provides *psychic income* that they can't get from most other advisors.

This works only if you naturally appreciate your clients and enjoy the same things they do. It's no fun faking interest or rapport where none exists. This is why it's so important to adopt those niches that make you feel comfortable. Your business can be a vehicle to build win-win relationships with people you enjoy. Many of your best clients will also become your friends as you achieve your goals together.

Meet Periodically to Service Your Clients

You should meet periodically with your best clients to review their financial progress, organize their financial affairs, make any appropriate changes to their accounts, strengthen your relationships, address concerns, solve problems, and encourage them to stay on their present prudent courses. This whole process works much better if you have a fee-based business.

I recommend you meet with your clients three or four times the first year. Then you can cut back to two or three times a year. These meetings should take from 60 to 90 minutes, but no longer. Your clients will usually need their financial planning and investment advice in small chunks. It makes it easier to digest, so it's less stressful.

As you get busier, have your customer service person meet with all of your "B" and "C" clients. You should meet with only the top 20 percent of your clients—your "A" list. Ideally, you'll have an administrative person who can handle the routine account service work.

Here are some ideas for making your clients ecstatic when they come in to your office for periodic performance review meetings.

1. Use a customer preferences form. In addition to the financial information you gather on your clients, you should also gather "soft" data. Create a form to keep track of important dates, names of family members and friends, favorite beverages, snacks, authors, places, flowers, pets, goals, dreams for the future, likes, dislikes, interests, etc. You'll use this information to determine how to personalize your business experience for each client.

2. Be prepared. Make sure you have any reports or other information ready well before your clients arrive at your office. Set aside some time the day before your meeting to review your notes and create an agenda. You can customize a standard agenda, if necessary. You'll feel more relaxed and your clients will feel secure that you have everything under control.

3. Greet clients with welcome signs. If you think your clients will respond well to such things, greet your clients with a sign in your lobby that says, "Welcome Jean and Bill Jones! We're happy to see you again." You'll make them feel special and appreciated.

4. Play their favorite music. Very few things can evoke as much positive emotion as a favorite song. Find out what music each client especially enjoys. Have it playing in the lobby when they arrive. This will make them feel at home.

5. Appeal to their sweet tooth. Stock special goodies for individual clients. Serve them their favorite snacks or sweets. Remember how they like their coffee. Food has a strong positive association for most people, especially sweets. They'll feel a slight "sugar buzz." Yet be aware that many people develop diabetes as they age. Do not offer sweets to these clients. Provide a variety of sugar-free snacks instead.

6. Be on time. Treat your clients like the important people they are, and they will reciprocate. Your professional role requires that you define the time frames of your interaction with your clients. Keep your meetings short and punctual. Stick closely to the key business at hand, but be friendly. Good time management and time for small talk makes your clients feel that you respect them.

7. Be cheerful. Everyone in your office must be cheerful and friendly. Tell staff members to smile when they talk with clients and to greet them like old friends. Let clients know they're more than just clients to you. If you do, they'll feel like part of your "family."

8. Find out what they have been up to. Start your meeting by asking about your clients' personal situations, especially anything fun that they have been doing. Listen to them talk about their lives and their goals. Focus the conversation on the future and look for ways you can support them to get what they want. Coach them on living a great life and what that means to them. They will feel understood and encouraged.

9. Ask about clients' family members. Talk about things friends talk about. Everyone has people in their lives who are close to them. Find out who's important to your clients. Often grandchildren are huge endorphin generators. Be sure you know about your clients' grandchildren and what they're doing. Ask about the granddaughter who's graduating from college or the grandson who just got his first real job. Your clients will feel as if you're part of their families.

10. Ask if any questions have come up since your last meeting. You're the key financial influencer and counselor in your clients' lives. Be sure to be accessible and helpful in educating your clients. They want you to educate them so they can become better investors and better consumers of your services. Debunk myths and simplify investments for them. You'll make them feel smart.

11. Ask about changes in their situations. You need to know if there have been any major changes in their financial situations. Ask them if they're considering or expecting any major changes in the near future. This is important because it may signal a need to change strategies, integrate other assets under your management, or resolve new problems. They'll feel well taken care of.

12. Reinforce their investment decisions and strategies. It's human nature for clients to worry about their money. Reinforce the fact that you work with the best and brightest minds in the industry. Educate your clients on the realities of the market and the volatility of all financial services. Explain how you have constructed their portfolios to minimize volatility and risk. Use every opportunity to show them that everything is on track and well within expectations. They'll feel in control, secure, and smart.

13. Compare investment performance to clients' goals—not market indexes. Don't compare your investment portfolio performance to investment indices. Have your clients set goals and track your performance relative to their goals. The benchmark should be their goals, not some abstract market index they don't really understand anyway. Graphs showing actual performance versus goals almost always look good after a few years. These graphs provide proof that you're adding value. Your clients will feel they're getting fair value for the money they spend for your services.

14. Systematically organize their financial lives. Each quarter, attack a different financial organizing task for your clients. You may start with wills and trusts and end up organizing their checkbooks. You should always have "something else" you're working on to organize and simplify your clients' financial lives. You should be able to go for years before you run out of things to organize and manage. Your clients will feel everything is under control.

15. Ask if there are any other issues they'd like to discuss. Conclude meetings by asking if there are any other issues that your clients would like to discuss as long as they're there. Answer any of their questions, then set up your next meeting and tell them what you plan to accomplish the next time you meet. Be open to any suggestions or questions they may have. If they need more of your time, set up a time to meet in the future. They'll feel heard and well taken care of.

16. Wash their cars. This is pushing the envelope a bit. For about $25 each, you can have your clients' cars washed while they're meeting with you. If your clients like the idea, have the car detail company spray the clean interior with your clients' favorite scents. They'll feel totally pampered and look forward to your next meeting.

Build Your Personal Relationship

In addition to periodic business review meetings, you should develop personal relationships with your best clients. Supplement your company and product-sponsor communication with a little personal "high touch." When it comes down to it, all business relationships are ultimately personal in nature. Here are some ideas for enhancing your personal relationships with your best clients and centers of influence.

1. Stay in touch. Frequent contact makes people feel secure. If clients never hear from you, they might start wondering if they're ever going to hear from their money. A regular flow of letters, invitations, and calls from you and those in your office makes clients feel connected to a successful, growing business where their money is safe.

2. Send a personal note or call them. You probably call your friends just to see how they're doing. Do this with your best clients and centers of influence, also. You can send personal notes, cards, articles, and e-mail. If you read something interesting, drop a personal note saying, "I just read this and thought you would find it interesting." They'll feel appreciated.

Two Keys to Becoming Client-Centered

What are the components of a business model that supports a higher level of service? There are two key things you need to do to make sure you're delivering the psychic income your clients are seeking.

MAKE YOUR CLIENTS ECSTATIC

When people think about you and your organization, what do they think of first? Do they think of mutual funds and insurance policies? Or do they think of playing golf with good friends and feeling that all is well?

If you create endorphins in your clients—making them feel passionate about your relationships with them—they will never leave you and they'll encourage their friends to become your clients. A superior service business is a superior relationship business. If you pamper your best clients, the word will get out. Everyone wants to be treated like royalty.

STAY ON THEIR MINDS

Out of sight, out of mind. Your best clients want to hear from you 15 or 20 times a year. The more they hear from you, the more opportunities they'll have to tell their friends about you. Constant communication is the way to keep the relationships strong.

Develop an effective client-communication process. Use a combination of telephone calls, notes, letters, reports, and special events to stay continuously on your prospects' minds.

3. Be responsive to their requests. Make your clients feel important by returning calls promptly. If you're out of the office or unavailable to return calls quite a bit, have someone on your team return client calls. Your service must be prompt and accurate. Your team members should anticipate and head off any client miscommunication problems.

If you don't return calls quickly, clients often feel unwanted and wonder what's happening. They may even get angry if they don't hear from you. By staying in contact, your clients will feel in control and well served.

4. Break bread with your best clients. Treat your best clients to lunch or dinner at least once a year. Birthdays are a great time to get together, but you don't need an excuse to meet. One way or another, get together occasionally for a social visit, not a business meeting. Suggest they bring along some friends. Their friends are going to be a lot like them. This is a great way to generate referrals. They will feel comfortable introducing their friends and associates to you.

5. Become their travel coach. Associate yourself with one of the biggest hot buttons for retired people—travel. One advisor sets up special investment accounts for clients. When they accumulate enough money, she tells them to pick a date to travel. She selects a vacation and books it through a travel agent. Many of her clients would never go on their own. But the advisor makes travel painless and fun. Try it yourself. Ask your clients to send you postcards. Post them in the lobby, and use them as conversation starters. Your clients will feel grateful.

6. Offer pet- and house-sitting services. Try this one out. When your wealthy clients travel, who watches their houses and takes care of their pets? Do they have pet sitters? Or do they take Rover and Fluffy to kennels? Would taking care of these chores be a highly valued service? Ask your best clients to find out how you can add value beyond your core products. How creative can you be?

7. Host fun and educational events. We covered this one in Chapter 18. Instead of mass marketing for new clients, fee-based advisors can concentrate most of their marketing activities on making their current clients ecstatic. Survey your clients and find out what types of events they would like to attend. Then sponsor fun events and occasional educational events. Invite some of your clients to help organize the activities. You'll create your own community, and many of your clients will want to be part of it.

Think "Outside the Box"

As the financial services industry becomes more and more competitive, it becomes harder to make yourself distinctive. Savvy financial professionals will push the limits of customer service to go far beyond their core products. You'll need to do the same to beat the competition. Pamper your clients like the concierge does at a fine hotel.

A client-centered business, by definition, is highly referable. A sales-centered business is not. The more expertise you have in specialized niches, the more attractive you'll be to people in those niches. Position your business to solve the problems that your ideal clients want help in solving. Make sure clients and centers of influence see your company as a professional organization with which clients are lucky to be doing business.

Chapter at a Glance

Remember that money has no value in itself. It's simply a means of exchange. Focus on meeting the emotional needs of your clients. Don't focus on just your products. Outstanding customer service is one of your most effective marketing strategies.

The easiest way to find out what your clients will pay for is to ask them. As you conduct your interviews, read between the lines. Watch their body language and listen to their voice intonation. Be sensitive to the things that create endorphins in their lives. Then set up your company to systematically associate your team with the things your clients want most from their money.

You must provide competitive financial products and sound financial advice. But that's just the baseline. Become a "lifestyle enhancer" and your clients will help you build your business. Some will even become your marketing apostles.

Chapter 19 Action Steps

Exercise 1: Create a simple form to collect information about new clients' favorite treats, music, and activities. Begin using it so you can regularly stock a few of these when they come in for meetings.

Exercise 2: Brainstorm with your staff on ways you can pamper your clients and make them ecstatic that they get to work with you and your firm.

Dream Big Dreams

You become as great as your dominant
aspiration . . . If you cherish a vision,
a lofty ideal in your heart,
you will realize it.

—**James Allen,** American self-improvement author,
As a Man Thinketh

ongratulations! You've come a long way! I'm impressed that you've read all the way to the last chapter. I know you've invested a lot of your time and concentration to get here. I worked hard writing this book, hoping you would read to this point. I also hoped you'd enjoy the journey and learn much about the art of effort-less marketing.

I set out nearly ten years ago to help transform this industry from one with a product-centered sales focus to one with a client-centered marketing focus. I knew this industry was going to evolve through the same three phases that all industries experience. I wanted to play a major role in helping the financial services industry grow. My goal has always been to elevate the industry to a higher level of win-win thinking.

I'm more excited today than ever because, as I complete this book in the last year of the twentieth century, the signs are clear that the transformation is in full bloom. Everyone is talking about relationships. They're talking about fee-based asset management. They're talking about putting clients first, and they're thinking about niche marketing.

As I travel around the country working with top executives in the investment industry, I'm seeing excitement and enthusiasm I haven't seen for years. There's a buzz that something big is in the air.

The industry is shifting its focus from products to people. The age of the transaction-oriented advisor is rapidly coming to an end. Active traders are quickly moving to the Internet, leaving Prudent Investors to the retail financial services industry.

More and more financial services organizations are starting up interdependent strategic partnerships to create win-win relationships for everyone. Many businesses in this new age are finding it's more beneficial to partner with other businesess than it is to compete with them. There's so much opportunity for bright, creative people now. They just need to think win-win to take advantage of all the incredible opportunities.

You've Become a Client-Centered Advisor!

I've given you a ton of information in this book. I've tried to package it in a useful and inspiring format. Every story in this book is true. Some of the stories I've simplified to make a central point easier to understand. But I didn't make anything up. That's something I didn't have to do. Client-centered advisors are very effective marketers. Prospects listen to them. Reporters quote them. Centers of influence refer to them. Most important, their clients love them. When you become a client-centered advisor, all of the things you dream about will come true for you.

You're obviously committed to building a super-profitable business and a wonderful life. You've discovered you *can* have it all. But you can't do it the old way. You need to do it the effort-less way.

Reading this book is the first step. A book like this isn't meant to be read just once. This book should serve as a useful reference for the rest of your career. Go back through the book, and identify key chapters that you want to read again. Do the exercises that will have the most impact on your business right now. Outline what you learn, then implement the appropriate lessons for your business.

Use this book to transform your business and your life. Identify additional resources that will help you build your client-centered business. By reading this book, you've started to focus on people, payoffs, and positioning. You've begun to ask the right questions, such as, "How do I best serve this group of people?" and "Where do I want to go personally?"

As you build your super-profitable business and your wonderful life, continue to ask the question, "How can I better serve these people?" And make sure that, in addition to your niche(s), one of the groups you aim to serve is your family.

Understanding the "Purpose Hierarchy"

One final tool I'd like you to be aware of before I end this book is the "purpose hierarchy." This is a very powerful tool you can use for yourself and with your clients to help you take your business to the next level.

The term *purpose hierarchy* comes from a fascinating book called *Breakthrough Thinking: The Seven Principles of Creative Problem Solving* by Gerald Nadler and Shozo Hibino (Prima Publishing, 1998). In the book, they explain that the objective of a purpose hierarchy is to expand your thinking about a problem, challenge, or opportunity. The best way to describe the power of the purpose hierarchy is to tell a story from the book.

A warehousing facility was having problems with breakage and loading errors when workers loaded trucks. It was such a big problem that they called in an industrial engineering consultant to help them identify the cause and recommend a solution.

After some evaluation, the consultant reported that the best way to eliminate the problems was to automate the loading process in the warehouses. The executives thought the analysis and recommendation made sense. A conveyer belt system would cost a little over $60,000 and would pay for itself in eight months.

But this particular company had 24 warehouses. Since the total solution was going to cost well over $1 million, they wanted one of their internal industrial engineers to review the project before moving forward.

Instead of rubber-stamping the plan, the young engineer assigned to the project examined the purposes of the loading dock. He started with the smallest purpose: *to load the trucks*. Then he thought out a series of additional purposes until he reached a much larger purpose: *to efficiently distribute products to the dealers*.

This larger purpose provided a wider scope than the original purpose. Now he was able to look at the problem from a number of new perspectives. It became clear that loading the trucks was just the tip of the iceberg of the total process of efficiently distributing products to the dealers.

The young engineer learned the warehouses had been built in the 1920s to circumvent a factory work force that was on strike. In their time, the warehouses solved a problem and served a valuable purpose. But today, having so many warehouses was an obsolete form of distribution. After evaluating the different options, he decided that the best solution was to sell 20 of the 24 warehouses. This eliminated the need for conveyer belts and created a much more efficient distribution system from the factory to the dealers. It was a much bigger solution to a bigger problem. It was a breakthrough.

Instead of spending over $1 million to automate the warehouses— which would have been the right solution to the wrong problem—the company took a totally different approach, freeing up millions of dollars in capital and saving hundreds of millions of dollars a year. The more efficient distribution method gave the company a huge advantage over competitors in its industry. Eventually, the company's more efficient system forced its competitors to change their distribution systems as well.

By developing the purpose hierarchy, the young engineer solved the loading problem, created a more efficient distribution system, and lowered the cost to the dealers. By asking the right questions he transformed his company and ultimately transformed the entire industry.

The Purpose of Investment Advice

We can use a purpose hierarchy to transform our industry. I have developed a simple hierarchy for financial advisors. It starts out with a small purpose and works its way up to a very large purpose. This purpose hierarchy has 12 levels divided into three sections.

The way to develop a purpose hierarchy is to identify a very small purpose and ask, "What is the purpose of that?" Your answer will take you to the next purpose, for which you ask, "What is the purpose of that?" And so on. This process moves you up the purpose hierarchy.

To start, ask, "What is the purpose of financial advice?" The smallest purpose is *to understand financial products and services.* And what is the purpose of that? *To design financial, investment, and estate plans.* What is the purpose of that? *To sell financial plans, investments, insurance, and other financial products and services.* And what is the purpose of that? *To earn commissions and/or fees.*

You can see that each larger purpose encompasses all of the smaller ones. I stopped at "earn commissions and/or fees" because this is the level at which many financial service companies and salespeople are working. Although they haven't stated it specifically, it's the unconscious default position for most individuals working in our industry today. This is where all traditional salespeople play the game.

It gets even more interesting as we continue. What is the purpose of earning commissions and/or fees? *To support a relationship to help your clients achieve their goals.* The purpose of that is *to help your clients simplify their lives and achieve (or maintain) financial independence.* The purpose of that is *to free your clients from the need to work (or worry).* The purpose of that is *to create positive options and choices for your clients.*

You can see that each larger purpose gets more interesting as we move away from the tangible products and services and start to focus more on the wants and needs of the clients. The people who play the game at this level—creating more positive options for their clients—are client-centered financial advisors. Their focus is implementing strategies that will create more positive options. That's much more inspiring to clients than helping you earn commissions or fees.

But what happens if we continue? The purpose of creating positive options for clients is *to enable your clients to do what they want, when they want, with whomever they want.* The purpose of that is to *empower your clients to fulfill their highest dreams and aspirations.* The purpose of that is *to create more joy in your clients' lives.* And the purpose of that is *to create a more joyful world for all.*

Where Do You Want to Play the Game?

It's important to note that there is no one right purpose, only bigger and smaller purposes. You can play the game at any level you choose. The last set of purposes is focused totally on quality-of-life payoffs for your clients. This is where coaches and counselors play the game. I believe this conversion from selling to advising to coaching is the future of our industry. Here's why.

Creating positive options and choices for your clients is a noble goal, but many of your clients don't know what they really want from their lives or their money. If you help them determine what will bring more joy and fulfillment to their lives, you'll be adding tremendous value. As people become more financially secure, they start asking different questions. Help them answer the important personal questions that will fill their lives with more purpose, meaning, and joy. That's much more valuable to them than simply managing investment portfolios and setting up estate plans.

It's clear to me that technology is commoditizing and driving down the value of financial advice, products, and portfolio management. Being able to help your clients determine what they really want out of life—and then helping them achieve their goals—is a much more valuable service than selling such commodities. Many financial professionals have already moved past the salesperson's role and become true advisors.

My father worked for 20 years at a career he hated until arthritis forced him to retire at an early age. Five years later he died. This is a common pattern. Many people spend their whole lives doing something they dislike hoping to retire eventually. But many of these individuals

What Is the Purpose of Financial Advice?

To construct a purpose hierarchy, we start by stating the most basic purpose we can think of for something. Once we have that down, we ask, "And what is the purpose of that?" Each time we answer the questions, we ask it again, gradually working our way up to the largest purpose we can imagine.

SALESPEOPLE PLAY AT THIS LEVEL

- Understand financial products, services, and the giving of advice.
- Design financial, investment, and estate plans.
- Sell financial plans, investments, insurance, and other financial products and services.
- Earn commissions and/or fees.

ADVISORS PLAY AT THIS LEVEL

- Support a relationship that helps clients achieve their goals.
- Help clients simplify their lives and achieve (or maintain) financial independence.
- Free clients from the need to work (or worry).
- Create positive options and choices for clients.

VISION COACHES PLAY AT THIS LEVEL

- Enable clients to do what they want, when they want, with whomever they want.
- Empower clients to fulfill their highest dreams and aspirations.
- Create more joy in clients' lives.
- Ultimately create a more joyful world for all.

never get to enjoy retirement—the stage of their lives when they have enough money and time to live their dreams. What would it be worth to your clients if you could help them experience more joy, happiness, and excitement in their lives right now? Is that a service that many wealthy clients would pay to receive? I encourage you to look beyond advising to coaching.

Take the time to ask yourself these important questions: *At what level on the purpose hierarchy am I currently playing the game? What is the current stated or unstated purpose of my business? What is the current stated or unstated purpose of the organization that employs me?*

Then ask yourself at what level you would *like* to play the game. You can play at any level you choose. By moving up the purpose hierarchy, you create more meaning and significance in the work you do for yourself, your staff, and for your clients.

One last question is the most important: *What type of relationship do my clients want to have with me?*

One of the easiest ways to find this out is to show the purpose hierarchy to your clients and ask them what level of relationship they'd like to have with you. Then ask them where they believe your competitors are playing the game. This is a very powerful positioning strategy for you, especially if you have clients with multiple investment advisors. Ask them where the other advisors are playing the game.

You can use a purpose hierarchy to define the ideal relationships you want to have with your clients and the type of relationship that will add tremendous value for them and your business.

Now is the perfect time to reevaluate what you stand for, what game you're playing, and how you're adding value for your clients. By using the purpose hierarchy for yourself and sharing it with your staff and your clients, you can transform your relationship with your clients and your business. Ultimately, by asking the right questions we can transform the entire financial services industry.

Vision for the Future

I see in the purpose hierarchy the natural evolution from trying to make a living to enhancing people's quality of life. If you're worried about feeding and clothing yourself, you generally don't think much about other people's needs. But as your own needs are met, you begin to focus on other people's needs.

Clearly, the only way to build a super-profitable business and a wonderful life is to create true, lasting value for your clients, yourself, and your family.

When I first got into the financial services industry in the early 1980s, a stockbroker told me the old joke about the investment executive commenting on a trade. He said, "Well, the broker made money and the firm made money. Two out of three isn't bad!"

That attitude and result is unacceptable today. It's based on scarcity thinking. But we live in a world of abundance. In the new era of partnerships in which everyone's goals are aligned to help each other achieve their highest aspirations, we can do much better than two out of three.

With comprehensive wealth management and prudent investment advice: 1) the clients will win, 2) the advisor will win, 3) the broker/dealer will win, 4) the investment sponsors will win, 5) the publicly traded companies that need stable access to capital will win, 6) the overall economy will prosper, and 7) ultimately, we will create a better world for all.

By my count that's seven out of three, instead of two out of three. By becoming client-centered and thinking win-win we can work together to create synergy. The whole will be greater than the sum of the parts.

I believe we can create synergy as we form partnerships with our clients and vendors. The Internet will help make this possible by making fundamental financial processes easily and cheaply available. Individual financial advisors are going to have to add more value through their ability to ask questions, clarify issues, organize and manage processes, and coach clients to help them clarify their own inspiring visions of the future.

Many of your clients will work 30 or 40 years at jobs they never like. They'll be focused on retirement. But they'll have no specific plans about what they'll do when they finally retire. It's a strange paradox that at a time of their lives when they have all the money and time they need, many of them will sit around watching daytime TV with no inspiring or exciting reason to live.

If you become your clients' vision coach and help them create their own inspiring vision of the future, you will have the power to enhance their lives. You'll become the ultimate financial advisor and lifestyle coach.

You'll help people identify what they want and help them get it. What could be more valuable in a society of tremendous abundance than someone who helps others pick and choose the opportunities that offer the most joy for them?

Financial advisors of the future will provide outstanding products and services—but these things will be considered baseline commodities. The true value of advisors will be in the creative ideas they generate for helping their clients use their prosperity in a fulfilling and meaningful way.

By creating a special environment for your unique niche, you'll keep your clients for life. You'll literally transform yourself and your business. You'll surround yourself with exactly the types of people you like—both on your staff and in your client base. Going to work every day will be a thrill. When you get up each morning, you'll be enthusiastic about the work you do and eager to tackle the opportunities in front of you. In fact, you'll have so many opportunities that you'll need to have a few assistants just to help you screen them so you can select the best ones.

You'll be a renowned expert in your niche(s) and will be known and loved by everyone around you. You'll be a master of your game, and you'll be playing the game at a high level. Not only will your marketing be effort-less, but your lifestyle will be effort-less, too.

I believe, if you've read this far, that you've always wanted to be client-centered. You were raised in an industry with a paradigm that said two out of three isn't bad. But in your heart you want to help your clients. Ultimately you want to leave a positive legacy by making a better world. You believed seven out of three is better than two out of three. But you needed someone to show you how to make it work, that it would be practical and profitable to be client-centered. You secretly wanted someone to give you permission to become client-centered so you could create an effort-less business and an effort-less life.

You've Always Had the Power

At the end of the *Wizard of Oz*, the Wizard gives the lion courage, the scarecrow knowledge, and the tin man a heart. Then he tells them all: "You don't need to be helped anymore. You've always had the power. . . . "

You have always had the power to be a client-centered, effort-less marketer. You already have the brains, courage, and heart. The only thing you haven't had was a book to show you how. Now you have the book and I, the "wizard" of client-centered, effort-less marketing, give you permission to become a client-centered advisor and an effort-less marketer.

And now it's time to begin. In the beautiful words of the German writer Johann Wolfgang von Goethe,

"Whatever you can do, or dream you can, begin it. Boldness has genius, power and magic in it. Begin it now."

Good luck as you build your super-profitable business and your wonderful life! I expect great things from you. I know the market forces will be with you.

Acknowledgements

A book like this takes a lot of time to write. It's definitely a group project. I'd like to acknowledge some of the key people who helped make this book a reality.

First and foremost is Valerie Frazee, who did an incredible job editing and organizing the material. Without Valerie I probably never would have gotten this book done. Deb Grandinetti initially helped me create the conceptual framework for the chapters and convinced me to take on this project. Karen Risch and Christen Heide did a wonderful job critiquing and editing the final manuscript.

Robert Mott, who designed this book, and Tom Klare, who created the whimsical illustrations that introduce each section, deserve special mention.

My team at American Business Visions has provided tremendous support and resources. First, I'd like to thank Teri Lynn Cleary, our head coach at ABV. She is personally responsible for many of the success stories shared in these pages. She is undoubtedly one of the world's most gifted coaches.

I'd also like to express my gratitude to Donna Dyer for her encouragement and patience. Donna constantly inspires me to keep going until I turn my dreams into reality. And finally, thanks to Cheryl Keough, who has taken care of millions of details for me so I'd have the time and mental focus necessary to complete this project. It's a privilege to work with such a talented and dedicated team.

We developed most of the ideas and techniques described in this book through our work coaching and consulting with financial advisors over the last ten years. Some of our clients played key roles in shaping our coaching program and methodology. I'd like to acknowledge a few of these individuals.

John Bowen, president and CEO of Assante Capital Management Inc., U.S., has been a good friend, fellow visionary, and client for many years. John's company funded and tested many of the ideas shared in this book.

Ben Bingaman, Ron Howard, and many other people at RWB Advisory Services, Inc., have encouraged me and helped me to refine many of my ideas. Andy Lank, Michael Nairne, Steve Friday, and Alan Cranfield of Equion (now with various companies in the Assante group) in Toronto have been great supporters and extremely instrumental in the development of our coaching program. They truly are some of North America's most progressive financial service professionals.

Larry Chambers, who made the switch from being a stockbroker to running a boutique public relations firm, created the original spark for this book more than six years ago. He called me one day after reading my column in *Registered Representative* magazine and said, "What would you think about doing a book together?"

Ed Bryant of Premium Financial Communications is a great friend and "investors' advocate." Ed's one of the most creative people I know. He developed the idea of the emotional lighthouse.

My friend, Bill Bachrach, an awesome speaker and excellent person, has inspired me over the years—particularly in the early years when we did many projects together.

Bud Elsea has been a great supporter from the IAFP. Nick Murray gave me valuable guidance and insights on early drafts of the book. Chip Roame from Tiburon Strategic Advisors provided valuable insights and research. Thomas Stanley, author of *Marketing to the Affluent* (Irwin Professional Publishers, 1988), first got me thinking that there may be a career in speaking and writing for financial advisors.

At *Investment Advisor* magazine, Bob Clark believed in me and let me create my dream column. Also, thanks to Charlie Stroller and David Smith for their encouragement, and to David Bumke, who makes sure all my articles in *Dow Jones Investment Advisor* magazine are politically correct.

I'd also like to acknowledge Dan Jamieson, editor of *Registered Representative* magazine, for giving me my start as a published writer. And thanks to Cheryl Cooper who handled the copyediting on my column with *RR*.

There are many other people, especially the financial advisors who participated in our Market Quest coaching program and Quantum Leap workshops. You've all contributed one way or another to my thinking and to refining the strategies in this book. Thank you all for your commitment to excellence, insights, and encouragement.

About the Author

For more than a decade, Steve Moeller has helped entrepreneurs build profitable and rewarding businesses. As president and CEO of American Business Visions, Steve is a sought-after speaker, consultant, business strategist, and writer for financial industry trade publications.

Steve started his career in the advertising industry. In the early 1980s, he entered the investment industry and soon became an award-winning salesperson and eventually a successful marketing executive. Today he focuses his considerable talents on American Business Visions, a publishing and training firm he founded in 1989. The company creates marketing tools and business development systems for financial advisors and investment companies.

His unique business development process, best defined as relationship-based niche marketing, has become known as the "Moeller Method." This turnkey system enables advisors to identify and attract clients who are both profitable and fun to work with.

Steve believes that evolving technologies and consumer expectations are creating huge opportunities and challenges in the retail investment industry. He is committed to helping financial advisors transform their businesses into highly competitive, client-centered organizations.

Steve lives in southern California with his wife, Brooke.

Looking for More Tools to Help You Build Your Business?

To find information about resources recommended by Steve Moeller, please visit the American Business Visions Website. You'll find descriptions of all the reading materials mentioned in this book and links to additional resources available online.

www.businessvisions.com

This is also the place to go to subscribe to the *free* e-mail newsletter, "Steve Moeller's Client-Centered Advisor." Biweekly e-mails will provide you with inspirational success stories and tangible, how-to information that will help you transform your business.

ORDER FORM

To use this form to order by mail or fax,
please photocopy and fill out completely.

LEARNING SYSTEMS & TRAINING PROGRAMS

QTY	PROGRAM DESCRIPTION	PRICE EA.	SUBTOTAL
	Steve Moeller's Client-Centered Advisor— **FREE E-Mail Newsletter** *Bi-weekly tips, tools, and action steps designed to help you create a highly profitable and satisfying financial services business. (E-mail address required.)*	**FREE**	**FREE**
	Effort-Less Marketing *For single copy orders, go to our Website at www.businessvisions.com. If you do not have Internet access, use this form to place your order. For bulk orders (24 or more), please call us directly for special rates.*	**$44.95***	
	Effort-Less Marketing Diskette *All of the forms, letters, and questionnaires that are described in Effort-Less Marketing are available on diskette (or downloadable from the Web). This makes it easier than ever to customize them for your own use.*	**$49.95**	
	Discover Hidden Wealth Learning System *This system presents research about the top 22 target markets for investment advisors. Take advantage of this information to more effectively target your markets and service your clients. Learn where to find hidden opportunities—and what each market is looking for from you. Use step-by-step exercises to identify your high-payoff niche markets.*	**$149.00**	
	Marketing to the Wealthy Learning System *Never cold call again once you learn how to get wealthy prospects to call you. Identify who the wealthy are, how to find them, how to position yourself as a "Millionaire's Advisor," and how to keep getting more of your "ideal" clients by establishing relationships with their centers of influence—accountants and attorneys.*	**$149. 00**	

*All prices listed in U.S. dollars.
(Continued next page)

QTY	PROGRAM DESCRIPTION	PRICE EA.	SUBTOTAL
	Creating Strategic Alliances with CPAs *Many advisors would like to establish profitable relationships with accountants but do not know how. This step-by-step system walks advisors through the process of establishing profitable strategic alliances with CPAs. Includes a diskette with all the tools you need to be successful.*	**$399. 00**	

UPS Shipping Charges
per item within the U.S.
(call for international rates):
Standard $10. 00
2nd day $20. 00
Next day $30. 00
(see our Website for book rates)

Sub Total	$
California residents add 7.5% sales tax	$ CA only
Shipping	$
TOTAL	$

PAYMENT METHOD

❏ My check for $_____(payable to **American Business Visions**) is enclosed. (*Please pay in U.S. dollars.)

❏ Please charge my credit card.

    ❏ AmEx ❏ Discover ❏ MasterCard ❏ Visa

CREDIT CARD #:_____ EXP. DATE:_____

SIGNATURE:_____

CUSTOMER INFORMATION

NAME_____

COMPANY_____

ADDRESS_____ SUITE #_____

CITY_____ STATE_____ ZIP_____

WORK PHONE (   )_____ FAX (   )_____

E-MAIL_____

For free industry resources as well as more information about our products and services, visit our Website at **www.businessvisions.com.**

For fastest ordering by credit card, fax this form to (714) 505-8035,
or call (800) 678-1701 • (714) 505-8030

Or mail with your check enclosed to

American Business Visions
1131 East Main Street, Suite 203 • Tustin, CA 92780